D1299270

URBAN TRANSFORMATION IN CHINA

To our families, and friends and colleagues at
The Chinese Economists Society (CES)

Urban Transformation in China

Edited by

AIMIN CHEN
Indiana State University

GORDON G. LIU
University of North Carolina-Chapel Hill

KEVIN H. ZHANG
Illinois State University

ASHGATE

Published by
Ashgate Publishing Limited
Gower House
Croft Road
Aldershot
Hants GU11 3HR
England

Ashgate Publishing Company
Suite 420
101 Cherry Street
Burlington, VT 05401-4405
USA

Ashgate website: http://www.ashgate.com

British Library Cataloguing in Publication Data
Urban transformation in China. - (The Chinese economy series)
    1. Urbanization - China 2. Cities and towns - China - Growth
    3. China - Economic conditions - 1949- 4. China - Social
    conditions - 1949-
    I. Chen, Aimin II. Liu, Gordon G. III. Zhang, Kevin H.
    307.7'6'0951

Library of Congress Cataloging-in-Publication Data
Urban transformation in China / edited by Aimin Chen, Gordon G. Liu and Kevin H. Zhang.
    p. cm. -- (The Chinese economy series)
    Includes bibliographical references and index.
    ISBN 0-7546-3312-8
    1. Cities and towns--China. 2. Urbanization--China. I. Chen, Aimin. II. Liu, Gordon G.
III. Zhang, Kevin H. IV. Series.

HT147.C48U723 2004
307.76'0951--dc22

2003056778

ISBN 0 7546 3312 8

Printed and bound in Great Britain by MPG Books Ltd, Bodmin, Cornwall.

Contents

LIST OF FIGURES

LIST OF TABLES

PREFACE

D. GALE JOHNSON
The University of Chicago

The further urbanization of China will present the citizens and policy makers of China with major political, social and economic issues over the next several decades. The process of rapid urbanization through the influx of rural people into cities has never been without turmoil anywhere in the world. But in the case of China the controls that have been maintained on rural to urban migration which have resulted in a very large income disparity may well present even greater difficulties than found elsewhere. For the past four decades China has attempted to control the degree of urbanization through the *hukou* system which was designed to limit rural to urban migration as well as migration in urban areas. This system is being relaxed and there has been increased migration in recent years. Thus it was very appropriate that the theme of the conference should be the urban transformation in China.

China has a smaller percentage of its population living in urban areas than would be expected for an economy at its level of income. This has occurred as a result of its deliberate policy of limiting the migration that normally occurs during a long period of economic development during which employment in agriculture declines from being the source of employment of the majority of the labor force to having a relatively small minority of the labor force so engaged. According to the 2000 Census, the urban population of China was 36.2 per cent of the total population. This represented a significant increase from the estimate of 30.9 per cent for 1999. The increase was apparently due to two factors. First, due to population growth certain communities that were classified as rural during the 1990s were now classified as urban, and, second, the definition of a permanent resident was changed by reducing the number of months an individual was required to have lived in a community to be counted in the place of residence. Prior to the 2000 Census an individual had to reside in an area for a year to be counted as a resident; in the 2000 Census that period was reduced to six months. So far as I know, it has not been indicated how much of the 69.5 million increase in the urban population between the end of

---

URBAN TRANSFORMATION IN CHINA, edited by Aimin Chen, Gordon G. Liu and Kevin H. Zhang

1999 and 1 November 2000 was due to these two factors. Some small part of the increase was due to natural growth of the population.

While to some degree the content of nearly every chapter in this volume has been affected by the *hukou* system of controlling migration, I want to draw special attention to two of them. The chapter by Fei-Ling Wang 'Hukou Systems and Migration Controls' is the best discussion of the system that I have ever seen. It provides a remarkable amount of detail of how the system is administered and how it is used to discriminate against the rural to urban migrants. It is noted that during the period grain was both highly subsidized and rationed in urban areas, the migrants were not given access to the low cost supplies but had to purchase their grain in the market at much higher prices. After noting that the urban migrants with rural *hukou*s had to pay for their children's education, Wang noted that when such children were ready for college they had to return to the location of their *hukou* to take the entrance examinations. Why was this important? Wang notes: 'To many the regional differential in college entrance examinations and admissions remains perhaps the most important state subsidy to selected urban populations especially in major metropolitan areas such as Beijing and Shanghai.' Why is this a subsidy? Because the required scores for admission to college are lower for the residents of Beijing and Shanghai to attend colleges in those cities than for, say, the residents of Sichuan or Guizhou. Actually this form of discrimination is principally discrimination against rural residents since a student with a *hukou* in Chengdu can be admitted to a college in Chengdu with a lower score than a student from a village in Sichuan.

In Chapter 7 Daniel Goodkind and Loraine A. West summarize the available and often confusing evidence on the size of the floating population – primarily those living in urban areas but without an urban *hukou*. They find that studies define the floating population in different ways. They note a special study for 1999 in which the floating population was defined as being away from the residence of their *hukou* for six months or longer and found that 63.8 million people were involved. In their chapter they note a recent change with respect to the education of children of temporary migrants, which are all those people who do not have a *hukou* in the city in which they reside regardless of how long they may have lived there. Cities are now required to provide schooling for children of migrants who have lived in the city for six months or more. However, the migrant children go to special schools, not the regular urban schools.

Aimin Chen and N. Edward Coulson analyze factors affecting the growth of the non-agricultural populations of Chinese cities. For those not very familiar with the organization of Chinese cities it may be noted that most Chinese cities above a certain size include an agricultural area of some size. Their study covered the period from 1995–98. They found that cities with a relatively large service sector grew most rapidly. Foreign direct investment was positive in encouraging inmigration. However, domestic investment did not encourage migration. They found, somewhat surprisingly, that the conditions of housing, transportation and government fiscal expenditures had little effect on migration.

Shuanglin Lin and Shunfeng Song analyzed the relationship between per capita GDP growth and investment, foreign direct investment, labor force growth, government expenditures and urban infrastructure of 189 large and medium sized cities for 1991–98. Their results were quite consistent with those obtained by Chen and Coulson, namely that while foreign direct investment was positively related to growth, total investment as a share of GDP was not and the share of government in GDP had a negative effect on growth. They found no evidence of convergence in per capita GDP among Chinese cities.

Mei Wen argues that the empirical evidence indicates that the development of rural industry may have stunted China's urban development. I believe that it is more accurate to say that the unwillingness to permit reasonably free migration from rural to urban areas encouraged rural development of industry and slowed the rate of urban development. I believe it is an unsettled question whether urban areas could have created the 100 million jobs that were created by township and village enterprises between 1984 and the mid-1990s in addition to the jobs that were created in urban areas over the same period. Is it not possible that the township and village enterprises were due to managerial and entrepreneurial resources and capital that would not have otherwise been mobilized?

Zouhong Pan and Fan Zhang analyze the effect of city size on productivity. They found that every doubling of city size resulted in a 8.6 per cent gain in firm productivity. Their result calls into question the long-term viability of my proposal to generate the majority of the jobs required by 2030 to reduce employment in agriculture to 10 per cent of total employment in small cities and towns in each county with the workers continuing to live in villages and commute on a daily basis to their work. There need to be 12 to 15 million new jobs created annually to accommodate the growth of the nation's labor force plus the number of workers who will transfer from farm to nonfarm jobs. I argue that is highly unlikely that cities will be willing to accept the huge numbers of migrants year after year that would be required if most of these new nonfarm jobs were to be found in existing cities. The advantage of creating a large percentage of the new nonfarm jobs in cities and towns near where people now live is the enormous capital saving in housing and creating new urban areas that would be required to serve the workers if they migrated to cities.

If the gains from agglomeration are of the size indicated, my proposal would be a transitional one. Gradually over time the workers would migrate to larger cities. But when they migrated the situation would be quite different from migration today. If the villages are made better places in which to live as I argue they should be, the education of workers coming from rural areas will approach that of urban workers. In addition, the workers who have held nonfarm jobs for a significant period of time – say a decade or more – will enter the urban labor markets with a significant level of skills. Both of these factors will make the transition to a largely urban economy much more manageable than it would be if most of the migration occurred over the next three decades.

And not all of the workers would leave the rural areas. In highly industrialized countries such as France and the United States approximately a quarter of the population continues to live in rural areas, with rural areas defined as living in communities with populations of less than 2,500.

The urban-rural income disparity in China is among the highest in the world and much higher than existed in other countries at the same stage of development. As a result the level of employment in rural areas is much greater than it would have been had there been no restrictions on migration in the past. Consequently if the restrictions on migration were now lifted the migration from rural to urban areas would be enormous. It could easily approach 4 per cent of the rural population or 30 million per year of whom nearly 20 million would be members of the labor force. I argue in my chapter that this is not going to happen – that the existing large cities are not going to permit the inflow of migrants that this would imply. Consequently I suggest that there should be a policy of encouraging the creation of rural nonfarm jobs in one or two towns in each county. If this were done, the employees of these enterprises could continue to live in the villages and commute to work on a daily basis if there were adequate bus service and quality roads. To make this a viable policy, life in the villages must be improved to include TV service, tap water, inside toilets and, above all else, improved schools.

China faces many decisions in the years ahead with respect to urbanization. How will the *hukou* system be further modified? Will it be eliminated? If restrictions on migration are eliminated, will policies be developed that will assist in achieving an orderly transfer of people from rural to urban areas?

If China does do anything it will be the only country that ever has. Above all else, the huge income disparity between urban and rural areas means that China faces a situation that is orders of magnitude greater than that faced by any other country, either in the past or currently.

There are other and equally interesting chapters in this volume that I have not commented upon. I recommend them to you. This volume provides a quite remarkable background of information and ideas about urbanization in China as well as a presentation of problems that China faces in the years ahead as it urbanizes further.

Introduction

AIMIN CHEN
Indiana State University

GORDON G. LIU
University of North Carolina

KEVIN H. ZHANG
Illinois State University

I   The Issue

China is an economy of vast size and is primarily rural. As such, China is in the midst of a most rapid urbanization and the Chinese government has made it a developmental priority to further urbanize. Urbanization refers to both aspects of urban population growth and urban place expansion. The latter is a spatial measure, which, in China, is indicated by the administrative adjustment of rural villages to townships and towns, and towns to urban cities. China has upgraded many towns into urban cities and rural townships into towns. The number of cities has increased from 450 in 1989 to 663 in 2000 (*China Urban Statistical Yearbook*, 1990–2001). The number of towns increased from 2176 at the beginning of the reform to 20,374 in 2001 (*China Small City Series I*, CCTV, 1 May 2002).

The substance of the spatial adjustment is the growth of the non-agricultural population, which is, therefore, the most important measure of urbanization. Since 1978, China has been experiencing the greatest rural-urban migration in the history of the world, and its urban population rate had doubled, from 18 per cent in 1978 to 36 per cent in 2000 and was nearly 38 per cent in 2001 (*China Statistical Yearbook*, 2002, p. 93). Despite the rapid increase in urban population, however, China's urbanization is said to have lagged behind the world's average urbanization rate of 50 per cent (*Xinhua News*, 30 October 2001, www.cnd.org/global/01/10/30) as well as China's own industrialization rate of 51.1 per cent (ibid., p. 52) and the rate of non-agricultural employment of 50 per cent in 2001 (ibid., p. 119). Moreover, many critical issues accompany

China's urban transformation. What accounts for urban population in China? What corrective policies must be implemented to accelerate China's urbanization? How would Chinese cities cope, economically, environmentally, and politically, with the rapid influxes of rural population into the cities? What mode of urbanization should China take? How large should Chinese cities be? How should Chinese cities' development yield agglomeration and scale economies? What role should the government play in the process?

Attempting to answer the questions of critical concern, this book intends to present the Chinese urbanization experience, to analyze the issues of theoretical and empirical importance, and to derive policy suggestions relevant for China, other centrally planned economies, as well as countries of similar economic development. The book deals with the following aspects of China's urbanization: 1) a general description and evaluation of China's urbanization situation and critical challenges facing the Chinese government; 2) changing patterns of China's urban population and their determinants; 3) spatial structures of cities and industrial distribution; and 4) urban productivity growth and roles of mega cities in national development.

II   The Background

Studies of China's urbanization are of importance for China's vast size, unique history, and exemplary impact. Academic issues and policy implications arising from China's experiences are relevant beyond China. The current book draws on, and extends from, the studies presented at the international conference, 'Urbanization in China: Challenges and Strategies of Growth and Development,' held June 2001, in Xiamen, China. The Chinese Economists Society (CES), a US-based academic organization of China-interest scholars from around the world, organized the conference. More than 150 scholars, policy makers, and business leaders from Australia, China (including Taiwan and Hong Kong), France, Singapore, and the United States participated or presented their work at the conference, reflecting well the importance and the urgency of the subject matter. The conference hosted over 90 paper presentations that were selected from over 160 submissions. The majority of the chapters are selected and adapted from the papers presented at the conference, with a few others solicited from scholars with expertise in the field and on topics of particular interest to complement the theme of the book. The book thus includes only the high-quality research that will illustrate the thematic issues in a comprehensive and coherent manner.

Compared with the available literature, this book stands out not only in its coverage of an important issue concerning a most important developing country undergoing market transition, but also in the comprehensiveness of its coverage of the history, characterization, theoretical modeling and empirical evidence, as well as the policy implications of China's urbanization. Moreover, the quality of the studies included and the prominence of many authors of these studies make the current volume still more significant. We hope to make a timely contribution to the understanding of China's urbanization not only for academics and students of China studies, but also policy makers and a broader audience who are interested in China's development.

III An Overview

The book's 15 chapters are organized as follows: Part I characterizes China's urbanization, Part II analyzes changing urban population, Part III investigates China's urban spatial structures, and Part IV deals with urban productivity and growth. In Part I, D. Gale Johnson[1] opens with his analysis of the effect of creating rural non-farm jobs on China's urbanization. He estimates that, to stop the widening of the current urban-rural income disparity, it will require approximately 15 million new non-farm jobs annually to provide for the number of workers that will need to leave agriculture and the growth of the nation's labor force annually over the next three decades. An alternative to migration of rural labor into large cities and to employment by TVEs that merits consideration is to create most of the new non-farm jobs in small cities and towns within commuting distances of the villages in which the rural workers now live. This would greatly reduce the enormous capital investment that would be required if the workers actually migrated to the locations where the new jobs were created. In Chapter 2, Kevin Zhang documents the evolution of the Chinese urban transformation in the last 50 years. He divides the period 1949–2000 into four stages based on China's urban policy and urbanization levels: the first stage of 1949–57, the second stage of 1958–65, the third of 1966–77, and the last stage 1978–2000. Reviewing salient features of China's urbanization and urban policy in the pre-reform and the reform periods respectively, he concludes that, relative to other developing countries at similar stages of development, China's urbanization since 1949 has been characterized by low levels and strict controls of rural-urban migration.

---

1   We are deeply saddened by the passing away of Professor D. Gale Johnson in April 2003. A great scholar and a kind friend to China, he will be remembered.

Yi Feng and Siddharth Swaminathan in Chapter 3 use a political economy model to study the relationship between urbanization and demographic change in China, based on data for the period 1960–95. The results show that while birth rates in the urban areas are affected by political stability and government capacity, birth rates in the countryside are not. The major policy implication of this discrepancy is that in order to sustain its economic development, China must urbanize the countryside demographically, economically and politically to produce a set of conditions that favor long-term growth. Chapter 4, by Qi Hong Dong, discusses why and how to carry out rural urbanization in China, based on the author's field research of urbanization in Fujian Province of China and her investigation of lessons from the US and OECD countries. She suggests that government rural policies should focus on privatization, cluster, comparative advantage, competition, and bottom-up development initiatives, which may raise rural income and ease the rural-urban migration pressure on cities to avoid industrialization-urbanization-Kuznets cycles.

The second part of the book starts with Chapter 5 by Aimin Chen and Edward Coulson in which they seek the causes of variation in the amount of migration to Chinese cities over the period 1995–99. Using a city fixed-effect model with lagged values of 'pulling' factors for each city, they find that while wage income shows no significant influence on migration, per capita gross city income does, suggesting that migrants seek returns above and beyond mere wages. Their regression results also show that cities with high ratios of manufacturing and service sectors grow most rapidly and that the developmental environment and the job creation potential of the private sector, indicated by the number of proprietors per capita, makes a significant difference in attracting migrants. Except for government fiscal expenditures, they find that the attributes of the quality of urban life, such as housing-market conditions and transportation, have little explanatory power. Jeff Xie and Kevin Zhang in Chapter 6 examine the link between urbanization and economic development in the period 1978–98 in both time-series and cross-section formats. The authors find that: 1) the rising national urbanization is basically caused by economic growth, and no feedback is observed; and 2) the level of urbanization in a province is too determined by its level of economic development, along with geographic and historical factors. Then Daniel Goodkind and Loraine West in the next chapter make an effort to define and measure China's floating population (*liudong renkou*) that comprises an important part of migrants and the impact of this population group on China's urbanization. The authors discuss the ambiguities and identify a variety of definitions that they think are pertinent. In the process, they analyze the major sources of data (censuses, migration surveys, and household registration lists) in terms of their analytical potential and methodological limitations, review existing studies, update statistics, and examine factors that have affected recent trends and are likely to affect future trends in migration and the floating population.

Chapter 8, by Fei-Ling Wang, discusses the unique nature of China's urbanization, the *hukou* (household registration) system as a highly institutionalized and deeply legitimized way of controlling the pace and size of China's urbanization. The author points out that after two decades of comprehensive economic reform, the *hukou* system has adopted several important changes of its own and has thus become fairly accommodating to the needs of labor mobility yet at the same time provides a strong support for China's political and social stability. China's urbanization, as a consequence, has been highly controlled, orderly, and slow.

Part III turns from the systemic structure of China's urbanization to the spatial structure. Shunfeng Song and Kevin Zhang in Chapter 9 investigate the spatial dynamics of China's city system by applying the Pareto law of city-size distribution. Based on 1985 and 1999 city-level data, they find that Chinese cities are quite evenly distributed and the intercity concentration declined in the 1980s and 1990s. They also find that the Pareto law fits the Chinese data quite well. Several factors have contributed to the rapid urban growth and changes in urban systems in the past two decades. The recent industrialization of China's economy has created many job opportunities in cities and attracted many rural workers to migrate into urban areas. The urban sector reform has relaxed many rural-urban migration restrictions and resulted in a huge influx of rural workers in cities. The open-door policy and foreign direct investment have also helped China to become more urbanized, especially in the coastal areas. The government's urban policy and the inclusion of many new cities have affected Chinese city-size distributions. Mei Wen in Chapter 10 investigates the coordination issue between China's industry and urban development. The author, through historical investigation on locations of two-digit manufacturing industries, suggests that it is desirable to develop large and medium sized cities for promoting the formation of new special-large and super-large cities and that Central and Western China need to develop satellite cities and transportation hubs to enhance their economic growth. The next chapter by Xiaobo Zhang addresses the question of how industrialization and urbanization affect land use. The author analyzes the determinants of land use by modeling arable land and sown area separately. An inverse U-shaped relationship between land use intensity and industrialization is explored both theoretically and empirically. The findings highlight the conflict between the two policy goals of industrialization and grain self-sufficiency. Several policy recommendations are offered to reconcile the conflict.

The final part of the book deals with urban economic growth, starting with Chapter 12 by Shuanglin Lin and Shunfeng Song. This chapter analyzes the relationship between per capita GDP growth and investment, foreign direct investment, labor force growth, government expenditures, and urban infrastructures based on the data for 189 large and medium sized Chinese cities for the period 1991–98. Cross-section analyses indicate that several factors, such as foreign investment, paved roads, and government expenditures on science and technology were positively related to per capita GDP growth, while the overall size of government, measured by total government spending share in GDP, appears negatively related to per capita GDP growth. Contrary to the literature on economic growth, total investment share in GDP was insignificantly related to per capita GDP growth. Also, there is no clear evidence of convergence in per capita GDP among Chinese cities. In Chapter 13, Zuohong Pan and Fan Zhang make an attempt to identify possible agglomeration economies in Chinese urban areas. Over 120,000 firm-level production data cross 28 industries from the Third National Industrial Survey, along with the urban population data of 200 cities are used. The results reveal strong and significant agglomeration economies in Chinese urban areas. The estimated average agglomeration elasticity is around 0.051, implying a 3.6 per cent gain in firm productivity for every doubling of the city size. The breakdown analysis suggests that the major source of the agglomeration advantage comes from localization effect – benefits from concentration of firms of the same industry within one geographical area, rather than urbanization effect – externalities from urban development itself. The Maximum size study also suggests that, while most of the Chinese cities have yet to grow to demonstrate the full strength of agglomeration economies, many Chinese industries have reached the 'optimal' industry size within a 'given' urban area.

Chapter 14, by Zhigang Tao and Richard Wong, examines how, along with its urban growth, Hong Kong has transformed itself from entrepôt to manufacturing during the period from 1951 to the late 1970s, and then from manufacturing to producer services since the late 1970s. In each case, the transformation was triggered by the change in Hong Kong's relations with mainland China. The former transformation was due to the sudden and dramatic decrease in China trade following the United Nations trade embargo; and the latter was a response to the open-door policy adopted in mainland China since the late 1970s. The last chapter by Hanchao Lu attempts to explain the phenomenon of rising Shanghai. The author first looks at the development of China's largest city in a historical perspective, then outlines Shanghai's major economic developments at the turn of the twenty-first century, including urban development, stock market, key industries, and mega business deals. This chapter compares Shanghai with New York City in the areas of commercial culture, tradition of cosmopolitanism and entrepreneurship, and their sizes in relation to the nation. The author suggests that Shanghai should be allowed more autonomy in business decision-making in order to be able to compete in global markets. Most importantly, Shanghai needs an institutionalized and transparent legal system that can warrant fair play in all business conducts. The author concludes that Shanghai's remarkable achievements in recent years have placed it facing an even greater challenge on its road toward 'China's New York City.'

IV   Acknowledgements

We thank all the participants of the international conference, Urbanization in China: Challenges and Strategies of Growth and Development, for contributing their quality research; we thank those involved in the organization of the conference for making it a success. We appreciate the research assistance that went into the studies collected in the volume as well as the editorial assistance in preparing the volume for publication. Finally, we are grateful to the Ford Foundation, the Asian Development Bank, Topsun Technology Company, Eli Lilly (China), Xiamen University, and the Xiamen Committee of Chinese People's Political Consultative Conference for their financial support.

PART I: CHARACTERISTICS OF CHINA'S URBANIZATION

CHAPTER 1

CAN AGRICULTURAL LABOR ADJUSTMENT OCCUR PRIMARILY THROUGH CREATION OF RURAL NONFARM JOBS IN CHINA?

D. GALE JOHNSON*
The University of Chicago

Abstract

If China's rural families are to participate fully in the future economic growth there must be a large reduction in the number of farm workers. In order to accommodate the reduction needed over the next three decades, there will need to be 12–15 million new non-farm jobs created every year. Township and village enterprises have provided roughly 100 million new jobs since 1985, but in recent years there has been little increase in such jobs. One problem is that these enterprises are very small-industrial enterprises with an average of about 11 workers. As the Chinese economy becomes more competitive, such small enterprises have experienced increasing difficulty in maintaining employment, let alone providing millions of new jobs each year. Where can the new jobs be provided? Due to continuing restrictions on migration, it is unlikely that many will become available in cities. An alternative is proposed, namely to promote the development of enterprises in one or two towns or small cities in each county. The workers could then continue to live in the villages and commute to their jobs on a daily basis. The advantage of this alternative is that it requires far less capital than if the same number of workers migrated with their families to cities.

This is a reprint of the original paper published in *Urban Studies* (http://www.tandf.co.uk), 39 (12), 2002.

The curse of being born on a farm in an economy that is undergoing economic growth is that the odds are great that you will have to choose to be something other than a farmer. Of course, an even greater curse would be that if significant economic growth did not occur, you would have little choice but to remain a farmer, and you would be poor all your life.

The people now living in rural China will face many difficult adjustments in the years ahead – many hard choices must be made. These choices will be based on emerging new opportunities; fortunately fewer and fewer will be faced with choices based on escaping poverty. Should one migrate to a large city? Would one be permitted to do so? Should one start a business in the village or a small town? Should one give up his or her land use rights? Should one try to find a job in a local TVE? And then give up farming? Or remain as a part-time farmer? These are not easy decisions, lightly made. It is not that only a few people will have to make such decisions but over the next three decades nearly every rural adult will face such decisions and more than three fourths of them, hopefully, will decide to leave farming entirely or in large part. This is what economic growth will require of the people of rural China over the next several decades if they are to share in it.

Labor Adjustment That Has Occurred

China has already undergone very significant adjustment of its rural labor force. In 1952 87.5 per cent of its population was rural; by 1978 the percentage had dropped only slightly, to 82.1 per cent. Since 1978 the adjustment has been much more rapid with a decline to 69.6 per cent (SSB, 1999). However, the shift in employment of rural people out of the primary sector has been significantly greater than the change in the rural population.[1] In 1952 employment in the primary sector was 83.5 per cent of national employment; in 1978 70.5 per cent and in 1998 49.8 per cent, according to the official data (SSB, 1999, p. 134). The official data significantly underestimates the decline in employment in the primary sector and thus in agriculture. But accepting the official data for the moment, approximately 35 per cent of the employment in rural areas was outside of the primary sector in 1998.

---

[1]   The primary sector includes somewhat more than farming, forestry, animal husbandry and fisheries. Presumably it also includes mining but employment in mining is only about a third of the difference between employment in primary industries in 1997 (347.3 million) and in farming, forestry, animal husbandry and fisheries (324.3 million) (SSB, 1998, pp. 126, 132 and 388).

If employment in agriculture (farming plus animal husbandry) is the same proportion as it is of value added in farming, forestry, animal husbandry and fisheries, then employment in agriculture as officially estimated in 1998 was 283 million or 61 per cent of total employment in the rural sector or 40.5 per cent of total national employment (SSB, 1999, pp. 377 and 380). But this estimate of agricultural employment is certainly an overestimate. The State Statistical Bureau still counts the millions of temporary migrants to the cities as employed in rural areas and probably in the primary sector.[2] It is now clear that agriculture no longer provides employment for the majority of the workers of China. Roughly speaking, it is highly probable that in 1952 agricultural employment was about 75 per cent of the total; today it is almost certainly less than 40 per cent.

Labor Adjustment Yet to Occur

In spite of the enormous adjustment in the distribution of labor that has already occurred, much remains to be accomplished if rural people are to share in China's economic growth in the future. Until quite recently, rural people have so far shared relatively equally in the benefits of economic growth during the reform period. Real per capita consumption has more than trebled (SSB, 1999, p. 72). While the increase in per capita income and consumption that occurred between 1978 and 1985 was due primarily to the improved productivity of agriculture and increases in real output prices, since 1985 a significant part of the improvement has been due to the increased importance of income from nonfarm employment and activities. In 1978 only 4 per cent of the income of farm households was attributed to nonfarm activities; in 1985 the nonfarm percentage had increased to 31 per cent and in 1998 the percentage had increased to 43 per cent. Transfer and property income accounted for

---

2   According to the State Statistical Bureau, in 1998 urban employment was 55.2 per cent of the urban population; in 1978 it was 54.5 per cent (SSB, 1999). There were very few temporary rural to urban migrants in 1978. We know that the temporary rural to urban migrants are still counted as rural residents, where they are registered. There is no way the urban employment data could include as many as 50 million employed migrants. The percentage of the urban population that was employed declined between 1990 to 1998 when the large increase in temporary migrants occurred; it would clearly have increased if the migrants were included in urban employment. It is possible that employment in agriculture (farming plus animal husbandry) is as low as 233 million if there are 50 million rural migrants on average throughout the year in cities.

approximately 6 per cent of total income in 1985 and 1998. Ignoring transfer and property income, it can be said that more than half of the increase in the income of rural people – perhaps as much as 55 per cent – came from nonfarm sources for the full 20 year period. Without the large increase in nonfarm sources of income for rural people, the improvement in farm productivity would have contributed little to their incomes.

The negative side of this positive story is that with nonfarm sources of income contributing more than half the increase in real income for rural people, the per capita consumption of urban households in 1998 was 3.3 times that of rural residents compared to 2.9 times in 1978 (SSB, 1999, p. 72); the ratio in 1952 has been estimated as 2.4 times. Thus the recent disparities in urban and rural consumption are probably greater than in 1978 and significantly greater than in 1952. These are comparisons in current prices. Thus the large adjustment in the sources of income and employment by rural people has approximately stabilized their position relative to the urban population. But was that a significant achievement? The really quite enormous changes in rural China – an increase of nearly 100 million jobs in the TVEs and more than 40 million jobs in private enterprises or self employment – was just sufficient to maintain approximately the same level of relative consumption or income. It is absolutely clear that the future prosperity of rural people does not rest primarily with agriculture but with finding more nonfarm jobs for workers now engaged in farming as well as for the new entrants to the rural labor force. The history of the past two decades makes it very clear that the transfer of labor out of agriculture must be even more rapid than it has been if the large differentials between urban and rural per capita consumption and income are to be significantly reduced.

I hasten to add that while more agricultural employment will not be the source of an increase in the relative incomes of rural people, increasing productivity in agriculture is essential to keep China's agriculture competitive in the world market and to expand food production to keep pace with demand.

I have projected that by 2030 farm employment will decline from about 41 per cent to 10 per cent of national employment (Johnson, 2000a). This assumes that as economic growth occurs that farm employment will decline by 3 per cent annually from an estimated level of 283.5 million in 1997. To accommodate the reduction in farm employment of 180 million plus the new entrants to the labor force in both rural and urban areas will require an average annual increase in nonfarm employment of 15 million (Johnson, 2000a, p. 329). This seems like an enormous task and it is, but the rate of nonfarm job creation required is 2.4 per cent annually, which is significantly less than the

5 per cent annual increase during the reform period though during the 1990s the rate declined to little more than 4 per cent (SSB, 1999, p. 134).

Urban-Rural Income Differences

The absolute levels, in current prices, of the series on urban and rural per capita consumption, income and living expenditures are given in Table 1.1; the ratios are found in Table 1.2. Regardless of which series you accept, the differences are large and there is little evidence that the past decade has seen any narrowing of the differences. The series on per capita consumption is the most inclusive, recognizing in-kind sources of consumption in both urban and rural areas. These nonmoney sources of consumption are much more important in urban than in rural areas. For example, in 1998 per capita living expenditures of urban households was 4,332 yuan while the total per capita consumption was 6,182 yuan or 43 per cent more. In rural areas the difference was much smaller – 1,895 versus 1,590 – a difference of 19 per cent (SSB, 1999, pp. 72, 326 and 341). Per capita data for the three series for urban and rural households are given in Table 1.1 while the urban to rural ratios are given in Table 1.2.[3]

Why are these series relevant to the topic of the location of new nonfarm job opportunities that will be needed for agricultural adjustment in the future? They are relevant because not only must the process of reducing the labor in agriculture offset the combined effects of the relative decline in demand for farm products and the more rapid rate of growth of labor productivity that is

---

3   Only the nominal data are given. For both per capita consumption and income SSB also presents series in 'comparable prices'. However, the price series are not described and they differ significantly between urban and rural areas. For example, the price series used to deflate consumption increases 25 per cent more in urban than rural areas from 1978 to 1998 while the deflator for income increases 35 per cent more. There are consumer price indexes for urban areas going back to 1978 but the rural price index is not available prior to 1985. But if it is assumed that rural prices would have changed as urban prices did between 1978 and 1985, then the index of urban prices increased by only 12 per cent more than rural prices. The price index used to deflate rural incomes increased only 11 per cent between 1978 and 1985 – this seems impossible because of the much greater increases in farm product prices. The grain price derived from the household surveys, for example increased by 52 per cent between 1978 and 1985 and grain accounted for 44 per cent of all food expenditures in 1978. If the 1978 expenditure weights were used, the increase in grain prices used in the household surveys would have increased consumer prices for rural households by 23 per cent if all other prices had remained unchanged, which they did not do. The purchase prices for wheat and rice, the main grains consumed by farm people, increased an average of about 70 per cent between 1978 and 1985 (SSB, 1986).

Table 1.1   Per capita consumption, income and living expenditures, urban and rural residents in current prices, 1978 to 2000, China (yuan)

Year	Consumption		Income[a]		Living expenditure	
	Urban	Rural	Urban	Rural	Urban	Rural
1978	405	138	344	134	n/a	116
1979	406	152	387	160	n/a	134
1980	496	178	478	191	n/a	162
1981	520	192	500	223	457	191
1982	526	210	535	270	471	220
1983	547	232	573	310	506	248
1984	598	265	660	355	559	274
1985	802	347	739	398	673	317
1986	833	351	900	424	799	357
1987	1089	417	1002	463	884	398
1988	1431	508	1181	545	1104	477
1989	1568	553	1376	602	1211	535
1990	1686	571	1510	686	1279	585
1991	1925	621	1701	709	1454	620
1992	2356	718	2027	784	1672	659
1993	3027	855	2577	922	2111	770
1994	3891	1118	3496	1221	2851	1017
1995	4874	1434	4283	1578	3538	1310
1996	5430	1768	4839	1926	3920	1572
1997	5796	1876	5160	2090	4186	1617
1998	6182	1895	5425	2162	4332	1590
1999	6996	1927	5854	2210	4616	1577
2000	–	–	6280	2253	4998	1670

Notes: a) The urban income measure is the per capita annual disposable income. The rural income measure is after payment of personal taxes. n/a = not available.

Sources: NBS (various years).

likely to occur in farming, it will be necessary for further reduction in farm labor to narrow the large difference in consumption and income between urban and rural areas. This adjustment is additional to what is required to keep the current urban-rural disparities from widening. I think one can easily argue that if all the next three to five decades hold for farm people is the maintenance of the current disparities, economic policy has failed to mitigate the current enormous urban bias.

Table 1.2 **Ratio of urban to rural per capita consumption, income and living expenditures in current prices, 1978–2000, China**

Year	Consumption	Income	Living expenditure
1978	2.93	2.57	n/a
1979	2.67	n/a	n/a
1980	2.79	2.50	n/a
1981	2.71	2.54	2.39
1982	2.50	1.98	2.14
1983	2.36	1.85	2.04
1984	2.26	1.86	2.04
1985	2.31	1.86	2.12
1986	2.37	2.12	2.24
1987	2.61	2.17	2.22
1988	2.82	2.17	2.32
1989	2.84	2.29	2.26
1990	2.95	2.20	2.19
1991	3.10	2.40	2.35
1992	3.28	2.58	2.54
1993	3.54	2.80	2.74
1994	3.48	2.86	2.80
1995	3.40	2.71	2.70
1996	3.07	2.51	2.49
1997	3.09	2.47	2.59
1998	3.26	2.51	2.72
1999	3.52	2.65	2.93
2000	n/a	2.79	2.99

n/a = not available.

Sources: NBS (various years).

It is not the objective of this chapter to discuss in detail the major factors responsible for such large differences in per capita consumption or income; I have dealt with this issue elsewhere (2000b). Very briefly, there have been three major policy areas that have adversely affected rural incomes. First, since 1960 there have been restrictions on rural to urban migration; the control of such migration has been the primary means by which the difference between urban and rural incomes has been maintained at such a high ratio. Second, rural education has been less accessible and of lower quality than urban education;

rural people possess less human capital than urban people and if in comparable situations, would produce less and have lower incomes.[4] Third, there has been an enormous urban bias in the allocation of investment and credit. In recent years there may have been a fourth factor, namely the heavy subsidization of state owned enterprises which permitted many of them to pay increasingly higher real wages while making losses and/or very low returns on capital.

The migration restrictions have greatly inhibited a major means by which rural people can adapt to economic growth, namely by migrating to cities as the relative demand for farm labor declines. This has been the primary process throughout the world and throughout history. Wage differences such as have existed between urban and rural China for the past half century would have resulted in high rates of rural to urban migration and did in the late 1950s, but the majority of the migrants were sent home during the Great Famine and not permitted to return to the cities.

Regardless of where the new nonfarm jobs required to absorb the labor force that needs to leave agriculture in the decades ahead are located, it is essential that rural education at the primary and secondary levels be brought up to the urban standards with respect to availability and quality. Rural people should be given the same access to the creation of human capital as urban people, no matter where the jobs are to be found. And, of course, if the new jobs are to be primarily in rural areas, the current discriminations in the availability of investment and credit must be eliminated.

Where Will Future Nonfarm Jobs be Located?

The majority of the new nonfarm jobs that has made it possible to reduce agriculture's share of national employment in China have been located in rural areas. Migration to urban areas has provided a significant number of

---

4   An indicator of the difference in quality of education between urban and rural areas is expenditure per pupil. In 1997 the expenditure per primary pupil in urban areas was 1,379 yuan compared to 316 yuan in rural areas; for junior secondary schools the expenditures were, respectively, 2,414 and 645 (SSB, 1998). In both cases, the urban expenditures per pupil were approximately four times the rural expenditures. Increasing both the amount and quality of rural education is very important to the future of China's economy. Due to the decline in urban fertility, nearly all of the net addition to China's labor force in the decades ahead will come from the rural sector. As of 1990 the rural labor force had 5.8 years of schooling compared to 9.5 years in urban areas (SSB, 1993). Thus the average years of schooling of the national labor force might actually decline in the years ahead unless rural education is significantly improved.

jobs, but a clear minority of the total nonfarm jobs to which farm workers have transferred. Most of the transfer to nonfarm jobs has occurred since the early 1980s.

The rapid development of rural nonfarm jobs in China since the early 1980s has been quite remarkable. The number of such jobs may have increased by more than 100 million between 1984 and 1998 according to the available and somewhat incomplete data. But it is disturbing to note that TVE employment in 1998 was little higher than in 1993 though self-employment and employment in private enterprises increased by 24 million over the same period (SSB, 1999, p. 137).[5] Another disturbing aspect of developments in 1999 and 2000 has been that rural household incomes have increased at a slower rate than urban household incomes. Part of the decline in relative incomes has undoubtedly been due to declining prices for many farm products but the slow pace of growth in rural nonfarm employment has undoubtedly had a role as well.

There are a number of reasons to doubt whether the future development of TVEs or rural nonfarm enterprises can depend on enterprises located primarily in the villages. Enterprises located in villages may suffer from a number of disadvantages. One is their small size – the average number of employees in all TVEs in 1998 was six workers; industrial TVEs had an average of about 11 employees. Enterprises of this size are simply too small to obtain the advantages of economies of scale or the productivity improvement due to specialization of the workers. A recent report of the Xinhua News Agency is a cause for concern about whether the Government of China comprehends the magnitude of the labor adjustment problem facing rural China: 'Over the next five years village-level enterprises hope to provide 10 million new employment opportunities as the government accelerates the industrialization and urbanization of the countryside' (China Online, 31 January 2001). If only 2 million new jobs are created in villages each year, nearly six times that number must be created elsewhere to accommodate the needed agricultural labor adjustment. There are two possible interpretations of the 2 million figures. One is that it represents what the government believes is feasible for the development of further rural nonfarm jobs in the villages and supports my conclusion that further expansion of such jobs is very limited. The other is that it is believed that the annual creation of 2 million new nonfarm jobs will make a significant contribution to the labor adjustment process and the incomes of rural people. There will be very little effect and if this is all or

---

5   It is possible that some of the increase in employment in private enterprises is due to a reclassification of TVEs to exclude some of the smaller enterprises that were privately owned but formerly classified as TVEs.

nearly all of the new nonfarm jobs available to rural people, the urban-rural income disparity will drastically increase over the next five years.

Such enterprises have an added disadvantage – cities have not become the dominant location of nonfarm enterprises, whether industrial, financial, advanced education and research and transportation, by accident but because there are advantages of agglomeration as well as of economies of scale. Cities make it possible for specialization to occur and be productive because in cities a firm can have ready access to a wide range of services and products while these require special and costly efforts for village enterprises to acquire or loss of productivity if they go without them.

The great success of the TVEs located in villages and the townships has been due to several factors, some of which may not prevail now or in the future. First, the low wage rate in rural areas, due primarily to the restraints on migration; the wage rate is low even after you account for differences in human capital between workers in urban and rural areas. Second, until the early 1990s the urban industrial structure, consisting primarily of SOEs, was inefficient and monopolized, permitting very high rates of profits for the newly emerging enterprises – the TVEs. This has now radically changed – virtually every industrial sector now has excess capacity and prices in most sectors are no longer monopoly prices. Third, the policy framework within which the TVEs functioned favored efficient and low cost producers. The majority of the TVEs operated with a hard budget constraint – in most cases, financial losses soon resulted in dissolution. This meant that inefficient and high cost TVEs were weeded out while such SOEs continued to be rescued by the government. The TVEs, including most of those owned by local governments, were forced to produce at low cost – this was not by choice but imposed by the conditions for survival.

Let me note now that there are many TVEs that can continue to operate in the villages and townships. Approximately 20 per cent of the workers are employed in construction and transportation and another 20 per cent in commerce, trade, catering and other services. It may well be that these TVEs either serve local customers or are not at a disadvantage due to the absence of economies of scale. But the industrial enterprises, which now employ about 60 per cent of the rural nonfarm workers, find themselves in precarious positions.

But even if the existing TVEs can be profitable and perhaps even slowly expand, if there are to be enough new rural nonfarm jobs to meet the growth of the rural labor force and of the workers who can no longer be profitably employed in agriculture, other sources of new nonfarm jobs must be found. Each year over the next three decades at least 15 million new nonfarm jobs must be found to permit the farm labor force to decline by 3 per cent annually and to provide jobs for the new entrants into the national labor force.

Can all or most of these new jobs be located in rural areas, not in villages solely or even primarily but in small cities and towns? This is a question that I wish to address.

An Alternative to Migration

The current policy of the government of China is to encourage the development of new nonfarm jobs in small cities and towns, including the enlargement of existing cities and towns as well as the development of new ones. There is some evidence, based on the experience in Jiangsu where the transfer of population from villages to smaller urban areas that it is intended that the workers and their families move to the urban areas as well. I wish to suggest that for the next few decades that an alternative approach should be considered, namely to locate many if not most of the new nonfarm job opportunities within commuting distance of the majority of village residents.

If the jobs, the workers and their families are moved from the villages, the capital investment required will be enormous. If 450 million new nonfarm jobs were all to be located in small cities and towns (the current number of TVE jobs would continue to be in the villages and townships), this would mean constructing housing for approximately 750 million people, since each worker has to provide housing for himself or herself plus an average of 0.65 dependents.

If the average number of residents per household were the same as the average size of rural households in 1998 – 4.3 – approximately 175 million houses would be needed to accommodate 750 million people. Based on the average cost of construction in 1997 of rural houses – not urban houses – of 24,000 yuan, the total cost would be 4.2 trillion yuan or 140 billion yuan annually for 30 years. This is just the cost of construction and does not include the public costs of creating new urban communities – roads, public utilities (water, sewer and electricity), schools and other urban amenities might well add a cost comparable to the cost of housing. Actually, housing acceptable in urban areas would probably cost significantly more than the figure used. In any case, an enormous investment would be required if the workers in the new nonfarm jobs moved from the villages to any urban area.

The investment in housing and urban facilities would be additional to investment required for production. Even at the present rate of fixed assets per worker in TVE industrial enterprises, the total investment over three decades would be about 11 trillion RMB; however, the investment per worker might have to be substantially greater than this if wages in the new jobs were to approximate the wages of the workers in the existing cities – perhaps double or treble the figure given.

The alternative to the transfer of populations from the villages to new or expanded small cities and towns would be for most rural workers to remain in the villages and for those with jobs outside the village, to commute to their jobs. If this alternative is to be a viable one and result in the narrowing not only of income differentials but to improve the quality of life and well-being of the villagers, the villages must be made more attractive places in which to live and work for both those who will remain employed in the villages and those who have jobs elsewhere. If this alternative is to be an attractive one, it would require, in addition, that every village would be on an all weather road and that bus service be provided that would permit the workers to commute at a reasonable cost in terms of time and money on a daily basis.

What would be required to make villages more attractive places in which to live? Most villages in China lack one or more of the amenities that urban residents in China now take for granted – tap water, inside toilets, reliable and affordable electricity, and quality access to television signals. In 1998 only 9 per cent of rural residents had refrigerators, 23 per cent had washing machines and 33 per cent had color televisions (SSB, 1999, pp. 347–8). One reason rural residents had fewer appliances than urban residents was because their incomes are much lower (see Table 1.2), but this does not explain most of the differences in appliances that require public amenities, such as reliable and low cost electrical service and tap water.

Justin Yifu Lin has made a strong case for improving the quality of life in China's villages by establishing ground television satellite receiving stations, establishing wells and water towers and the distribution network to provide tap water in every village home, and radically improving the electricity supply and delivery network while lowering its cost (Lin, 2000). He has proposed these changes to meet a dual objective – to improve the quality of life in the villages and to eliminate excess industrial capacity in a number of industries producing home appliances as a means of stopping the deflation in China and better utilization of existing resources. He notes the very large difference in the price of electricity between urban and rural areas – prices are three to five times higher in rural than urban areas. Such a disparity in prices has a significant adverse effect on consumption in villages. La Mai has noted the large difference in electricity consumption between urban and rural areas:

'Rural power grids have outdated equipment and operate under irrational management systems. Although electricity is basically available throughout the country, average per-capita consumption of electricity in rural areas is merely one ninth that in urban areas …' (La, 2000, p. 42).

Above all else, the rural educational system must be transformed to provide the same opportunities, at the same cost, to rural students as is available in urban areas.[6] As of 1990 rural workers had approximately four years less schooling than urban workers (SSB, 1993). If earnings are to be equalized, this differential in schooling must be eliminated. And the quality of rural schools must be upgraded to equal those of urban schools. If many of the new nonfarm jobs are located in county seat and other small cities and every village is on an all weather road, then the majority of secondary schools in rural areas no longer will need to be boarding schools. The secondary schools can be in the employment centers in each county and the students can ride buses, just as the workers do. By itself, equalizing the amount and quality of schooling between rural and urban areas, in the absence of unrestricted migration, will not equalize labor earnings but it is a necessary condition for such equality.

It is also essential that the credit system provide access to sufficient credit for the establishment of the new enterprises needed to provide nonfarm employment for the rural residents. The current system appears not to be capable of doing so. It lends very little to private enterprises and has a strong urban bias, providing relatively little credit to rural areas. Only when banks are required to be profitable and are not imposed upon by politicians and governmental officials to make loans that have little prospect of being repaid will the types of enterprises involved in providing the new jobs receive adequate credit.

Concluding Comment

If rural people are to share fully in economic growth over the next several decades, millions of new nonfarm jobs must be created every year. Farm employment must decline as demand grows slowly and labor productivity increases at a significant rate and nonfarm jobs need to be available to facilitate

---

6   While nearly all rural children now graduate from primary school, only about 81 per cent graduate from junior secondary school and less than 3 per cent of all children complete senior secondary school. In urban areas, approximately one-third of the children complete senior secondary school and about 30 per cent of the students in counties and towns (SSB, 1999).

this employment decline as well as for new entrants to the labor force. The number of new nonfarm jobs that need to be created each year is enormous – of the order of 15 million over the next three decades. It is questionable whether the township and village enterprises located in villages can create many of the new jobs. One alternative is to develop policies that will encourage the development of industrial enterprises in small cities and towns that would permit many of the rural workers to continue to live in villages and commute to their jobs. This would greatly reduce the investments needed to accommodate the transfer of workers out of agriculture if that transfer were to occur through migration from rural areas to cities.

References

China Online (2001), 'Villages to Produce 10M New Jobs in Five Years,' 31 January 2001.

Economic Research Service (1973), *Farm Population Estimates 1910–70*, US Department of Agriculture, Statistical Bulletin No. 523. Washington, DC: US Department of Agriculture.

Ge Yenfeng (2000), 'Policy Suggestions on Alleviating the Contradictions of Income Distribution during the Tenth Five-Year Plan Period,' *China Development Review*, 2 (4), p. 73.

Johnson, D.G. (2000a), 'Agricultural Adjustment in China: Problems and Prospects,' *Population and Development Review*, 26 (2), pp 319–34.

Johnson, D.G. (2000b), 'Reducing the Urban-Rural Income Disparity,' Office of Agricultural Economics Research, The University of Chicago, Paper No. 00-07, 6 November 2000.

La, M. (2000) 'More Efforts for Development of the Rural Market,' *China Development Review*, 2 (1), pp. 39–45.

Li, T. and Zhang, J. (1998), 'Returns to Education under Collective and Household Farming in China,' *Journal of Development Economics*, 56, pp. 307–35.

Lin, J.Y. (2000), 'The Current Deflation in China: Causes and Policy Options,' China Center for Economic Research, Peking University, Working Paper Series, No. E2000002, February 2000.

State Statistical Bureau (1986, 1993, 1997, 1998, 1999), *China Statistical Yearbook*, Beijing: China Statistical Press.

Yang, D.T. (1997), 'Education in Production: Measuring Labor Quality and Management,' *American Journal of Agricultural Economics*, 59 (3), pp. 764–72.

Yang, D.T. (2000), 'Education and Allocative Efficiency: Household Income During Rural Reforms in China,' unpublished paper.

CHAPTER 2

THE EVOLUTION OF CHINA'S URBAN TRANSFORMATION: 1949–2000

KEVIN H. ZHANG*
Illinois State University

Abstract

Compared with other developing countries at similar stages of development, China's urbanization since 1949 has been characterized by low levels and strict controls over rural-urban migration. This chapter intends to document the evolution of the Chinese urban transformation in the last half of the twentieth century. Four stages in the period 1949–2000 may be identified based on China's urban policy and urbanization levels. The first stage (1949–57) and the last stage (1978–2000) are similar in terms of rapid urban growth and the strong link between urbanization and industrialization. The second stage (1958–65) witnessed sharp fluctuations in both urban policy and urban populations. Anti-urban bias and falling urbanization levels were the main features in the third stage (1966–77).

Keywords: Urbanization, industrialization, anti-urban bias, and household registration

JEL classification: R11 and O53

1   Introduction

China is in the throes of the historic transition from an agriculturally rural society to an industrially urban one. In more than two decades since 1978, it has

*   Correspondence: Kevin H. Zhang, Department of Economics, Illinois State University, Normal, IL 61790–4200, USA. Tel: (309) 438–8928; Fax: (309) 438–5228; Email: khzhang@ilstu.edu.

been experiencing a rapid urbanization and the greatest rural-urban migration in the history of the world, and its urban population rate had doubled, from 18 per cent in 1978 to 36 per cent in 2000. Despite the rapid increase in urban population, however, studies have shown that China's rate of urbanization has lagged behind its economic development, and the Chinese government has made it a developmental priority to further urbanize, especially following China's WTO entry that will displace millions of Chinese farmers from their land. How Chinese cities cope with such rapid influxes of population has thus become a question of critical concern. While cities offer agglomeration and scale economies and numerous externalities (skilled workers, cheap transport, social and cultural amenities), the social costs of urban unemployment, a progressive overloading of housing and social services, as well as increased crimes, pollution, and congestion, may outweigh the urban advantages, especially when urbanization outpaces the development of necessary urban infrastructures. A successful urban transformation is, therefore, not only important for a sustainable economic growth, but also instrumental for narrowing income disparities and reducing poverty.

Studies of China's urban transformation are of importance due to China's vast size, unique development experiences, and exemplary impact. While much work has been devoted to exploring a variety of aspects of China's urbanization at particular periods (for example, Song and Zhang, 2002; Zhang, 2002; Zhang and Song, 2003), comprehensive studies of China's urban transformation in the past 50 years since 1949 have been limited. With 1,266 million people, China has the largest urban population (458 million) in the world, although its urban population share remains as low as 36 per cent in total population. This chapter intends to document the evolution of China's urban transformation in the last half of the century. The focus is to show how important the constraints of grain supply and urban unemployment were in China's urbanization. The next section builds an analytical framework, in which benefits and costs of urbanization are discussed. In section three, the evolution of China's urban transformation is explored through identifying main features of four different stages over the 50 years. We summarize the main points in the last section.

2   Analytical Framework of Urban Transformation

Urbanization is a process of relative growth in a country's urban population accompanied by an even faster increase in the economic importance of cities relative to rural areas. There is a worldwide trend toward urbanization. In most countries it is a natural consequence and stimulus of economic development based on industrialization. Thus urbanization and industrialization have moved in tandem and both are positively related to each other. The trend toward urbanization with industrial development is evident today in cross-country comparisons. As average income of a country grows from about $750 per capita to $7,500, both in terms of the manufacturing workforce share and the urban population share grow (Perkins et al., 2001).

What causes urbanization as industrialization proceeds? To a large degree cities are formed because they provide cost-reducing advantages to producers and consumers through agglomeration, economies and numerous external economies: (a) cities with large populations reduce firms' costs of recruiting labor of all kinds, especially skilled workers and technicians; (b) cities offer better infrastructure, including industrial sites, electricity, water, sewers, roads, and railroads; (c) health and education facilities are also more highly developed in cities; (d) each firm benefits from the economies of agglomeration that result from the presence of many other firms in urban areas, because a wide range of necessary inputs (repair and other industrial services) and services (financial markets, financial intermediaries, and communications) become available.

Urbanization is not a costless process but subject to many conditions. Obvious problems with cities include overcrowding, unsanitary conditions, displacement due to rural migration, and crime. More fundamental challenges are urban unemployment, and the supply of food necessary to feed the rising urban dwellers. While rural-urban migration was viewed as a natural process in which surplus labor is withdrawn from the rural sector to provide needed manpower for urban industrial growth, it is now clear from the recent experiences of many developing countries, that rapid urbanization may not be beneficent as rates of the migration exceed rates of urban job creation and surpass greatly the absorption capacity of both industry and urban social services. In particular, too much migration may disproportionately increase the growth rate of urban job seekers relative to urban population growth; and urban job creation is generally more difficult and costly to accomplish than in rural areas because of the need for substantial complementary resource inputs for most jobs in the industrial sector.

3   Urban Transformation in China: 1949–2000

Urbanization is usually measured by the share of urban residence in the total population. The main sources of a rise in a country's urbanization level include rural-urban migration, fast population growth in urban areas relative to rural areas, and the emergence of new cities. Like other countries, rural-urban migration is the main source of urbanization growth in China.

Figure 2.1 and Table 2.1 reflect the time trend of China's urbanization over the period in the study. When the People's Republic of China was created in 1949, only 10.6 per cent of China's 542 million people were in urban areas. The urban population share almost doubled to the level of 19.8 per cent in 1960. Then in the following years until 1978, the level of urbanization did not increase but fell a little to 17.6 per cent in 1977. Urban population has increased significantly in the reform era since 1978, with 36 per cent of the urban population share in 2000.

Four different stages of urbanization in China may be identified over the period 1949–2000, based on urbanization levels, rural-urban migration, economic development, and government urban strategies, as suggested in Table 2.2 and Figures 2.2 and 2.3:

1949–57: the stage of initial expansion;
1958–65: the stage of fluctuation;
1966–77: the stage of stagnation;
1978–2000: the stage of rapid growth.

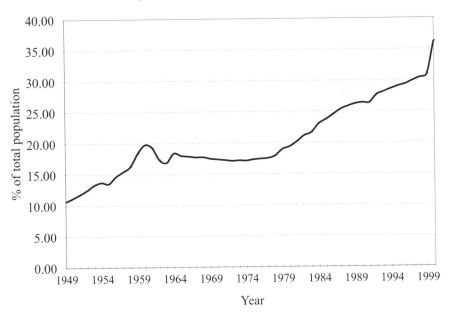

Figure 2.1   The level of urbanization in China: 1949–2000

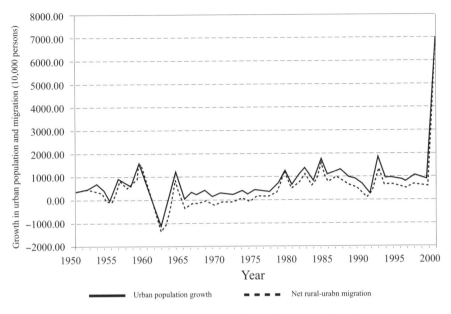

Figure 2.2   **Urban population growth and net rural-urban migration: 1950–2000**

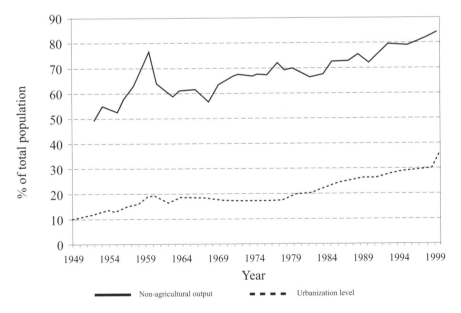

Figure 2.3   **Links between urbanization and industrialization: 1949–2000**

Table 2.1   Total population, urban population, and urbanization in China: 1949–2000

Year	Total population (millions)	Urban population (millions)	Share (%)	Year	Total population (millions)	Urban population (millions)	Share (%)
1949	541.67	57.63	10.64	1975	924.20	160.26	17.34
1950	551.96	61.71	11.18	1976	937.17	163.44	17.44
1951	563.00	66.32	11.78	1977	949.74	166.68	17.55
1952	574.82	71.62	12.46	1978	962.59	172.50	17.92
1953	587.96	78.26	13.31	1979	975.42	184.94	18.96
1954	602.66	82.50	13.69	1980	987.05	191.39	19.39
1955	614.65	82.85	13.48	1981	1000.72	201.75	20.16
1956	628.28	91.85	14.62	1982	1016.54	214.79	21.13
1957	646.53	99.50	15.39	1983	1030.08	222.70	21.62
1958	659.94	107.24	16.25	1984	1043.57	240.17	23.01
1959	672.07	123.73	18.41	1985	1058.51	250.94	23.71
				1986	1075.07	263.66	24.53
1960	662.07	130.76	19.75	1987	1093.00	276.74	25.32
1961	658.59	127.04	19.29	1988	1110.26	286.56	25.81
1962	672.95	116.62	17.33	1989	1127.04	295.40	26.21
1963	691.72	116.49	16.84				
1964	704.99	129.51	18.37	1990	1143.33	301.91	26.41
1965	725.38	130.42	17.98	1991	1158.23	305.43	26.37
1966	745.42	133.13	17.86	1992	1171.71	323.72	27.63
1967	763.68	135.48	17.74	1993	1185.17	333.51	28.14
1968	785.34	139.48	17.76	1994	0098.50	343.01	28.62
1969	806.71	141.17	17.50	1995	1211.21	351.74	29.04

Table 2.1 cont'd

Year	Total population (millions)	Urban population (millions)	Share (%)
1970	829.92	144.24	17.38
1971	852.29	147.11	17.26
1972	871.71	149.32	17.13
1973	892.11	153.44	17.20
1974	908.59	155.91	17.16

Year	Total population (millions)	Urban population (millions)	Share (%)
1996	1223.89	359.49	29.37
1997	1236.26	369.89	29.92
1998	1248.10	379.42	30.40
1999	1259.09	388.93	30.89
2000	1265.83	458.48	36.22

Sources: China Statistical Yearbook 2001 (SSB, 2001); Comprehensive Statistical Data and Materials on 50 Years of New China (SSB, 1999)

In the first stage (1949–57), China experienced an initial development of urbanization with steady growth from 10.64 per cent in 1949 to 15.39 per cent in 1957. The urban population grew at a rate three times as much as that of total population. The majority of urban population growth (70 per cent) came from city-ward migration, with an average annual migration of 3.64 million (Table 2.2). The social and political stability after the damage of the Japanese invasion and the civil war resulted in a good recovery of economic development, and an expansion of urban population. Real per capita income increased rapidly, with average growth rate of 6.78 per cent. The share of industrial output in GDP rose from 21 per cent in 1952 to 30 per cent in 1957 (SSB, 1999). The main features of the stage are rapid urbanization, the dominant contribution of migrants to urban growth, and the strong link between urbanization and industrialization. In sum, China's urbanization at this stage was not dissimilar to the developing world at the initial stage of industrialization.

The second stage (1958–65) first witnessed the Great Leap Forward, in which a large amount of city-ward migration was encouraged by the government. Then the Great Famine reversed the direction of migration. During the two years of the Great Leap Forward, there was a massive mobilization of the peasant population for labor-intensive local industrialization resulting in thousands of commune centers with tens of thousands of people. The level of urbanization reached its peak of nearly 20 per cent in 1960 and then quickly fell to below 17 per cent three years later. The overall pace of urbanization was slow relative to the previous stage. The contribution of migration fell and became less than the natural urban population growth. Institutional factors played a key role in shaping the directions of migration, which was the main source of fluctuations in urbanization. The rapid urbanization in the late 1950s was closely associated with the failure of the massive commune experiments and the sharp fall in agricultural production, which drove many people from the countryside into towns and cities. In fact, both industrial and non-agricultural output as a proportion of GDP shrank in most years since 1959.

The third stage (1966–77) concurred with the Cultural Revolution, in which China experienced an urban containment, with slight falls in the levels of urbanization. The main feature of this stage is industrialization without urbanization, which obviously diverged from the normal pattern of urbanization. The share of industrial output in GDP grew by 9 percentage points, from 38 per cent in 1966 to 47 per cent in 1977. But the share of urban population actually fell, and the growth of major cities was curbed as some manufacturing plants and workers were shifted to smaller cities in inland areas. The city-ward migration was restricted through the household registration

Table 2.2   Urbanization, migration, and economic growth in China: 1949–2000

Period averages (annual growth rate (GR) or average annual changes (AC))	1949– 57	1958– 65	1966– 77	1978– 2000
Urbanization				
Total population (GR) (%)	2.24	1.36	2.23	1.25
Urban population (GR) (%)	7.06	2.84	2.06	4.54
Urban population (AC) (millions)	5.23	4.42	3.30	13.26
Urbanization levels (AC) (%)	0.59	0.25	–0.03	0.83
Urbanization levels (GR) (%)	4.72	1.27	–0.16	3.25
Composition of Urban Growth				
Natural urban growth (AC) (millions)	1.60	2.42	3.25	2.63
Share of natural growth (AC) (%)	30.48	54.81	98.48	19.84
Net rural-urban migration (AC) (millions)	3.64	2.00	0.05	10.63
Share of migration (AC) (%)	69.53	45.19	1.52	80.16
Economic growth				
Real per capita GDP (GR) (%)	6.78*	0.49	3.01	8.12
Non-agriculture sectors in GDP (AC) (%)	2.05*	–0.55	0.74	0.55
Industrial share in GDP (AC) (%)	1.76*	–0.27	0.83	0.12

*   The periods are 1952–57. The share of natural urban growth is defined as percentage of natural growth of urban population in total urban growth in persons. The remaining part of total urban growth is the share of net migration.

Sources: Computed from *China Statistical Yearbook 2001* (SSB, 2001) and *Comprehensive Statistical Data and Materials on 50 Years of New China* (SSB, 1999).

(*hukou* in Chinese) system that was formally introduced and implemented in the early 1960s. Moreover, several million city youths were transferred to rural areas in the 'rustication' campaign. The urban population grew at the rate of 2 per cent, which is lower than the total population growth (2.23 per cent). City-ward migration played no role in urban growth. The resulting level of urbanization was maintained at around 17 per cent during the period, with a slight fall from 17.86 per cent in 1966 to 17.55 per cent in 1977.

The fourth stage (1978–2000) witnessed the most rapid growth in urban transformation as a result of the relaxation of administrative controls of rural-urban migration, due to the remarkable success in economic reforms and economic growth (real per capita income grew at a rate of 8 per cent). With rural industrialization, urban industrial expansion, and the relaxation of institutional controls on city-ward migration, China's urbanization level grew dramatically, from about 18 per cent in 1979 to 36 per cent in 2000. The role of rural-urban migration was restored and contributed 80 per cent of urban population growth, with an average annual amount of 13 million migrants (Table 2.2). This stage resembles the pattern and pace of urbanization in other developing countries, although some pre-reform features were kept, such as restricting the entitled population and encouraging new non-agricultural employment in rural enterprises. The elimination of grain rationing (a crucial component of the urban household registration system) in the cities further weakened whatever practical constraints the registration system may have had on urban growth.

Changes in numbers and types of cities reflect similar features of the four stages as well. The current classification of city size in China consists of four categories: mega cities with a population of more than one million, large cities (0.5–1 million), medium cities (0.2–0.5 million), and small cities (under 0.2 million). Table 2.3 shows the pattern of China's cities in the period of 1949–2000. Except for a significant increase in the early 1950s, the total number of cities did not change much (from 184 in 1958 to 193 cities in 1978) in the pre-reform era because of the control on migration. Changes in the post-reform urban policy have brought about a substantial rise in the number of cities, largely as a result of rural to urban migration. The number of cities increased by more than threefold, from 193 in 1978 to 663 in 2000.

Cities have witnessed rapid expansion and city-size distribution has changed since 1949. The number of mega cities has grown from five in 1949 to 40 in 2000, and from seven to 53 for large cities. Together the share of mega and large cities in all cities increased from 9 per cent to 14 per cent. The largest increase took place in medium cities (from 18 in 1949 to 218 in 2000), representing a growth of 12 times, in contrast to an increase of about three times in small cities (from 102 to 352). The share of medium cities rose from 14 per cent to 33 per cent, and the share for small cities fell from 77 per cent to 53 per cent.

China's urbanization in the past 50 years may be characterized in two ways. First, the level of urbanization has been low relative to other developing countries at the same development levels. Second, the process of urbanization has been controlled to a large extent by the state and influenced by the nation's development strategy. Low urbanization appears to be the result of administrative controls on rural-urban migration through the system of food rationing and household registration. But the fundamental factors behind China's anti-urban bias were cities' limited ability to absorb huge amount of rural migrants and the Soviet-style heavy industrialization strategy.

Table 2.3 Number and types of cities in China: 1949–2000

Year	All cities	Mega cities (>1 million)		Large cities (0.5-1 million)		Medium cities (0.2-0.5 million)		Small cities (< 0.2 million)	
		Number	*Share*	*Number*	*Share*	*Number*	*Share*	*Number*	*Share*
1949	132	5	3.79	7	5.30	18	13.64	102	77.27
1958	184	10	5.43	18	9.78	48	26.09	108	58.70
1965	168	13	7.74	18	10.71	42	25.00	95	56.55
1978	193	13	6.74	27	13.99	60	31.09	93	48.19
2000	663	40	6.03	53	7.99	218	32.88	352	53.09

Sources: Cities of New China for 50 Years (SSB, 1999); *China Statistical Yearbook 2001* (SSB, 2001).

China is the most populous country in the world. The majority of its people live in rural areas, and per capita arable land is lower than the average in the developing world. These features together have made China's urbanization unique in absolute magnitude of rural-urban migration, and thus provide a challenge in dealing with rapid urban growth. The limited absorbability of cities has been largely a result of huge amount of surplus rural labor and a shortage of food production. The heavy industrialization strategy, under which higher industrial output did not create employment growth, further reduced cities' ability to offer jobs to rural migrants. In this strategy, heavy industrialization was organized and enhanced by central government and peasants were expected to develop agriculture to support urban industries. The heavy industrialization strategy was thus not designed to induce massive urbanization because capital-intensive heavy industries did not raise the labor-absorption capacity of cities and therefore failed to help relieve rural surplus labor pressure. Therefore, in most of the time since 1949, the Chinese government has had to find a way to reduce the pressure from the increasing urban population. The controls of urban population were mainly conducted through household registration system and grains ration, which were introduced and implemented in 1958.

The reform period since 1978 marks a new phase in China's urbanization, in which the urban population has expanded rapidly and the level of urbanization has doubled in the two decades. Compared to the pre-reform period, the major policy changes involved the gradual loosening up of the strict controls over urban growth. Gradual changes in urban policies took place once reforms filtered down. For instance, after people's communes were dissolved in the early 1980s, food rationing and job allocation also became less effectively regulated. In the 1990s, large flows of city-ward migrants became common in all cities, especially metropolitans such as Shanghai, Beijing, and Guangzhou. The changes in urban policies were largely the result of an increase in the supply of food and a rise in labor-intensive manufacturing and city-service industries. With higher productivity in agricultural sector and imports of grains from international markets, a shortage of food has no longer remained a constraint to urban growth. However, controls on rural-urban migration have not been abandoned and the household registration system still remains, since large job creation in urban areas still cannot match the potential pace of city-ward migration. As a result, urban population growth has not been consistent with industrialization and economic development, resulting in an obvious urbanization lag even in post-reform China.

4 Summary and Concluding Remarks

This chapter examines China's urbanization in the last half of the century since 1949 by documenting the evolution of urban transformation into four stages and assessing China's urban policies. To some extent, what happened in the reform period (1978–2000) resembles what was seen in the first stage (1949–57), with rapid urban population growth through city-ward migration, along with rapid industrialization. The second stage (1958–65) first suffered over-urbanization, and then experienced a sharp fall in the urbanization level. A strong response to what happened at this stage led to a so-called anti-urbanism strategy adopted in the third stage (1966–77), under which not only was rural-urban migration not permitted, but also opposite direction migration was encouraged. As a result, industrialization did not lead to urbanization, and the share of urban population shrank during this period.

Comparative insights are drawn from the four stages with respect to cities' absorptive ability and urban policies based on the nation's development strategy. Urban growth was largely constrained by shortages of food supply and limited job creation in the cities. The heavy industrialization strategy not only discouraged agricultural productivity but also reduced urban job creation. Even after rapid urbanization for the two decades since 1978, the proportion of urbanized population in China is still behind many developing countries at similar development levels. Now China is in a dilemma: urbanization could become a critical driving force in China's economic development in the following two decades through efficient allocation of the labor force and cities' agglomeration and economies of scale. But too much urbanization or over-urbanization may lead the economy and the society to collapse, as cities cannot absorb too large a number of rural migrants.

How to accommodate rural migrants in China has now become a controversial issue not only at the academic level but also at the political and administrative levels, due to its relevance both in quantitative and qualitative terms. The current system of household registration and controls over city-ward migration are incapable of dealing with growing number of the floating rural population. In the last ten years since the early 1990s, the state monopoly in the provision of urban infrastructure and services has been proving to be unsustainable and the surging migrant influx has become an impetus for further reforms in urban policies. The Chinese government is now considering completely abandoning the household registration systems and other discriminatory treatment of rural migrants. This of course would be a big step in the process of China's urbanization, and its success would largely depend on how cities absorb the huge number of rural migrants. It would be helpful if more resources were allocated to labor-intensive industries and services, and more unskilled labor could also be employed to work in exporting to the world market if China becomes the world factory.

A comprehensive strategy may be developed to deal with the challenge and opportunities facing China. Several policy instruments that appear to be the consensus of most economists emerge as follows (Todaro and Smith, 2003): (a) Reducing population growth as a fundamental policy should be continuously implemented, since any long-term solution to China's employment and urbanization problems must involve a lowering of the current rate of population growth; (b) appropriate labor-intensive technologies of production should be chosen. While advanced technologies definitely are more efficient in production through adoption of typically labor-saving machinery and equipment, they inhibit at the same time the success of the long-term program of employment creation both in urban industry and rural agriculture. Efforts thus may be made to develop small-scale, labor-intensive rural and urban enterprises; (c) the composition of the national output should be adjusted toward small-scale, labor-intensive industries to create employment opportunities. Expansion of such industries may be accomplished in two ways: directly through government investment and incentives, particularly for activities in the urban informal sector, and indirectly, through income distribution to the rural poor whose consumption structure is more labor-intensive than that of the rich; (d) factor-price distortions should be eliminated. Evidence from other developing counties suggests that correcting factor-price distortions through eliminating capital subsidies and curtailing the growth of urban wages by market-based pricing may be helpful in increasing employment opportunities and making better use of capital resources; and (e) finally, the appropriate rural-urban balance should be created to ameliorate both urban and rural unemployment problems and to avoid over-urbanization by slowing the pace of city-ward migration. Such efforts may be linked to activities such as the development of the rural sector, encouragement of small and modest-sized cities, and the spread of small-scale and labor intensive industries.

References

Perkins, D., Radelet, S., Snodgrass, D., Grills, M. and Roemer, M. (2001), *Economics of Development*, 5th edn, New York: W.W. Norton & Company.

Song, S. and Zhang, K.H. (2002), 'Urbanization and City-size Distribution in China,' *Urban Studies*, 39 (12), 2317–27.

State Statistical Bureau (SSB) of China (1999), *Comprehensive Statistical Data and Materials on 50 Years of New China*, Beijing: China Statistical Press

State Statistical Bureau (SSB) of China (2001), *China Statistical Yearbook 1995, 2000*, and *2001*, Beijing: China Statistical Press.

State Statistical Bureau (SSB) of China (1999), *Cities of New China for 50 Years*, Beijing: China Statistical Press.

Todaro, M.P. and Smith, S.C. (2003), *Economic Development*, 8th edn, Boston, MA: Addison Wesley.

Zhang, K.H. (2002), 'What Explains China's Rising Urbanization in the Reform Era?,' *Urban Studies*, 39 (12), 2301–15.

Zhang, K.H. and Song, S. (2003), 'Rural-urban Migration and Urbanization in China: Evidence from Time-series and Cross-section Analyses,' *China Economic Review*, forthcoming.

CHAPTER 3

POLITICAL CAPACITY AND DEMOGRAPHIC CHANGE: A STUDY OF CHINA WITH A COMPARISON TO INDIA

YI FENG*
Claremont Graduate University

SIDDHARTH SWAMINATHAN
La Sierra University

Abstract

This chapter uses a political economy model to study birth rates in China and compare them to those in India. The model identifies government capacity as a crucial factor that shapes people's decision regarding the number of children they will have. As population growth and economic growth are interrelated, a government can use the political process to achieve its economic objectives. The implications of the model are tested against China's and India's data for the period 1960–95. The result shows that the birth rates in both countries confirm the theoretical conclusion. The major policy implication is that in order to sustain its economic development, China and other populous developing countries must urbanize the countryside demographically, economically and politically to produce a set of conditions that favor long-term growth.

Keywords*:* Economic development, demography, political systems

JEL classification: J1, N3, N4, O2, O4, R5

---

*   Correspondence: Yi Feng, School of Politics and Economics, Claremont Graduate University, 170 East 10th Street, Claremont, CA 91711.

This research is supported by a grant from the National Science Foundation (SBR-9730474). Kristin Johnson provided editorial assistance. Siddharth Swaminathan wrote the discussion on political capacity in India in Section 4 of this chapter.

URBAN TRANSFORMATION IN CHINA, edited by Aimin Chen, Gordon G. Liu and Kevin H. Zhang

1   Introduction

This chapter uses a political economy model to study birth rates in China and compare them to those in India. The model identifies government capacity as a crucial factor that shapes people's decision regarding the number of children they will have. As population growth and economic growth are interrelated, a government can use the political process to achieve its economic objectives. The implications of the model are tested against China's and India's data for the period 1960–95. The result shows that the birth rates in both countries confirm the theoretical conclusion. The major policy implication is that in order to sustain its economic development, China and other populous developing countries must urbanize the countryside demographically, economically and politically to produce a set of conditions that favor long-term growth.

The growth of population in China has responded to a strategic policy process that has been implemented to control the increase in population particularly in cities across China. This essay focuses on government capacity as the political determinants of birth rates in China and extends it to a comparison with India.

Theoretically, I posit a political model of demographic change. The foundation of the theoretical model can be found in Feng, Kugler and Zak (2000, 2001). The formal model in this work demonstrates that policy choices have important consequences on a country's development path through the impact of birth decisions across generations. The fundamental model integrates political systems with demographic change and economic development, deriving a set of necessary conditions for development. The formal model shows that at the equilibrium level, births decrease with political stability, political capacity, income, and education. In this chapter, I focus particularly on political capacity and conduct a comparative study of China and India.

Section 2 presents a set of views on sources of demographic changes in China. Section 3 offers empirical observations of politics and births in both China and India. Section 4 conducts a statistical analysis. Section 5 concludes this chapter with policy implications.

2   Alternative Views of Demographic Change

This study is placed in a set of alternative theories of demographic change. There perspectives are cultural, economic, sociological and political. Below I use China as a template for those theories.

The Cultural Perspective

The cultural perspective attributes demographic change to cultural characteristics of the nation. For instance, Zhao (1997) maintains that Chinese culture played a critical role in the success of the government's family planning program. 'These [cultural] elements are the traditional values concerning the relationship between state, family, and individual, and the related social norms. In contrast to Western countries where individualism has its origin, the interests of the state and the family were strongly emphasized in historical China' (Zhao, 1997, p. 731). Similarly, Wu and Jia (1991) and Zou (1993) point out that Chinese people follow the government's family planning program and willingly carry it out as the result of traditional Chinese values regarding the relationship between the state and the family. Such a theory argues that population growth in China will decline rapidly as a response to government's family planning policy and particularly so in the regions where Chinese culture and tradition have held the most influence.

The Modernization Perspective

The modernization thesis holds economic development as the universal key to demographic change regardless of cultural elements. For instance, Whyte and Parish (1984) ascribe the decline in birth rates in China to the processes of modernization, which is universal and common to all countries. They believe that political or cultural factors in determining demographic change are irrelevant and maintain that industrialization, urbanization, and other forms of modernization are all part of outcomes of worldwide industrial revolution and transformation. Those factors facilitate birth control in China.

This argument is partly supported by Lavely and Freedman (1990) who find that health, education, and urbanization in China possibly initiated a fertility rate change in urban areas without much government intervention. However, they also find an anomaly: 'It is more difficult, however, to explain the precipitous subsequent declines in both urban and rural areas and the rapid rise in family planning among illiterate rural women by appealing to these developmental factors' (Lavely and Freedman, 1990, p. 366).

The Sociological Perspective

The sociological view regards demographic change as a dynamic response to short-run social conditions. For instance, Coale (1984), Chen (1984) and

Poston (1992) focus on population change in China during one specific period, namely, the late 1950s to early 1960s. They point out that the famine experienced in China during and immediately after the Great Leap Forward campaign led to serious conditions of subfecundity as well as to disruptions for many couples in their patterns of normal married life. The significant increases in births in the early 1960s took place in conjunction with the economic recovery in China, and were also a result of the 'the restoration of normal married life, from an abnormally large number of marriages, and from the unusually small fraction of married women who were infertile because of nursing a recently born infant' (Coale, 1984, p. 57). It should be noted this perspective is a limited description of China's population trend, as it focuses on a short period.

Other explanations for the population change during this period show that 'the political climate of the 1950s and the 1960s was generally favorable to high fertility. The socioeconomic system characterized by the 'iron rice bowl' encouraged large families by making childbearing easier. For an individual family the cost of bringing up a child might have been even lower than before' (Zhao, 1997, p. 753). Wolf (1986) ascribes the rise in China's fertility and birth rates in 1962–63 to 'superhuman effort demanded of the population' during the years of the Great Leap Forward (Wolf, 1986).

The Political Perspective

This view of demographic change looks into political efficacy as an explanation of demographic change. The theory in this chapter focuses on one political variable as a major driver for population growth. As in the model (Feng et al., 2000, 2002), political actors face several constraints when making government spending decisions. Foremost among these is maintaining public order so that the ruling regime remains in power (Alesina et al., 1997; Arbetman and Kugler, 1995; Magee et al., 1989). *Political capacity* implies the effectiveness of the government in implementing policy (Arbetman and Kugler, 1997) so that the government increases its chance to remain in power. This political imperative limits the allocation of the remaining tax revenue. The discretionary portion of tax revenue therefore indicates a government's ability to affect its goals. For this reason I denote this variable as a country's political capacity. Once the government's survival is assured, its next objective is to increase the 'size of the pie' by stimulating the accumulation of physical capital. A larger physical capital base raises private incomes as well as tax revenue, both of which lead to great public support for the government, further ensuring its survival. Political capacity decreases births since government policy raises economic efficiency, increasing individual incomes.

A representative individual in the model maximizes expected utility during adulthood, subject to a budget constraint. During young adulthood, he works for firms and pays part of his labor income to the government in the form of taxes; his remaining income is spent to fund his own, and his children's consumption, and to save for retirement.

In addition to the amounts of consumption and savings during young adulthood, he also decides how many children to have. In this model, children acquire human capital from their parents and join the labor force when they enter adulthood. Human capital, along with physical capital changes over time as the result of choices made by individuals, firms and the government.

Capable governments raise the productivity of private firms by setting policies leading to economic efficiency. Arbetman et al. (1997) demonstrate that politically capable governments promote a wide range of economic activities such as investment, trade, and price stability. Because my focus is development, the model restricts political capacity to a single effect, namely raising labor productivity.

Such a model shows that births decrease as human capital and physical capital rise since an individual's labor income is a function of both types of capital. Also, an increase in political instability increases births since it reduces labor income and subsequently the opportunity cost of raising children. Political capacity decreases births since government policy that raises economic efficiency increases individual incomes.

The model predicts that births decrease when political capacity rises. The model provides an explanation for earlier empirical findings (e.g., Organski et al., 1984) by deriving the joint dynamics of fertility, politics and economic growth. Politically capable governments enhance human capital accumulation by spending on public investment, raising productivity, and thus labor incomes. As a result, capable governments unwittingly initiate demographic transitions, leading to low birth rates, a stable population, and sustained economic development.

Those predictions are strongly confirmed in the cross-country time series data of more than 100 countries during the period of 1960 to 1990 (Feng, Kugler and Zak, 2002). Studying China as a particular case, Feng, Kugler and Zak (2002) also find that while urban birth rates support the model, rural data do not. Their policy implication is that China has to urbanize its countryside not only economically, but also politically in order to facilitate rural demographic change in line with China's long-term development goals. They also point out that in a cross-county setting, China's rural data may still support their theory when compared to other developing countries' data. In this chapter, I will conduct an empirical analysis of the effect of political capacity on birth rates in both China and India.

3   Empirical Observations

The political theory of demography has been supported by anecdotal evidence of different policy practices across countries. For instance, Wolf (1986) compares India's and China's family planning programs. 'Birth control programs like those initiated in the early 1960s and 1970s would have had no more chance of success in China than Indira Gandhi's ill-fated efforts in India. As in India, the resistance would have barricaded itself behind the walls of village solidarity …. The Chinese program succeeded where the Indian program failed because the great collectivization program of the 1950s had already leveled those walls, putting the government in firm control of the communities they once sheltered' (Wolf, 1986, p. 114). This theory ascribes the success of China's family planning to government's control and influence in the countryside.

Figure 3.1 shows the crude birth rates (CBR), defined as births per thousand people, in China and India for the period of 1960 to 1998. The birth rates data are from Basic Data of China's Population compiled by Yao Xinwu and Yin Hua (1994) and China Population Information Center (1999). The Indian data are from the United Nations. While both countries evince a downward trend in population growth, they also demonstrate different patterns. The demographic decline in India seems to be smoother than that in China where the birth rates started to decline from 37.97 per cent in 1954, all way to 18.62 per cent in 1961, and then increased rapidly in 1962 and peaked in 1963 (43.37 per cent). Then they started to decline again. During the period of 1967 through 1971, the drop in population growth was stalled. The decline resumed after 1971. From 1977 to 1991, China's birth rates assumed a W shape, ranging from 17.82 in 1979 to 23.33 per cent in 1987. From 1991 to 1998, they steadily dived to 16.03 per cent.

Figure 3.2 and Figure 3.3 display disaggregate crude birth rates in the urban and rural areas in the two countries. Yao Xinwu and Yin Hua (1994) and the China Population Information Center (1999) provide the Chinese data. The Indian Census Bureau provides the Indian data. The selection of years was determined by the availability of the data for both countries. Again, China's demographic decline seems to be more dramatic than that of India.

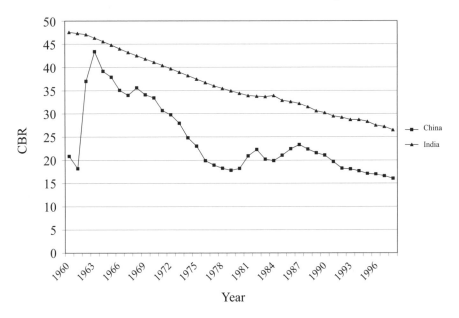

Figure 3.1   National crude birth rates, 1960–98

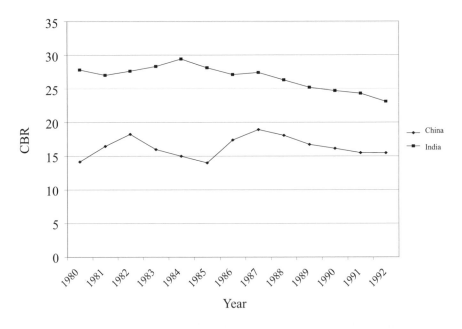

Figure 3.2   Urban crude birth rates, 1980–92

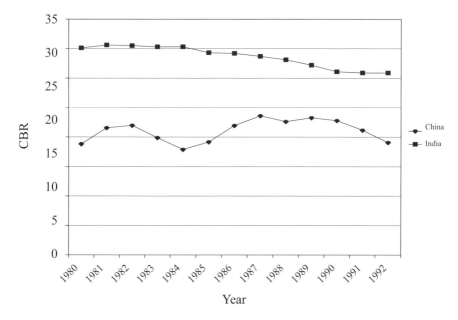

Figure 3.3   Rural crude birth rates (CBR) in China and India, 1980–92

4   Statistical Analysis

The test of this political theory of demographic change requires the operationalization of the political capacity variable. Because of the difficulty of consistently determining the various policies that make up political capacity, I use the government's budget constraint to estimate political capacity using information on tax receipts and implicit political effectiveness. The conception advanced by Organski and Kugler (1980, p. 74) lays the foundation for the measurement of relative political capacity. As governmental operation depends upon resources extracted from the population, governments cannot survive – let alone govern – without such resources.

Taxes are exact indicators of governmental presence. Few operations of governments depend so heavily on popular support – or on fear of punishment. Revenues affect so directly the lives of most individuals in society, and few are avoided so vigorously. Without some form of tax revenue, there is no national unity, and no control. Failure to impose and extract taxes is one of the essential indicators of governmental incapacity to obtain and maintain support.

Guided by this theoretical principle, Arbetman and Kugler (1995) create a measure of relative political extraction (RPE) obtained in three steps. First, an Ordinary Least Squares regression is run on the following model for less developed countries:

$$\frac{Tax}{GDP} = \beta_0 + \beta_1(time) + \beta_2\frac{(\text{Mining})}{GDP} - \beta_3\frac{(\text{Agriculture})}{GDP} + \beta_4\frac{(\text{Exports})}{GDP} + \varepsilon;$$

while for developed countries the regression is

$$\frac{Tax}{GDP} = \beta_0 + \beta_1(time) + \beta_2\frac{(\text{Mining})}{GDP} - \beta_3\frac{(GDP)}{Population} + \beta_4\frac{(\text{Exports})}{GDP} + \varepsilon.$$

In the second step, the predicted value for the tax ratio is obtained using the parameter estimates derived from the first step. In the third step, the following ratio is calculated:

$$Relative\ Political\ Extraction = \frac{Actual\ Government\ Revenue}{Predicted\ Government\ Revenue}.$$

Third, if the above ratio is larger than one, then the government is defined as 'strong' since it collects more taxes than otherwise predicted, based upon economic factors. Such a government is also regarded as politically capable and efficient. If the ratio is less than one, then the government fails to collect the taxes it is supposed to obtain on economic grounds, and it is regarded as politically incapable.

It has been noted government capacity varies in China in response to government's strategy of political mobilization or economic development (Feng and Li, 1997). The relative political extraction (RPE) data are available for the PRC for the period of 1960–95. The relative political extraction of the People's Republic of China was high from 1964 to 1971, where the ratio of actual over expected taxation is above one. The year 1972 marked a low government capacity level. From 1973 to 1983, the ratio varies between 1.16 to 1.25, lower on average than the first 'high' period. After 1984, it declined to below one, indicating low government capacity. From 1988 to 1991, China's government capacity surged again before it drifted lower.

Government capacity responds to government strategy and priorities. The plateaus in Figure 3.4 correspond to the Cultural Revolution, the power transition around Mao's death, and the ascendancy of Deng Xiaoping. The

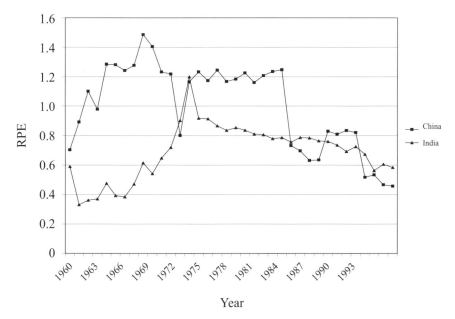

Figure 3.4   Relative political extraction, 1960–95

three troughs correspond to the periods of economic reconstruction in the early 1960s, the aborted return to the pre-cultural revolution 'normalcy' in 1972, and the deepening of economic reforms. Political movement requires political mobilization and resource extraction. An economic program toward a market economy requires decentralization and market incentives. Given this dichotomy of political mobilization and economic decentralization, the role of government capacity in reducing population growth may be ambiguous in China. In the case of China, economic development, which generally reduces population growth, may require concomitant low government capacity. The decrease in government capacity, however, results in an increase in population growth. Thus, the combination of high economic growth and low government capacity may create a counterbalancing effect on population growth.

During the period 1960–65, India fought two wars: a border war with China in 1962 and the second Kashmir war with Pakistan in 1965. Typically, wars are periods of increased mobilization. From the period from 1966 to 1975 there is a steady increase in India's RPE. The 1971 war with Pakistan over the creation of Bangladesh led to the mobilization of the Indian population which the Congress Party, especially Indira Gandhi, capitalized on as a vehicle for electoral success. The dominance held by the Congress Party began to slowly crumble and opposition parties began making grounds in 1977. The early

1970s witnessed a deepening of economic problems within India exacerbated by the international oil crisis and severe drought. The resulting severe food shortages and spiraling prices were accompanied by increasing political unrest and violence. Most importantly, the suspension of democratic rights with the declaration of the national emergency in 1975 greatly undermined the Congress Party's likelihood of success in later elections. In 1977, the high degree of unity among the opposition parties resulted in a lesser degree of vote fractionalization in the federal elections (Butler, 1992).

Since 1975 there has been a steady decline in the capability of the government. Economic policy in India until 1991 was based on the Soviet style model of planned development. With emphasis on investment goods specifically in heavy industry and import substitution industrialization, private industry benefited from protective tariffs or the total prohibition of imports. Two major developments in India's electoral scene since 1989 have been the emergence of a multiparty system and the rise of regional parties. The weakening of the Congress Party's position has been accompanied by the improved showing of opposition parties. While no single party has been able to secure a majority in parliament, the national parties have formed coalitions with the support of regional parties. In the 1980s and 1990s, India also witnessed a substantial instability resulting from ethnic, religious and separatist violence. Hindu-Muslim clashes have been a major of instability within the country. Since 1989 India has been preoccupied with the separatist movement in Kashmir leading to the 1999 Kargil and 2002 standoffs over infiltration of terrorists in Indian-held Kashmir. While the likelihood of war is relatively low (Kugler et al., 2001) the military buildup and political instability generated by the separatist movements diverts resources from pressing domestic priorities such as education and health.

The statistical model on the time series data for China and India is

$$Ln(B_t) = \beta_0 + \beta_1 Ln(RPCt) + \beta_2 Ln(GDP_t) + \beta_3 Family + e_t$$

where t indicates the year, B is the crude birth rates, RPE is relative political capacity measured by relative political extraction and GDP is real GDP per capita. I also include a dummy variable $FAMILY$ that takes the value of one for the years 1971-1995 and zero otherwise. Wolf (1986) and Zheng (1995, pp. 238–9) document that China's birth rate stayed at a high level (with the exception of the late 1950s and the early 1960s) until 1971 when the Chinese government was determined to implement a national program to control births. The inclusion of the family planning program dummy variable is particularly important in the test of the Chinese case. Government strength matters in addition to policy content. The theoretical model predicts a positive effect of political instability on population growth and negative effects of government capacity and income on population growth.

The Chinese and India data has been pooled, using maximum likelihood (ML) autoregression as the estimation method, which corrects for various orders of serial correlation that tend to inflate statistical significance. With regard to the data affected with serial correlation, autoregressive correction produces more robust results than Ordinary Least Squares (OLS) estimation, as it uses conservative variances for the parameter estimates.

The dependent variables in the three regressions are national, urban, and rural crude birth rates, respectively. One reason for distinguishing them is that significant differences in birth rates exist between cities and the countryside. As Feng, Kugler and Zak (2002) find, urban and rural demographic transitions respond to political variables in a very different way.

Table 3.1 shows the regression results. Note that the rural and urban regressions do not have the family planning variable, as the Indian data start in 1980 in the sample. The economic perspective of demographic change is supported by the data. Real GDP per capita is statistically significant in the national and urban regressions, though it is not in the rural regression. Political capacity is not statistically significant in all regressions and even has a wrong sign in the rural and national regressions. The family planning variable is negative, but lacks statistical significance.

The absence of support for the theoretical model may result from the pooling of the Chinese and Indian data. The ambiguous results could signal the difference in the parametric structure of the Chinese and Indian models. Using the Chow test, we find that the F statistics are 11.334 for the national model, 2.998 for the rural model, and 5.046 for the urban model. At the 0.05 per cent error level, the null hypothesis of no parametric difference is rejected for the Chinese and Indian data. Indeed, country-specific regressions should be used. Based on the Chow test results, I re-run the model separately on the Chinese and Indian data. Table 3.2 shows the regression results from Chinese data.

Across the three regressions, the best performing variable is the family planning dummy variable. It should be also pointed out that the magnitude of the parameter estimate on this variable is twice as large in the urban areas as in the rural areas. The modernization thesis finds support in the national data and the urban data. The impact of national wealth on birth rates is weak in the countryside. This result may reflect the increasing gap of wealth between

Table 3.1   Maximum likelihood estimation of autoregressive models on pooled data

Variable	National (1)	Rural (2)	Urban (3)
Constant	5.563**	4.443**	5.256**
	(1.007)	(1.366)	(1.336)
Political Capacity	0.027	0.107	−0.119
	(0.075)	(0.126)	(0.136)
GDP per capita	−0.326**	−0.163	−0.323*
	(0.148)	(0.200)	(0.199)
Family	−0.065	−	−
	(0.074)	−	−
Total $\bar{R}^2$	90.1	78.6	80.1
σ	0.104	0.128	0.138

Notes: **: Significant at the 0.05 error level, one-tail test. *: Significant at the 0.10 error level, one-tail test. Numbers in the parentheses are standard errors. Total is the R-square using autoregression that corrects for serial correlation.

Table 3.2   ML estimation of autoregressive models on Chinese data

Variable	National (1)	Rural (2)	Urban (3)
Constant	4.567**	4.275**	4.637**
	(0.834)	(1.109)	(0.701)
Political capacity	0.065	0.139	−0.384**
	(0.140)	(0.162)	(0.150)
GDP per capita	−0.186*	-0.139	-0.219*
	(0.148)	(0.178)	(0.113)
Family	−0.240*	−0.210*	−0.412**
	(0.074)	(1.142)	(0.090)
Total $\bar{R}^2$	80.8	75.6	80.1
σ	0.138	0.152	0.144

Notes: **: Significant at the 0.05 error level, one-tail test. *: Significant at the 0.10 error level, one-tail test. Numbers in the parentheses are standard errors. Total is the R-square using autoregression that corrects for serial correlation.

the urban and rural areas in China as pointed out by Johnson in Chapter 1. Most interestingly, the urban supports the political theory of demographic change. The effect of political capacity on birth rates in the urban areas in China is negative and statistically significant. The magnitude of its impact on birth rate reductions is three times as large as that for the countryside. This result strongly supports the in findings Feng, Kugler and Zak (2002). As will be discussed later, the comparison of the difference between the urban and rural phenomena offer important policy implications: In order to reduce the population pressure facing the nation, it is imperative to urbanize the Chinese countryside politically.

Table 3.3   ML estimation of autoregressive models on Indian data

Variable	National (1)	Rural (2)	Urban (3)
Constant	7.004**	6.493**	5.506**
	(0.230)	(0.249)	(1.038)
Political capacity	−0.017	−0.048	−0.059
	(0.028)	(0.052)	(0.222)
GDP per capita	−0.498**	−0.432**	−0.323*
	(0.036)	(0.038)	(0.157)
Total $\bar{R}^2$	97.6	94.0	0.319
σ	0.027	0.020	0.082

Notes: **: Significant at the 0.05 error level, one-tail test. *: Significant at the 0.10 error level, one-tail test. Numbers in the parentheses are standard errors. Total is the R-square using autoregression that corrects for serial correlation.

In contrast, the demographic trend in India is well explained by the modernization thesis. The level of income per capita has a salient negative impact on birth rates across the national, rural and urban regressions. Noticeably, the magnitude of the impact on births of wealth in the Indian data is twice as large as that in the Chinese data. The predominant determinant of demographic change in India is the level of income. Political capacity consistently has a negative sign, though it is not statistically significant. The lack of significance may result from the lack of data or from the lack of political mechanism to channel the government's family planning program as pointed out by Wolf (1986). The impact of political capacity in India is much weaker than that in the Chinese urban data. The magnitude of the effect of political capacity on births in India is about only 10 per cent of that of the effect of political capacity on births in the Chinese urban data.

5   Policy Implications and Concluding Remarks

This essay introduces a political model of demographic change and economic development. Particularly, I argue that government capacity is an important determinant of birth rates under certain circumstances. Empirically, I test this theory at three levels of birth rate – national, rural and urban – and against the data of both China and India, the two most populous nations. While the pooled data show ambiguity, the individual time series does provide strong evidence of the impacts of government capacity on birth rates. China's urban birth rates are predicted well by the theoretical model, though the rural birth rates and subsequently the national birth rates do not produce strong evidence for the model. For the Indian data, the most important variable is real GDP per capita. While the political perspective of demographic change explains the urban birth rates in China, the modernization thesis accounts for the Indian data largely.

Compared to urban areas, the influence of the political mechanisms on birth control in rural areas has been relatively weak, particularly in China. This result does not support the cultural perspective of demographic change, as Chinese culture and values definitely permeate the countryside. Similarly, the Chinese rural data do not support Wolf's (1986) theory of political efficacy. Ironically, the finding here shows that the penetration of China's government in the countryside to push for its family planning program is limited and does not produce intended results.

As noticed widely, the gap of wealth has increased in China between its urban and rural residents. The reduction of rural population is conducive to a reduction in the gap of wealth. While a reduction in population in the countryside decreases the pressure on the need to create nonfarm jobs, the creation of nonfarm jobs will also facilitate the reduction of population in the countryside. The enormous challenge of creating millions of nonfarm jobs every year in the next several decades can be significantly muted by the reduction of rural birth rates.

A government can devise an economic policy to generate incomes so that the population growth can be reduced. Or a government can politically influence its demographic structure to maximize the economic growth rate of the country. In other words, population reduction can happen because of the modernization process, or it can be the generated in a political and policy process. A stable and capable government has the option of promoting long-term development through controlling demographic transition. Therefore, instead of leaving population decline to modernization, a government can take the initiative to manage population growth so that economic growth can be accelerated and sustained.

References

Alesina, A., Ozler, S., Roubini, N. and Swagel, P. (1996), 'Political Instability and Economic Growth,' *Journal of Economic Growth*, 1, pp. 189–212.

Arbetman, M. and Kugler, J. (1995), 'The Politics of Inflation: An Empirical Assessment of the Emerging Market Economies,' in Thomas, D. Willett, T.D., Burdekin, R., Sweeney, R. and Whilborg, C. (eds), *Establishing Monetary Stability in Emerging Market Economies*, pp. 81–100. Boulder, CO: Westview Press.

Arbetman, M., Kugler, J. and Organski, A. (1997), 'Political Capacity and Demographic Change,' in Arbetman, M. and Kugler, J. (eds), *Political Capacity and Economic Behavior*, pp. 193–220. Boulder, CO: Westview Press.

Butler, D. (1992), 'The Predictability of Indian Election Results,' in Mitra, S.K. and Chiriyankandath, J. (eds), *Electoral Politics in India*, New Delhi: Segment.

China Population Information Center (1999), *Population and Family Planning Key Data Manual.* Beijing: State Commission of Family Planning.

Chen, S. (1984), 'Fertility of Women during the 42-year period from 1940 to 1981,' in China Population Information Center, *Analysis on China's National One-per-Thousand Sampling Survey*, pp. 32–58. Beijing: China Population Publishing House.

Coale, A.J. (1984), *Rapid Population Change in China, 1952–1982*, Washington DC: National Academy Press.

Feng, Y., Kugler, J. and Zak, P. (2000), 'The Politics of Fertility and Economic Development,' *International Studies Quarterly*, 44, pp. 667–93.

Feng, Y., Kugler, J. and Zak, P. (2002), 'Population Growth, Urbanization and Role of Government in China: A Political Economic Model of Demographic Change,' *Urban Studies*, forthcoming.

Feng, Y. and Li, J. (1997), 'Internal Constraints and International Competitiveness: A Research Note on China,' *Journal of Contemporary China*, 6, pp. 377–87.

Johnson, D.G. (2001), 'Can Agricultural Labor Adjustment Occur Primarily through Creation of Rural Nonfarm Jobs in China?,' paper presented at the Conference on Urbanization, Xiamen, China, 27–28 June.

Kugler, J. and Arbetman, M. (1997), 'Relative Political Capacity: Political Extraction and Political Reach,' in Arbetman, M. and Kugler, J. (eds), *Political Capacity and Economic Behavior*, pp. 11–46, Boulder, CO: Westview Press.

Kugler, J., Tammen, R. and Swaminathan, S. (2001), 'Power Transitions and Alliances in the 21st Century,' *Asian Perspective*, 25 (3), pp, 5–29.

Lavely, W. and Freedman, R. (1990), 'The Origins of the Chinese Fertility Decline,' *Demography*, 27, pp. 357–67.

Organski, A.F.K., Kugler, J., Johnson, T. and Cohen, Y. (1984), *Birth, Death and Taxes: Political and Economic Transition*, Chicago: University of Chicago Press.

Organski, A.F.K. and Kugler, J. (1980), *The War Ledger*, Chicago: University of Chicago Press.

Poston, D. (1992), 'Fertility Trends in China,' in Poston Jr, D.L. and Yaukey, D. (eds), *The Population of Modern China*, New York: Plenum Press.

Website http://www.censusindia.net/ 'Vital Statistics in India.'

Wolf, A. (1986), 'The Preeminent Role of Government Intervention in China's Family Revolution,' *Population and Development Review*, 12, pp. 101–16.

Wu, C. and Ji, S. (1991), 'Chinese Culture and Fertility Decline,' *China's Population Science*, 5, pp. 7–12.

Yao, X. and Hua, Y. (1994), *Basic Data of China's Population*, Beijing: China Population Publishing House.

Zhao, Z. (1997), 'Deliberate Birth Control under a High-Fertility Regime: Reproductive Behavior in China before 1970,' *Population and Development Review*, 23, pp. 729–67.

Zheng, X. (1995), *China's Female Population and Development*, Beijing: Beijing University Press.

Zou, Q. (1993), 'China's Family Planning and the Chinese Culture,' in Bing, D., Lim, S. and Lin, M. (eds), *Asia 2000: Modern China in Transition*, pp. 92–107, New Zealand: University of Waikato Printery.

CHAPTER 4

STRUCTURE AND STRATEGY FOR *IN SITU* RURAL URBANIZATION

QI HONG DONG*
Barat College/DePaul University

Abstract

After inspecting the rural urbanization in the Fujian Province of China, and studying the lessons about rural urbanization of the America and OECD countries, the author discusses why and how to carry out in situ *rural urbanization in China. The process of China's urbanization is a topic that has rarely been touched upon. Government rural policies should focus on privatization, cluster, comparative advantage, competition, and bottom-up development initiatives, which may raise rural income and ease the rural-urban migration pressure on cities to avoid industrialization-urbanization-Kuznets cycles.*

Keywords: structure, strategy, rural urbanization, Kuznets cycle

JEL classification: R11

1   Introduction

In China, the gap between the rural and urban income is larger than at any time since the 1949 revolution, and is among the highest in the world today. Chinese experts believe that some 10 million farm workers could be thrown out of work due to the effects of the World Trade Organization (WTO). If the

---

*   Correspondence: Qi Hong Dong, Associate Professor of Barat College, DePaul University at Lake Forest, Il. 60045. Tel: (847) 574-4314; Email: qdong@barat.edu.

The author thanks the Chinese Economic Society (CES) for giving her the great opportunity to inspect the rural urbanization in the Fu Jian Province of China in June, 2001. All the opinions and errors are the author's.

rural crisis were to result in widespread unrest, it would slow the full range of economic reforms underway ...(*Financial Times*, 8 October 2001).

Facing this challenge, some scholars suggest eliminating the 'hukou system', and letting farmers be free to migrate to the big urban cities. Can this solve China's rural problems? Theory and evidence can answer this question.

2   Industrialization-Urbanization-Kuznets Cycles

Since the Industrial Revolution, urbanization and industrialization have moved in tandem. The urban population in the leading areas of western and northern Europe exceeds 80 per cent. In the twentieth century, when economic growth spread to Asia, change was seen there, too. Less than 10 per cent of the population was urban at the start of the century; it has grown to more than 30 per cent today. Since China's economic reform of 1978, the urban population has also increased dramatically. For example, in Shanghai, the number of migrants rose more than tenfold in one decade; from 0.26 million in 1981 to 2.81 million in 1993 (Wang and Zuo, 1999).

The continuing concentration of economic activities and population in already overcrowded major cities can generate economic inefficiencies. While large cities offer economies of scale and benefits of agglomeration, these advantages could eventually be more than offset by negative externalities: worsening pollution, congestion, crime, and other ill effects. The benefits of the urban setting are taken into account in location decisions by businesses and households while the negative externalities do not fully enter in their costs. This, along with the average cost pricing of urban public provisions, could lead many large cities into an inevitable state of over-expansion (Riew, 2001). The historical experience of the developed countries has shown that urbanization proceeded as an irregular wave erupting intermittently in a financial crisis and collapse. These long swings in economic growth are commonly termed Kuznets cycles, in recognition of Simon Kuznets' pioneering work. During these cycles, real investment typically occurred in a two-stage sequence consisting of the needs for industrialization and urbanization. Industrialization induced tremendous investment in new production technology, while urbanization attracted excessive investment in urban infrastructure. According to Kuznets, the results of these events would lead to huge borrowing and when interest rises, financial crisis and collapse would be unavoidable. In free market economies of the past, this urbanization process occurred in Kuznets cycles, averaging 15–25 years in duration (Easterlin, 2000). Is the 1997–98 Asian financial crisis a possible rebirth of the Kuznets cycles? Will China follow the same pattern? Is it possible to avoid this industrialization-urbanization-Kuznets cycle? Maybe *in situ* rural urbanization is the answer.

3   *In Situ* Rural Urbanization

Today's America and OECD countries face the same challenges in rural areas as China faces. Data collected from the America and OECD countries make it clear how inadequate a single sector definition of rural areas is. Even among the most rural regions of OECD countries, only one out of five jobs are in the agricultural sector (including forestry and fisheries), and employment shares of the industrial sector (including mining and construction) are higher than those of agriculture (Drabenstott, 2000). Rural areas are no longer synonymous with agriculture, and agriculture is no longer the backbone of rural areas. Rural areas in the America and OECD countries also suffer from the out-migration of both young and highly skilled workers, leaving behind an aging population and strained public services. In addition, most rural areas have difficulty mustering the critical mass of capital and infrastructure to encourage and sustain new rural entrepreneurs. Yet, sustained development has been observed in some American and OECD rural areas. Economic structural and production technical changes have brought their incomes closer to non-farm incomes. The factors of success are the following (Pezzini, 2000, p. 47):

a) Manufacturing and service industries begin to relocate to suburban and rural green fields where land is more plentiful and cheaper. The availability of more diverse employment opportunities serves to increase population movements from urban to rural areas.
b) Sustained endogenous development has also been observed. This has involved both intermediate and remote regions. In these areas, growth in local industries has reversed patterns of economic decline and out migration.
c) Residential location decisions place increasing emphasis on quality of life factors, including proximity to open countryside and natural amenities. This has resulted in people moving from cities to rural areas. A pollution-free, easily accessible, and natural environment attracts them, and improved transport links make residence in rural areas feasible.

In order to achieve *in situ* rural urbanization, China's rural areas need to change their structure.

3.1 The Structure

3.1.1 Privatization Rural development should encourage privatization, as many of the current firms in China are still state or collectively owned. Power and responsibility do not go together. In order to show their achievements, some managers have been investing blindly with government's capital as the only source. Rural policy should encourage and support partnerships, as well as privately owned firms, to go public so as to raise money for further expansion, rather than relying on the government for capital. Inspecting the northern Fu Jian Province, I found different levels of government agencies from all over the country own most hotels in those resort areas. They have the privilege of getting land usage, and if they are not financially successful they can rely on the government. All of these hotels' halls are splendid, but the restrooms inside are not adequate and clean, thus attracting few tourists. It is a typical example of 'Da Guo Fan'. Nearby, I found some half-built constructions owned by the local residents that had been abandoned due to lack of capital. An individual's ability to compete with the government is lean. One important characteristic of a market economy is that equal entities compete. If there is no equality, there is no market economy. Therefore, no single reform is more important than the separation of government from enterprises. The government should not be involved in any competition, but should focus on structural change, policy adjustment, natural monopoly resource allocation and education.

3.1.2 Cluster Industrial cluster will enhance the process of industrialization and urbanization in an original agricultural area (Zhao and Deng, 2001). Rural development should focus on the regional rather than the individual sector. OECD governments are recognizing that economic regions are more meaningful than traditional policy boundaries, and attempts are being made to align the two. At the state level, this structure requires creating new interministerial working groups. At the local level, it often means forming new partnerships among various public departments and agencies, as well as, including the private and nonprofit sectors (Shortall and Shucksmith, 1998). From the case studies of OECD countries, it is believed that clusters are sources of competitive advantages for regional economies. Here, the author means to cluster in certain rural areas, rather than to cluster in big cities. In China, a unique development pattern of cluster-industrialization-urbanization has emerged in the Jinjiang of Fu Jian Province – a pattern called the 'Jinjiang Model' (Zhao and Deng, 2001), but a big specialized market has not been formed in the northern Fu Jian Province. Due to the backward distribution system, the comparative advantage products like bamboo, wood and related goods, and various agriculture goods are still produced by each individual family. Repeat and low level investment is everywhere, natural resources have not been contributed efficiently, and comparative advantage becomes comparative disadvantage, as economies of scale have not been achieved.

3.2 The Strategy

3.2.1 Comparative advantage Each rural area should find its own comparative advantage. Agricultural policies have traditionally cast the countryside as a homogenous space, yet evidence shows that rural areas are experiencing divergent development trajectories shaped by their regional contexts (Lowe and Ward, 1998). Each rural area should specialize in its comparative advantage. According to Stauber (2001), there are basically four types of rural areas in America: a) urban periphery-rural areas within a 90-minute commute of urban employment, services, and social opportunities; b) high amenity-rural areas of significant scenic beauty, cultural opportunities, and attraction to wealthy and retired people; c) sparsely populated-rural areas where the population density is low and often declining and therefore the demand for traditional services, employment, and social opportunities are limited by isolation; and d) high poverty-rural areas characterized by persistent poverty or rapid declines in income. China's rural areas can be similarly divided. A 'one size fits all' rural policy is infeasible. Urban periphery areas should take advantage of their locations to create new market demands and linkages so as to increase regional competitive investments. High amenity-rural areas should search for local rural features that can spur new growth, such as scenic amenities, environmental virtues, or unique products that reflect the cultural heritage of a particular region. Sparsely populated and high-poverty rural areas should get enough funds from the government for their initial development and use new technology to overcome remoteness to create infrastructure that expands competitive advantage. In other words, the government should create special immigration and support programs that recruit people to targeted rural areas and then assist them in creating new, successful enterprises.

3.2.2 Competition Competition should substitute subsidies and prioritize the building of 'competitiveness' in rural areas to meet the needs of the global economy. Ongoing subsidies dull incentives and create an attitude of dependence. Firms' attention will focus on renewing subsidies rather than creating true competitive advantage. Once started, a subsidy is difficult to stop

(Porter, 1990, p. 640). For rural manufacturing to continue as a significant economic engine, it must adopt new approaches to create and maintain a competitive advantage. For example, in the northern Fu Jian Province, I found that the local residents have little knowledge about how the market economy works. Local farmers, satisfied with one family's own production, lack of capacity for competition, only know how to produce goods and services and do not know how to sell them (see Appendix). Rural policy should help rural businesses, including family farmers to survive changes that have occured after China's entry into the WTO. Rural policy should divert resources from programs, which focused on subsidies and instead support education, training, and increasing the attractiveness of areas for new enterprises.

3.2.3 Bottom-up Rural policy should support 'bottom-up' development initiatives. Strategic goals are most likely to be achieved by encouraging rural communities to shape their own futures. Development is something that individuals and groups do, not something done for them. Put the development agenda in local hands and create a much stronger link between decisions and their consequences. In the inspection of Fu Jian Province, I was very interested in the 'Hearing Hall' of Jiao Mai City, located in the southeast of Fu Jian Province. The top leaders of this city have visited American and European countries several times. Coming back, they did not imitate the western countries and build tall buildings, but learned how to manage a city democratically. They have carried out a 'bottom-up' policy: the 'Hearing Hall' composed by the local residents have made every important decision. All rural residents should play a critical role in deciding future priorities and strategies, not just those residents with the most economic and political influence.

4   Concluding Remarks

There is no agreement on what the rural policies should be, but there is a broad consensus that rural areas will need new policies if China is to reach its full potential in the twenty-first century. Government policies should focus *on privatization, cluster, comparative advantage, competition, and bottom-up* development initiatives. None of my answers to the rural urbanization in China are adequate, yet they illustrate the approaches the Chinese government should take. These rural policies may raise rural income and ease the rural-urban migration pressure on cities to avoid industrialization-urbanization-Kuznets cycles.

References

Drabenstott, M. (2000), 'Beyond Agriculture: New Policies for Rural America – A Conference Summary,' *Economic Review*, 85 (3), pp. 39–45.

Easterlin, R.A. (2000), 'Locational Restructuring and Financial Crises,' *Structural Change and Economic Dynamics*, 11, pp. 129–38.

Financial Times, 8 October 2001.

Lowe, P. and Ward, N. (1998), 'Regional Policy CAP Reform and Rural Development in Britain: The Challenge for New Labor,' *Studies*, 32, pp. 469–75.

Pezzini, M. (2000), 'Rural Policy Lessons from OECD Countries,' *Economic Review* – Federal Reserve Bank of Kansas City, 85 (3), pp. 47–57.

Porter, M. (1990), *The Competitive Advantages of Nations*, New York: Free Press.

Riew, J. (2001), 'Toward a New Urban Development Policy: With Focus on Developing Countries,' in the International Conference of Urbanization in China, Challenges and Strategies of Growth and Development Proceedings, (3) 186.

Shortall, S. and Shucksmith M. (1998), 'Integrated Rural Development: Issues Arising from the Scottish Experience, European Plan,' *Studies*, 6, pp. 73–88.

Stauber, K.N. (2001), 'Why Invest in Rural America – and How? A Critical Public Policy Question for the 21st Century,' *Economic Review*, 86 (2).

United Nations Department of Economic and Social Affairs Population Division, 1997 and 1998.

Wang, F. and Zuo, X. (1999), 'Inside China's Cities: Institutional Barriers and Opportunities for Urban Migrants,' *American Economic Review* (May), pp. 276–80.

Zhao, B. and Deng, L. (2001), 'A Cluster Based Approach to Industrialization and Urbanization: The Case of Jinjiang (China),' in the International Conference of Urbanization in China, Challenges and Strategies of Growth and Development Proceedings, (2), 150.

Appendix

(A dialogue with a fruit-sale couple in the Wu Yi Mountain Areas on 2 July 2001).

Q: How is your life today?
A: Better than our parents. They have been working hard for their whole life; still have not enough to eat.

Q: How long do you sell fruits every day?
A: More than 12 hours a day, from morning about 7 o'clock to midnight 1 o'clock. We are very tired. (Their 6 years old son is playing around there all day long.)

Q: Why doesn't one of you try to find a job somewhere else?
A: Husband: I went to Zhejiang Province to do business long time ago. Because I was not familiar with the environment, the local residents took me in. Last year I went to Shenzhen to sell electric parts, because I did not know the technology, I lost several thousands yuan. Today as a farmer I cannot earn any money, and I cannot do business, therefore I am selling fruits.
Wife: Also it will be hard to do this business just by myself. Every morning we need buy the fruits from farmers and then transport the fruits here, and the business is getting harder to do now, various fees like manager fee, clean fee, spot fee … We earn about 1000 yuan/month and fees are about 200 yuan/month.

Q: How do you think somebody spent about 1000 to 2000 yuan just for one meal?
A: Wife: We are not used to eating that kind of meal and we never want to eat that kind of meal.

Q: Have you ever thought about buying stocks?
A: We do not believe that kind of stuff, which can make you become a beggar within an hour.

Q: What do you work hard for?
A: Our kid can study more and have a better life in the future.

P.S. Because I took some of their time, I bought one watermelon from the husband. The watermelon is 3.5 jiao/jin, and total is 8 jin. I gave him 5 yuan (10 jiao/yuan) and said 'no change'. He said, 'Oh, we can not accept that'. When I insisted, he asked his wife, who was dealing with another customer at that time, and at last she said, 'OK' and both thanked me again and again. I felt embarrassed. How pure and honest these farmers are. They deserve to have good rural policies.

PART II: CHANGING URBAN POPULATION

CHAPTER 5

DETERMINANTS OF URBAN MIGRATION

AIMIN CHEN, PhD*
Indiana State University

N. EDWARD COULSON, PhD
Penn State University

Abstract

This study seeks the causes of variation in the amount of migration to Chinese cities over the period 1995–99. We use a city fixed-effect model with lagged values of 'pulling' factors for each city. While wage income shows no significant influence on migration, per capita gross city income does, suggesting that migrants seek returns above and beyond mere wages. Our regression results show that cities with high ratios in the manufacturing and service sectors grow most rapidly. We find that the developmental environment and the job creation potential of the private sector, indicated by the number of proprietors per capita, makes a significant difference in attracting migrants. Except for government fiscal expenditures, we find that the attributes of the quality of urban life, such as housing-market conditions and transportation, have little explanatory power.

Keywords: urbanization, migration, pulling factors

JEL classification: R23, J60

---

*   Correspondence: Aimin Chen, Associate Professor, Department of Economics, Indiana State University, Terre Haute, IN 47809. Tel: (812) 237–2175; Email: ecchen@isugw.in dstate.edu.

This is a reprint of the original article published in *Urban Studies* (http://www.tandf.co.uk), 39 (12), 2002.

URBAN TRANSFORMATION IN CHINA, edited by Aimin Chen, Gordon G. Liu and Kevin H. Zhang

1   Introduction

This research examines the determinants of urban migration that has contributed to China's urban population growth, an important aspect of an economy's urbanization. Our focus is on the differential growth rates of Chinese cities as a result of cities' receiving in-migrants.[1] Thus we ask why some cities have received more migrants, and thus have grown faster, than others.

The literature on population migration and growth in China is reasonably rich. One type of study has focused on the definition of urban population and policies on the *hukou* system. Cheng and Selden (1994) examine the origins and the development of the Hukou system and its social implications in the creation of spatial hierarchies and the consequences in defining the position of villagers in the Chinese social system. Wu (1994) and Wu and Zhou (1996) discuss the measurement of population in urban China and the difficulties of defining China's urbanization in light of these data problems. Chan (1994) focuses on the growth of urban population as a result of both the reclassification of newly urbanized areas as well as the in-migration during the period 1978-1992. Liang and Chen (2001) study the pattern of China's urbanization, its unique experiences, and the impact of migration, providing insights into unique growth experiences of Chinese cities.

Another type of migration research focuses on the migration of rural population into the cities. These studies have evaluated the pushing factors that have caused out-migration of rural population to cities and the factor that have 'pulled' the migrants back to their rural origin (Hare, 1999; Zhao, 1999). They have also considered the dynamic role of returnees as agents of information transfer, entrepreneurship, and change in previously isolated rural localities (Murphy, 2000). These studies are based either on surveys of rural migrants or on case studies and qualitative analysis without the support of statistical evidence. Their focus is on the rural migrating population.

Seeborg, Jin, and Zhu (2000) analyzed several factors that have affected the new rural-to-urban labor mobility in China from both urban side and rural side. The urban-side factors are identified as the 'iron triangle of constraints' (i.e., the residency requirements, state controlled work units, and secret personnel

---

1   The spatial measure of the China's urbanization can be indicated by the administrative adjustment of rural towns to urban cities. This development is well captured by the time series data at the macro-level. China has upgraded many rural towns into urban cities. The number of cities has increased from 450 in 1989 to 479 in 1991, 517 in 1992, 570 in 1993, 622 in 1994, 640 in 1995, 666 in 1996, and 668 in 1997 and 1998, and 667 in 1999 (*China Urban Statistical Yearbook*, 1990–2000).

files), the effects of certain economic reforms, especially the development of the contract wage system in SOEs, and the effects of privatization and rising unemployment on the floating population. The rural-side forces are the gap between urban and rural incomes, agricultural market reforms (including the development of the household responsibility system), the development of industries in the rural areas, and the pool of surplus labor in agriculture. Seeborg, Jin, and Zhu provide no data analysis and empirical evidence to the claimed relationship between the explanatory and dependent variables, however.

The research described here fills a void in the literature by concentrating on the city 'pulling' forces using pooled time-series and cross sectional data over the period 1995–99, the most recent period for which data are available. Our city pulling factors include a more comprehensive set of variables than in Seeborg, Jin, and Zhu. Realizing that city data naturally exclude conditions of the rural sectors[2] and that rural pushing forces are also important in city-bound migration decisions, we use a city-specific fixed-effects model to control for both city and local rural variables that are time-invariant. We also include a time trend to control for any nationwide trends in urban and rural conditions.

The paper is structured as the follows. In Section 2, we describe our model and provide data and variable specifications. Section 3 presents the empirical regression results as well as policy implications. Section 4 concludes the chapter.

2   Modeling Issues and the Data

Our regressions take the form

$$\Delta\ln Lit = \Sigma_j \beta_j Xijt - 1 + w_i + v_{it} \tag{1}$$

where i indexes the city, t, the year of the observation and j indexes the right-hand side variables. $\Delta\ln Lit$ represents the growth rate of urban non-agricultural population, and Xijt is an independent variable j for city i, with weight β_j, which, in order to circumvent problems of simultaneity, is generally lagged by one year. We will usually include a city-specific fixed effect, w_i, in the equation. The time-varying part of the unobserved portion of city growth is given as v_{it}.

---

2   At the provincial level, data can include both city pulling and rural pushing effects, but it will be difficult to single out the migration effect on urban growth that, at the provincial level, may very well be caused by changing statutory towns into cities.

2.1   *Dependent Variable*

Our dependent variable is the growth rate of urban non-agricultural population minus the natural growth rate (births minus deaths) of the urban population. (We exclude agricultural population in order to capture the effect of industrialization.)

This variable is effectively the migration rate, for the following reasons. At the national level, total urban non-agricultural population can grow as a result of reclassifying many rural towns into urban cities. The number of urban cities in China has increased from 479 in 1991 to 667 in 1999, adding many residents previously in rural towns to the classification of urban resident. At the city level, however, the growth of urban non-agricultural population must come from three sources: 1) the natural growth (births minus deaths); 2) statistical reclassification within a city; and 3) migration into the cities.

The statistical reclassification within a city takes place when new policies allow people to change their Hukou (or household registration) status from agricultural population to urban non-agricultural population. This happened when non-agricultural Hukou status became de-linked with the 'grain source' to include those who resided in urban cities and lived primarily on non-agricultural income regardless of whether they were entitled to receiving 'commodity grain' (Wu, 1994). As a result, peasants setting up businesses in small cities and towns have been granted urban non-agricultural Hukou provided that they are responsible for their food grain. People also change their Hukou status when they retire from military service and remain legally in the cities, when rural students go to college and never return to their hometown, and when city limits expand to include areas that are previously rural. While it is considered as statistical reclassification, this is essentially a weaker form of migration in which people moved from rural to urban areas over a long period of time through occupation or income source changes.

Direct migration that becomes part of the growth of urban non-agricultural population also involves statistical reclassification. Starting from the third national census in 1982, the new definition of urban population has included all persons who have lived for one year or more within the officially defined cities, including those newly classified, and also those who have lived there less than one year but have been absent from their place of *hukou* registration for one year or more (Wu, 1994). These are migration of rural residents into the cities in a stricter form.

2.2   Independent Variables

The independent variables include measures of factors that enhance productivity or that improve the quality of urban life. All variables are either in per capita or percentage terms.

- Gross City Product: This is like a per-capita Gross Domestic Product (GDP) only at the city level. We expect a positive influence of the per capita value of this variable since migration would flow from lower to higher income areas.
- Salary: The average level of salary is also expected to exert income effect.
- Employment Rate: This is labor force employment rate in the cities. A higher unemployment rate is expected to provoke more active lobbying against rural migrants and set barriers. We are, however, skeptical about the outcome of this variable in explaining its effect on urban migration because of the data reliability problem as will be discussed later.
- Proprietors: These are private single-owner businesses measured as a ratio to per 10,000 people in the city. A higher value of this variable indicates a more conducive growth environment for private businesses as well as a greater source to absorb migrant labor. In China, private businesses have become the major source for creating new jobs and absorbing surplus labor from the state as well as the rural sectors. These private businesses have been less discriminatory against rural migrants than state enterprises that must bear the burden of supporting the currently employed labor force, of which a considerable number have been made redundant. Moreover, a greater value of this variable also indicates a better survival environment for those who migrate to settle in the city. Furthermore, setting up a new business is a sufficient condition for a rural resident to become an urban resident, thus directly contribute to the rate of urbanization.[3]
- Second Sector and Third Sector: These variables give the shares of labor force employed in the second sector (including mining, manufacturing, construction, and the production and supply of electricity, water and gas) and the third sector which consists of service industries including transportation, telecommunications, wholesale and retail trade, banking and insurance, TV broadcasting, education, sports, etc. These are expected

---

3   This variable, however, is lagged one period in our regressions to reflect the existing 'survival condition' for migrants and to avoid potential endogeneity problem between it and the dependent variable.

to be positive pulling factors for a city, as opposed to employment in the first sector which consists primarily of agricultural employment.[4]

- FDI: Foreign direct investment. This variable is expected to positively pull migration into the cities because of its effect on creating employment opportunities and boosting income. Moreover, this variable also strongly correlates with a city's location, policy treatment, and historical development. The coastal cities in China have received most FDI because of their location and policies that establish the coastal Open Cities to create more conducive environment for foreign direct investment.

- Housing Investment: This indicates urban housing market development that should influence the decision making of potential migrants. China had had tight administrative controls of housing allotment in the cities, which had served as a means by the government to restrict population mobility. Higher investment in housing by the market amid housing reform indicates a greater supply and availability of private housing to facilitate in-migrants. This variable is thus expected to have positive influence on the dependent variable.[5]

- Public Transportation: The availability of public transportation should indicate effectively the quality of urban life in China. It is measured by per capita number of passengers. Good public transportation also makes the city more accessible to the first-time migrants. We, therefore, expect this variable to show positive effect.

- Fiscal Expenditures: This variable of local government fiscal expenditures is included to show an effect of quality of urban life as well, assuming that higher expenditures correlate with better public amenities, health care system, schools, and local governments' ability to facilitate migrants.

2.3   The Data

Our data come from two sources of various issues of the China Urban Statistical Yearbook and Urban Construction Annual Report. Covering the period

---

4   Cities in China, depending on their administrative ranks, include counties and rural townships. The cities in our data include administratively townships, but not counties. Under the administration of townships are villages where major production activities are agricultural.

5   We expect the variables of rent and price of ownership housing to be more direct indicators of housing market reform and facilitating condition of urban floating population, because the higher is the cost of housing, the more difficult it is for migrants to settle in the city. These variables, however, may not duly reflect their expected effect on urban migration as a result of data irregularity as will be discussed later in the data section.

1995–99, the data set includes 223 cities out of a total of 667 in 1999. These included cities that are generally larger in size and are more economically developed.

It can be seen from Table 5.1 that a little over a third of the cities are from the Central region of China and about one-sixth are from the relatively sparsely populated Western region, leaving about a half of the observations from the more developed Eastern region. While this region tends to have the largest cities, this (as will be seen) does not translate into differences in growth rates. For lack of data, Tibet is excluded from the set. Since not all variables are available for all years and all cities, the effective number of observations is much smaller than the full size of the data set. Table 5.1 will present how many observations are in each regression.

Table 5.1   Variables and summary statistics

Variable	Mean	Standard dev.
Migration rate	0.010432	0.093932
Population (non-agricultural, 10,000 people)	107.2808	122.6131
Central (=1 if city is in central region)	0.368469	0.482607
West (=1 if city is in western region)	0.162162	0.368766
Gross city product (yuan per capita)	11,689	9,368
Average salary (yuan)	6803.093	2227.031
Employment rate (%)	97.41985	2.743145
Proprietors (number per 10,000)	4.739827	6.935045
Second sector (%)	46.50	15.3045
Third sector (%)	38.85	17.3497
FDI (USD per capita)	120.68	290.40
Housing investment (yuan per capita)	518.81	772.77
Public transportation (trips per capita)	26.84	31.13
Fiscal expenditures (yuan per capita)	916.78	1010.87

Sources: *Urban Statistical Yearbook of China*, 1996, 1997, 1998, 1999, and 2000; *Urban Construction Annual Report*, 1996, 1997, 1998, 1999, and 2000.

Means and standard deviations for the variables we use in the regressions are also presented in Table 5.1. An overall glance at the table speaks to the extraordinary diversity in the data, which will pose a challenge for any empirical model. For a number of the variables the standard deviations are several times the mean of the data, indicating substantial skewness (as might be expected).

For example, the migration rate (defined as population growth rate minus the 'natural growth rate' derived from births and deaths) has an average of about 1 per cent per year, but the standard deviation is around 9 per cent.

We find the data on housing variables to be least available and most unreliable. For about half of the cities we have some data on housing prices and rents, but serious irregularities exist. In Chengdu, the capital city of Sichuan Province, for example, reported rental space in the market went up from 41,600 square meters in 1998 to 228,900 square meters in 1999, but reported rental revenue went down from 7,222,500 yuan to 1,188,900 yuan. As another example, all cities in Fujian Province, in order to fulfill requirements, provided exactly the same set of data in 1999 as in 1998 on number of houseless households and the floor space constructed. We are, as a result, least confident that housing variables will have their rightful explanatory power in our regressions.

Moreover, we have little confidence in the employment rate data. As can be seen from Table 5.1, China had an average (registered) employment rate of 97.4 per cent, or an unemployment rate of less than 3 per cent, with very little variation. The data reflect poorly the jobless situation, which is estimated elsewhere to be 7–8 per cent percent in the late 1990s and about 25 per cent if disguised unemployment is included (Chen, 1999). This data series became unavailable in 1999, perhaps due to Chinese officials realizing this problem.

3   Empirical Results

Our goal is to empirically characterize the variation in migration experienced by cities in China. Since migration is both cause and effect of any number of other economic and social characteristics of the city in question, all of our regressions use one-year lags of all of the causal variables. All of these regressors are in either per capita terms or in percentages, as appropriate.

We classify these variables into two groups. First, there are variables that speak to the quality of life in the city. Among these are the housing market variables, including the (per capita) amount of housing investment in the city,[6]

---

6   For about half of our observations we have some data on housing prices and rents, which (for this limited sample) had no explanatory power for migration. It is possible in any case that housing prices may be endogenous even when lagged, since they can be very forward-looking. The interaction between the housing and labor markets in China remains a topic of future research.

the (per capita) fiscal expenditures in the city, which is a measure of the extent of the provision of local public goods, and the extent of the public transportation system (as per capita numbers of passengers).

The second category has to do with labor market conditions. It includes three direct measures: average salary of workers, per capita gross city product, and employment rate. It also includes variables that represent the city's acceptance, or openness, to more 'modern' or 'open' ways of doing business. There are substantial differences in the character of city-economies and their orientation toward more liberal markets. Our intent here is to try and use these variables to get at the more long-term prospects of potential migrants than would be available from current (expected) compensation. Among the variables that would fulfill this role are the (per capita) level of foreign direct investment, the (per capita) number of (self-employed) proprietors, and the percentage of the workforce employed in second and third sector firms.

The major lacuna in our data is the absence of rural wage or quality of life indicators. Since so much of migration in China is rural-to-urban in character, this omission is less important to the extent that similar conditions exist in all rural areas of the country or that rural-to-urban migration is not spatially contiguous. In case these conditions do not hold, we can to some extent control for cross-city differences in nearby rural conditions through city-specific fixed effects (which of course also control for unmeasured time-invariant city attributes). We also have a time trend included in our regressions to control for any nationwide trends in rural conditions (or urban conditions, for that matter).

An alternative to city fixed effects would be a regional dummy variable, but this location measure is evidently not fine enough a measure of regional differentiation. In column (1) of Table 5.2 (which also contains all of the subsequent regression results), it can be seen that regional dummy variables for the Central and West regions of China do not have significant t-ratios, even when no other variables are included. Thus, while the coefficients indicate that the cities of the interior regions have, on average, slower growth rates than the more developed East, these differences are not important in explaining the city-to-city variation in population growth. An underlying explanation for this result may lie in the very nature of the data set that contains cities instead of provinces. Comparing provinces, it has been a stylized fact that most migration has flowed toward the east coast. However, the cities of the Central and Western regions included in our data set are relatively more important within their provinces than many of the cities in the Eastern region and so may attract more intra-province migration, thus blurring the effect of inter-province migration.

We then present, in succeeding columns of the table, results of fixed effect regressions using the two groups of variables discussed above. Column (2) includes all of the variables. Turning first to the compensation variables, we find that neither the employment rate nor the average salary has much of a conditional correlation with migration. Both have coefficients with t-ratios less than 0.5. This is not entirely surprising because of the data problem that we discussed earlier. The 'compensation' variable that does matter is per capita gross city product, which has the expected positive sign and a t-ratio in the usual rejection range. The correlation coefficient between salary and per capita GDP is only around 0.05; therefore these two variables are capturing different elements of the city economy, and only those elements associated with the latter are important for attracting migrants.

The additional variables with explanatory power are those that indicate the 'character' of the city economy. The proprietors variable has a positive sign, along with a t-ratio of 4.475, suggesting that cities with a better developmental environment of private businesses attract more migrants. Also significant are the second and third sector employment shares, suggesting that orientation towards third sector (and to a lesser extent second sector) employment may encourage migration above and beyond the wages commanded in these sectors, because of the future prospects of such firms. The only variable in this group that does not appear to be significant is the level of foreign direct investment (FDI), which has a t-ratio less than 0.5.

Thus it appears that the structure of a city's economy, as much as anything, attracts migrants. Cities with high levels of proprietorial self-employment and high percentages of service sector jobs are the ones that attract people to their area. The 'compensation' variables provide further confirmation: what is important is the overall income (per capita) in the city, not salary. The lack of explanatory power of FDI, on the other hand, may be a result of its correlation with per capita GDP (r = 0.52).[7]

The next set of variables includes those dealing with 'quality of life'. These are basically all insignificant. The public transportation variable has

---

7   We find that lagged GDP per capita is significant in a regression with current FDI as the explanatory variable, but not vice versa. On that account, one might say that GDP causes FDI, at least more so than the reverse. FDI flows to cities of high GDP and superior investment environment so that the contribution by FDI to GDP apparently has a weaker impact than the direct effect of GDP itself. The significant effect of lagged GDP (per capita) supports our inference. Moreover, the insertion of domestic investment in place of, or alongside FDI caused no change in any of the results here. The coefficient of this variable had a t-ratio less than 0.5.

Table 5.2   Determinants of urban migration

	OLS (1)	Fixed effects (2)	Fixed effects (3)	Fixed effects (4)	Fixed effects (5)
Intercept	0.0131				
	(2.48)				
Central Region	-0.0061				
	(0.873)				
Western Region	-0.0029				
	(0.316)				
Year		-0.187**	-.0176**	-0.184**	-.0155**
		(-3.381)	(-3.258)	(-3.404)	(-2.907)
Salary		-4.95×10^{-6}	-3.77×10^{-6}	-5.28×10^{-6}	-3.99×10^{-6}
		(-0.762)	(-0.599)	(-0.311)	(-0.623)
Gross city product.		6.717**	8.536**	6.822**	
		(2.693)	(4.066)	(2.892)	
Employment rate		-4.76×10^{-4}	5.367×10^{-4}	-6.27×10^{-4}	-7.77×10^{-4}
		(-0.234)	(-0.266)	(-0.311)	(-0.383)
Fiscal expenditures		3.14×10^{-4}		3.12×10^{-4}	4.76×10^{-5}**
		(1.497)		(1.587)	(2.413)
Housing investment		2.04×10^{-6}			9.71×10^{-6}
		(0.216)			(1.088)
FDI		1.03×10^{-5}	1.26×10^{-4}	1.03×10^{-5}	1.44×10^{-5}
		(0.409)	(0.512)	(0.418)	(0.575)
Second sector		0.0015**	0.0014**	0.0014**	.0011
		(2.179)	(2.059)	(2.03)	(1.649)
Third sector		0.0015**	0.0015**	0.0015**	0.0015**
		(2.307)	(2.39)	(2.40)	(2.397)
Proprietors		0.589**	0.573**	0.577**	0.598**
		(4.475)	(4.701)	(4.739)	(4.803)
Observations	877	792	798	798	799
R-squared	<.01	.092	.086	.090	.080

** indicates significance at .05 level (two-sided).

a negative coefficient, and its t-ratio is less than 0.05, as is the t-ratio for the housing investment variable, although this coefficient is positive. The fiscal expenditures coefficient, however, has somewhat more explanatory power than the others and is expectedly positive, although with a t-value of 1.50, it is still impossible to reject the zero null at the usual significance levels. The lack of significance of these variables might be a result of China's long controlled population mobility that has created a severe urban-rural income disparity, making the quality of life in the cities at the current stage of migration far less important than income and potential job opportunities. Data problems as afore-analyzed are another explanation.

Finally, we note that the time trend is negative. In one sense this is puzzling; one might have expected the opposite sign. However, given that the dependent variable is a rate of change, it is perhaps not surprising that the rate has slowed over the sample period, especially under the ceteris paribus condition that all of the other variables have been held constant through the years of the sample.

We turn again, then, to the question of whether some of the insignificant t-ratios are generated through collinearity.[8] Removal of one or more of the variables may strengthen the conditional correlation of other variables with the dependent variable and on that account we present some alternative specifications. It turns out that little change is effected by these specification changes: the elimination of housing investment and/or fiscal expenditures does not bring about the significance of FDI, as seen in column (3), nor does the simple elimination of housing investment bring about the significance of fiscal expenditures, as displayed in column (4). Furthermore, the removal of gross city product (per capita) does not bestow significance on FDI, but does raise the t-value of fiscal expenditures into the rejection range, as can be seen in column (5).

We performed several regression diagnostics for these regressions. We performed RESET tests on all of the above regressions, to test for the presence of omitted variables in our regressions.[9] RESET uses the multiple correlation coefficients between the error terms and powers of the fitted values of the dependent variable, where a lack of correlation fails to reject the hypothesis of no omitted variables. We use (as is standard) second, third and fourth powers and find no significant correlation. We also regress squared error terms on these polynomials as a test for heteroskedasticity, and in all cases find no significant correlation. Thus to that extent the regressions appear to be well specified, in spite of the wide variation in the data.

---

8   As it happens, there is a strong degree of correlation between fiscal expenditures level of proprietorship ($r = .43$), between the fiscal expenditures variable and FDI ($r = .58$), between fiscal expenditures and housing investment ($r = .73$), and, correspondingly, between housing investment and FDI ($r = .41$). There is also, naturally enough, a strong correlation between FDI and gross city product ($r = .52$), and between these two variables and fiscal expenditure ($r = .58$ and $r = .85$). All other bivariate correlations are substantially smaller than this.

9   The original derivation of the RESET test is Ramsey (1969).

4. Conclusions

The regressions analyzed above show an overriding result that the industrial structure of a city is most important in affecting migration. Cities with higher ratios of employment in the manufacturing and service sectors have experienced higher growths of urban non-agricultural population from migration. Moreover, the number of proprietors (per capita) also has a significant effect on migration, suggesting an important fact that the development of private businesses not only provides a welcome environment to rural migrants but also sources of their employment. Such results point to a strong policy directive that nurturing the developmental environment for private businesses is crucial to China's urbanization. Furthermore, our results show that while per capita wage level (salary) exerts no significant influence on migration, per capita gross city product does, indicating that migrants do not simply flock to cities for higher wages and that broader economic opportunity is the greater attraction.

On the other hand, city quality of life variables in our regressions show little influence on migration, except the variable of local government expenditures that has a marginally significant effect. We interpret this result in two ways. First, at the relatively early stage of China's rural-to-urban migration, the overwhelming concerns of the migrants are income and potential employment opportunities rather than city quality of life. Second, it is possible that the absence of better quality-of-life measures is to blame, especially those that relate to the housing market. Further studies of the effects of quality of life are most necessary when data become more available.

References

Chan, W.K. (1994), 'Urbanization and Rural-Urban Migration in China since 1982,' *Modern China*, July, pp. 243–81.

Chen, A. (1999), 'Analysis of Unemployment and Labor Market Development in China,' presented at the International Symposium on 21st Century China and Challenge of Sustainable Development, 3–5 September, Washington, DC.

Cheng, T.J. and Seldon, M. (1994), 'The Origins and Social Consequences of China's Hukou System,' *The China Quarterly*, September, pp. 664–8.

Fan, C.C. (1996), 'Economic Opportunities and Internal Migration: A Case Study of Guangdong Province, China,' *The Professional Geographer*, February, p. 45.

Glaser, E., Scheinkman, J. and Shleifer, A. (1995), 'Economic Growth in a Cross-Section of Cities,' *Journal of Monetary Economics*, 36, pp. 117–43.

Hare, D. (1999), '"Push" versus "Pull" Factors in Migration Outflows and Returns: Determinants of Migration Status and Spell Duration among China's rural population,' *The Journal of Development Studies*, February, pp. 45–72.

Harris, J.R. and Todaro, M.P. (1970), 'Migration, Unemployment and Development: A Two-Sector Analysis,' *American Economic Review*, 60 (1), pp. 126–42.

Liang, Z and Chen, Y.P. (2001), 'Urbanization in China: Historical Overview and Emerging Patterns in the 1990s,' paper presented at annual meetings of Population Association of America, Washington, DC, 29–31 March.

Ramsey, J. (1969), 'Tests for Specification Errors in Classical Linear Least-squares Regression Analysis,' *Journal of the Royal Statistical Society*, 31, pp. 350–71.

Seeborg, M.C., Jin, Z. and Zhu, Y. (2000), 'The New Rural-urban Labor Mobility in China: Causes and Implications,' *Journal of Socio-Economics*, 29 (1), pp. 39–56.

Shen, J. (1999), 'Modeling Regional Migration in China: Estimation and Decomposition,' *Environment and Planning*, July, pp. 1223–338.

Murphy, R. (2000), 'Return Migration, Entrepreneurship and Local State Corporatism in Rural China: The Experience of Two Counties in South Jiangxi,' *Journal of Contemporary China*, July, pp. 231–47.

Statistical Yearbook of China, China Statistical Publishing House, various issues, Beijing.

Urban Construction Annual Report, 1996–99, Ministry of Construction, Beijing.

Urban Statistical Yearbook of China, 1996–99, China Statistical Publishing House, Beijing.

Wu, H.X. (1994), 'Rural to Urban Migration in the People's Republic of China,' *The China Quarterly*, September, pp. 669–98.

Wu, H.Y. and Zhou, L. (1996), 'Rural to Urban Migration in China,' *Asian Pacific Literature*, 10 November, pp. 54–67.

Yang, X. (2000), 'Determinants of Migration Intentions in Hubei Province, China: Individual versus Family Migration,' *Environment and Planning*, May, pp. 769–87.

Zhang, Y. (1999), 'Burdensome Population a Headache for China,' *Beijing Review*, 21 June, pp. 19–21.

Zhao, Y. (1999), 'Labor Migration and Earnings Differences: The Case of Rural China,' *Economic Development and Cultural Change*, July, pp. 767–82.

CHAPTER 6

URBAN POPULATION IN THE REFORM ERA

JEFF KEJING XIE
Huazhong University of Science and Technology

KEVIN HONGLIN ZHANG*
Illinois State University

Abstract

China's process of transforming itself from a rural to an urban economy has been accelerated since 1978 when economic reforms were initiated due to rapid economic growth. This chapter examines how the Chinese urban population was related to economic development in the reform era in both time-series and cross-section formats. We find that (i) the rising national urbanization is basically caused by economic growth, and no feedback is observed; and (ii) the level of urbanization in a province is too determined by its level of economic development, along with geographic and historical factors.

Keywords: Urbanization, and economic development

JEL classification: R11 and O53

The slow urban growth in China during the Maoist era (1949-77) has been recognized as a sharp divergence from a 'normal' pattern of world urbanization. Urban policies at that time tended to discourage the growth of large cities,

---

*   Correspondence: Kevin H. Zhang, Department of Economics, Illinois State University, Normal, IL 61790–4200, USA. Tel: (309) 438–8928; Fax: (309) 438–5228; Email: khzhang@ilstu.edu.

Yu Chen provided excellent research assistance. Any errors are ours.

and a variety of administrative measures were adopted to control the rural-to-urban migration. While the share of industrial output in GDP grew steadily, the urban population share did not increase correspondingly because of the control on population mobility and in particular rural-urban migration. The control of urban population growth was mainly through the household registration system, in which job provisions and low priced food rations entitled only to registered urban households acted as a highly effective barrier separating rural from urban and agricultural from non-agricultural populations. As a result, the aggregate urban population in the country grew slowly and even shrank in some years.

The economic reform initiated in 1978 has inevitably steered the urban policy and thus marks a significant growth of the Chinese urban population. Cities were again viewed as centers of regional and national development, in contrast to the anti-urban bias of previous decades. The strict administrative measures used in the pre-reform period to control urban growth began to loosen up. Along with the rapid economic growth and changes in the industrial structure, China's process of transformation from a rural to urban society has been accelerated. Urban population rose substantially by 285 million from 173 million in 1978 to 458 million, in 2000, and the corresponding urban population share in the total population increased from 18 per cent to 36 per cent in the period 1978–2000 (SSB, 2001).

What explains the timing and the extent of China's rising urban population? How does China's economic development interact with its urbanization? There is a growing body of literature on China's urbanization. The recent studies include Becker and Morrison (1999), Chang (1995), Chen and Parish (1996), Kojima (1995), Song and Timberlake (1996), Song (2001), Song and Zhang (2001), and Zhang and Zhao (1998). However, empirical analyses of its national and regional urbanization patterns have been limited. In particular, we are still uncertain about some critical issues concerning the Chinese experience in urban growth, such as measures of regional urbanization and factors behind the rapid national and regional urban growth. This chapter aims to study how China's urban population and urbanization are linked to its economic development in the period of economic reforms since 1978. The emphasis is on describing major features of the urban growth at both national and regional levels, and on explaining these features from time-series and cross-section data. In particular, we intend to close the gap in the literature by: (a) constructing measures of urbanization for each province based on a reasonable procedure; (b) identifying interactive links between national urbanization and economic development through time-series analyses; and

(c) assessing from cross-section data factors that determines regional patterns of urban population.

The results of the study are summarized as follows. While the Chinese urbanization has been associated with its economic development, the direction of the causal link runs from economic development to urbanization, not *vice versa*. The regional urbanization is shaped in general by the patterns of provincial development levels and sectoral structures, along with geographic and historical factors. Surprisingly, foreign trade and foreign investment seem to have little impact on regional urbanization.

1   Patterns of Chinese Urban Population and Urbanization

Though there were problems of inconsistencies and ambiguities in official data on the urban population due to frequent changes in definitions of urban areas, the recent efforts made by the Chinese government have led to its urban statistics at national levels being more realistic. For instance, the adjusted data on Chinese urban population and the levels of urbanization in *China Statistical Yearbook 2000* (SSB, 2000) have no significant differences from what had been suggested by several studies (Wu, 1994; Zhang and Zhao, 1998). Therefore some key characteristics of China's urban population and urbanization may be derived from the update official publications.

The pattern of the Chinese urbanization may be studied at both national and regional levels. Table 6.1 presents some major indicators of urbanization and economic development during the period 1978–99 for China. Table 6.2 displays regional patterns of urbanization and economic development, in which the provinces are ordered by level of urbanization in 1998. Before moving on, we need to mention how the regional urbanization levels are constructed. So far there are two major sources of data on the Chinese regional economy: *China Regional Economy: A Profile of 17 years of Reform and Opening-Up* (SSB, 1996) and *Comprehensive Statistical Data and Materials on 50 Years of New China* (SSB, 1999). While the former contains data on urban population by province from 1978 to 1995, the information seems not to be reliable because the corresponding levels of urbanization in most provinces as well as the nation are much overstated. In fact the Chinese government has realized the problem and stopped using the data in its later publications. In the second source, no data on urban population are provided but non-agricultural population data are included. While the information on the non-agricultural population that is taken from the household registration system is more accurate, national urbanization levels are understated by 13–28 per cent as only non-agricultural population is treated as urban population. To obtain the urban population share of a province for each year in 1978–99, we thus first calculate the ratio of the national urban population share to the non-agricultural population share over 1978–99. If the ratio at the national level is thought to be same for each province, which is quite reasonable, we can construct annual regional urbanization levels in the period by multiplying the non-agricultural population share of the province in a year with the national ratio in that year. The resulting levels of regional urbanization seem to be reasonable and are consistent with the estimations made in the existing studies (e.g., Zhang and Zhao, 1998).

Some characteristics of China's urban population and urbanization emerge from Tables 6.1 and 6.2.

First, increases in the absolute magnitude and the share of national urban population are unprecedented. While total population grew at an average rate of 1.29 per cent per annum during 1978–99, the rate for urban population is 3.79 per cent, almost three times of the former. The level of urbanization increased by 13 percentage points in 21 years from 18 per cent in 1978 to 31 per cent in 1999, or about two-thirds of a percentage point per year. In terms of urban population growth, each year more than 10 million people were urbanized, and the total increase of urban population in the two decades is of the order of 222 million. Two single years, 1984 and 1992, witnessed the largest increase in the urban population, with 17 and 18 million persons, respectively.

Second, Chinese urbanization is positively linked to economic development at both national and regional levels. (a) As indicated in Table 6.1, real per capita GDP grew at the average rate of 8.17 per cent per year during 1978–99, and the urban population rose at a rate of 3.79 per cent, resulting in an increase in the urban population share from 18 per cent in 1978 to 31 per cent in 1999. At the same time, the agricultural employment share, another indicator of economic transformation from rural to urban society, decreased from 70.5 per cent to 50 per cent. (b) The regional pattern shown in Table 6.2 is in general consistent with the national pattern in terms of the positive link of urbanization to economic development. For instance, Shanghai, Beijing, and Tianjing, the three municipalities possessing provincial status, enjoy highest levels of both per capita income and urbanization. Provinces in northwest and southwest with low-income levels generally have small shares of urban population. (c) The positive link between urbanization and economic development may also be seen from correlations between growth rates of the two indicators in Table 6.2. Those provinces with higher growth rate of income (e.g., Guangdong, Jiangsu, Shandong, Zhejiang, and Henan) experienced fast growth in urbanization.

Table 6.1   Urbanization and economic development in China: 1978–99

Year	Total population (10,000)	Urban population (10,000)	Urban population share (%)	Urban growth in persons (10,000)	Share of agricultural employment (%)	Real percapita GDP (1978 = 100)
1978	96259	17250	17.92	582	70.53	100.00
1979	97542	18494	18.96	1244	69.80	106.09
1980	98705	19139	19.39	645	68.75	113.02
1981	100072	20175	20.16	1036	68.10	117.40
1982	101654	21479	21.13	1305	68.13	126.22
1983	103008	22270	21.62	791	67.08	137.95
1984	104357	24017	23.01	1746	64.05	156.87
1985	105851	25094	23.71	1077	62.42	175.52
1986	107507	26366	24.53	1272	60.95	188.16
1987	109300	27674	25.32	1308	59.99	206.58
1988	111026	28656	25.81	982	59.35	226.22
1989	112704	29540	26.21	884	60.05	231.90
1990	114333	30191	26.41	651	60.13	236.97
1991	115823	30543	26.37	352	59.70	255.51
1992	117171	32372	27.63	1829	58.50	288.20
1993	118517	33351	28.14	979	56.40	323.34
1994	119850	34301	28.62	950	54.30	360.23
1995	121121	35174	29.04	872	52.20	393.72
1996	122389	35949	29.37	776	50.50	426.79
1997	123626	36989	29.92	1040	49.90	459.67
1998	124810	37942	30.40	953	49.80	490.47
1999	125909	38893	30.89	951	50.10	520.36
Annual average growth and shares						
1978–88	1.44	4.79	0.79	1199	−1.74	8.51
1989–99	1.11	2.79	0.47	1024	−1.82	8.42
1978–99	1.29	3.79	0.65	1058	−1.64	8.17

Sources: Computed from *China Statistical Yearbook 2000* (SSB, 2000) and *Comprehensive Statistical Data and Materials on 50 Years of New China* (SSB, 1999).

Urbanization in those with lower growth rate of income (e.g., Tibet, Shanghai, Qinghai, Tianjing, Beijing, and Guizhou) grew slowly.

Third, although the rate of urbanization is determined by economic development, large regional variations across provinces arise due to historical and geographic factors, as suggested in Table 6.2. (a) The levels of urbanization in three northeastern provinces (Liaoning, Heilongjiang, and Jilin) may be higher than would be expected from their respective incomes in 1998. This may be explained by the historical fact that the industrial development in these provinces was already relatively advanced in the 1930s during the Japanese

Table 6.2   Urbanization and economic development by province: 1978–98

Provinces	Level of urbanization			Real per capita GDP		
	1998 (%)	1978 (%)	Growth rate (%)	1998 (Yuan)	1978 (Yuan)	Annual growth rate (%)
Shanghai*	80.12	66.39	0.94	23722	8065	5.54
Beijing*	72.43	60.52	0.90	15200	4052	6.83
Tianjing*	67.01	55.93	0.91	13149	3705	6.54
Liaoning*	55.13	35.87	2.17	8793	2193	7.19
Heilongjiang	53.72	39.86	1.50	7070	1813	7.04
Jilin	52.24	34.67	2.07	5548	1238	7.79
Xingjiang	43.40	30.51	1.78	6019	1029	9.23
Inner Mongolia	41.58	28.67	1.88	4788	1033	7.97
Guangdong*	38.21	18.37	3.73	10439	1184	11.50
Ningxia	34.80	19.38	2.97	3981	1186	6.24
Hubei	33.85	16.54	3.65	5905	1072	8.91
Jiangsu*	33.06	14.10	4.35	9440	1387	10.06
Qinghai	32.61	27.09	0.93	4121	1383	5.61
Shandong*	31.95	9.90	6.04	7631	1022	10.57
Shanxi	31.91	18.37	2.80	4753	1179	7.22
Hainan*	30.40	16.54	3.09	5489	1008	8.84
Shaanxi	26.82	16.58	2.43	3618	950	6.91
Jiangxi	26.05	16.31	2.37	4161	887	8.03
Zhejiang*	25.04	12.92	3.36	10539	1071	12.11
Fujian*	24.13	15.48	2.24	9505	879	12.64
Hunan	23.61	12.08	3.41	4651	924	8.42
Anhui	23.19	12.08	3.31	4272	785	8.84
Gansu	22.95	15.09	2.12	3251	1132	5.42
Hebei*	22.88	12.36	3.13	6101	1175	8.58
Sichuan	22.08	9.13	4.52	4083	819	8.36
Henan	21.71	9.11	4.43	4404	748	9.27
Guangxi*	21.13	11.96	2.89	3833	724	8.69
Yunnan	17.98	11.84	2.11	4076	725	9.02
Guizhou	17.27	12.87	1.48	2167	563	6.97
Tibet	16.59	16.36	0.07	3407	1206	5.33
Nation	30.40	17.92	2.68	6019	1231	8.37

Notes: An asterisk (*) after the name of a province indicates that province to be in the coastal region. Real per capita GDP for each province is measured in 1995 prices, and annual growth rate is average rate for the period of 1978–98. The level of urbanization for each province is constructed as follows, since no accurate data on provincial urban population are available. First, we compute the share of non-agricultural population in total population, which is close to but understates the urban population share. Then we adjust the share with the ratio of the national urban population share to the national nonagricultural population share.

Sources: Authors' computation based on SSB (1999) and SSB (1996).

colonialism, and was further promoted in the 1950s during the honeymoon of China and the former Soviet Union. Their relative low per capita income in 1998 may reflect the slow economic growth due to difficulties in reforming the state-owned enterprises that dominated the three provincial economies. (b) Some of the poor provinces in northern China (Inner Mongolia, Ningxia, Qinghai, and Xingjiang) rank unusually high in urbanization, which may reflect local geographic conditions of desert and dry land, and high costs of living in distant areas because of water scarcity. (c) On the other hand, several rich coastal provinces (Zhejiang, Fujiang, Jiangsu, Guangdong, and Shangdong) have lower urban population shares than would be expected from their income levels. This may partly reflect good geographic conditions for agricultural production in these areas so that the pressure for rural people to move to cities is relatively small. More importantly, the relatively low urbanization levels may be simply a statistical artifact: large fraction of rural people who work in non-agricultural sectors, such as village and township enterprises, still retains agricultural registry and is treated as non-urban population.

Fourth, the level of urbanization in coastal areas has grown faster than that in inland areas during the period 1978–98. The column for annual growth rate of urbanization in Table 6.2 suggests that most of provinces in coastal areas (e.g., Shandong, Jiangsu, Guangdong, Zhejiang, Hebei, and Hainan) enjoy higher growth rates of urbanization (3.09–6.04 per cent) than the national average (2.68 per cent). This is probably because the provinces in coastal areas were offered highly favorable opening-up policies such as establishment of special economic zones, open economic regions, and open cities. These policies promote exports by these provinces (Zhang and Song, 2000; and Zhang, 2001c) and encourage large flows of foreign direct investment (FDI) into the coastal areas (Zhang, 2001a). Larger exports and FDI inflows are expected to change the economic structure toward a higher level of urbanization.

2   Empirical Analyses

It is well known that urbanization is a natural and inevitable consequence of economic development, because economic development entails a massive shift of labor and other inputs from rural agricultural sectors to urban industrial sectors (Hamer and Linn, 1987; Mazumdar, 1987). The fall of labor force share in agriculture and the rise in industry and services during economic development involve two phenomena: demand shifts and supply shifts resulting from capital accumulation and technological change. On the demand side, a large share of income is spent on food at low-income levels, but that share falls and income shares spent on industrial products and services rise as income increases (so called Engel's law). The effect of the demand shifts is to raise returns to labor and other inputs in industry and services relative to those in agriculture so that labor and other inputs are induced to move from rural agriculture to urban industry and services. On the supply side, the costs and prices of industrial products may fall relative to those of agricultural products, due to faster technical progress and larger benefits from capital accumulation, scale economies, and highly educated labor force in industry than in agriculture. Along with international trade, cost reductions in industry are likely to cause large inflows of labor in that sector and thus increase urbanization (Williamson, 1988).

2.1 Explanations to the Rising National Urbanization

The hypothesis of positive link between urbanization and economic development over time may be described as a logistic function of the following form: $U^{-1} = \alpha_0 + \alpha_1 e^{g(Y)}$. U is the percentage of population urbanized; g is a function of Y, the per capita income; e is the base of natural logarithm; and α_0 and α_1 are parameters to be estimated. The key characteristics of the logistic function is that the urbanization responds slowly to economic development (indexed by per capital income) at low development levels, then responds rapidly, and again slows down at higher levels. The preference for the logistic function is based on confusion between urbanization as a function of time and as a function of economic development. It is reasonable to expect urbanization to be a logistic function of time, because both urbanization and economic development are likely to start slowly as a country struggles to escape from low-level traps, then accelerates, and finally decelerates in high development levels (Mills and Becker, 1986).

Taking natural logs on both sides and rearranging terms, the logistic function becomes $\ln(U^{-1} - \alpha_0) = \ln\alpha_1 + g(Y)$. Given this equation to be linear in all parameters except α_0, we can estimate the equation by running linear regressions for a large number of α_0 values and choosing the α_0 value that maximizes R^2. Mills and Becker (1986) have conducted some experimentation of estimating the above equation, and they found that the best and simplest functional form to estimate this logistic function may be the following:

(1) $U_t = \alpha_0 + \alpha_1 A_t + \alpha_2 Y_t + \alpha_3 T + \varepsilon_t$

where two more explanatory variables are added in the regression model: the share of agricultural employment (A) and the time trend (T). Since the output of both industrial and services production is mostly sold outside the urban areas, both the industry and services influence (but are not influenced by) the urban population. There is thus a case for including the share of industry and services together among the explanatory variables. Alternatively, one can use the share of agricultural employment. The time trend variable (T), which takes values 1 through 22 from 1978 to 1999, may capture effects of an upward trend in the level of urbanization that cannot be explained by other variables in the model.

Equation (1) is estimated with national time-series data. Annual data on the urbanization (U_t), real per capita GDP (Y_t), and agricultural employment share (A_t) are computed from information in *China Statistical Yearbook 2000* (SSB, 2000) and *Comprehensive Statistical Data and Materials on 50 Years of New China* (SSB, 1999).

As presented in Table 6.3, estimates of equation (1) suggest significant and positive effects of economic development (Y) on the Chinese urbanization (U). The coefficient of agricultural employment share (A) is significant and has correct negative sign, indicating that shifts of rural agricultural labor force to urban industry and service sectors enhance urban growth. This finding is consistent with not only theoretical predictions, but also a widespread belief that China's rapid economic growth and sectoral changes toward industry and services foster its urbanization. The positive coefficient of T indicates an upward time trend in the level of urbanization, which may be due to factors other than income growth and sectoral changes.

We should be cautious in interpreting results from equation (1), since it is unclear whether or not the model is subject to simultaneity bias. One may argue that a feedback from urbanization to economic development may be likely to exist. The standard Granger-causality test is conducted, and the results are reported as follows. The statistic for the test of the null hypothesis that the Chinese economic development (measured by logarithm of per capita income) does not Granger-cause urbanization is 2.97, which rejects the hypothesis at 5 per cent of significance. The hypothesis of the exogeneity of urbanization cannot be rejected due to the small value of the statistic for that test (0.21). This finding not only complements our results from the structural model of equation (1), but also suggests that China's urbanization in the last two decades is likely to be a consequence of its rapid economic growth.

Table 6.3   Link between urbanization and economic development in China

Independent variables	Coefficients	t-statistic
C	37.34***	9.58
A	−0.26***	−4.81
Y	0.02**	7.84
T	0.67***	11.58
R^2	0.99	
F-statistic	1309.47***	

Notes: Dependent variable of the level of urbanization (U) is measured in percentage. The
sample size is 22 from 1978 to 1999. C is a constant. Explanatory variables include per
capita GDP (Y), agricultural employment share (A), and time trend (T). Two lags are
taken in the each of estimations of Granger tests. The asterisks ***, **, and * indicate
levels of significance at 1%, 5%, and 10%, respectively.

2.2 Explanations to Regional Patterns of Urbanization

The estimation of equation (1) is useful for a better understanding of national
urbanization. However, the specification with time-series data is of limited use
in revealing patterns of regional urbanization. In particular, we are interested
in knowing how regional characteristics such as special geographic-historical
factors and foreign trade and investment affect provincial urbanization,
along with the economic development and sectoral structures. The resulting
specification of regional urbanization model with cross-section data is given
as

$$(2)\ \ U_i = \beta_0 + \beta_1 Y_i + \beta_2 A_i + \beta_3\left(\frac{X_i}{GDP_i}\right) + \beta_4\left(\frac{FDI_i}{GDP_i}\right) + \beta_5 D_i + \mu_i$$

where U_i, Y_i, and A_i are the level of urbanization, per capita GDP, and
agricultural employment share in province i. The share of exports in GDP (X_i
/GDP_i) and the share of inward FDI flows in GDP (FDI_i/GDP_i) in province i
are included in the model to indicate effects on urbanization of the privileges
enjoyed by the coastal provinces in promoting exports and attracting FDI.
The regional dummy variable (D) is expected to capture geographic and
historical influences on regional urbanization. The dummy takes value of one
for provinces of Liaoning, Heilongjiang, Jilin, Xingjiang, Inner Mongolia,
Ningxia, and Qinghai, and zero for the rest.

All data are obtained from *Comprehensive Statistical Data and Materials on 50 Years of New China* (SSB, 1999) and *China Statistical Yearbook 2000* (SSB, 2000). The data on the agricultural employment shares for 5 provinces (Tianjing, Inner Mongolia, Shangdong, Guanxi and Gansu) in a few years are taken from *China regional Economy: A Profile of 17 years of Reform and Opening-Up* (SSB, 1996) since they are missing in the first source. To see whether or not changes over time take place in determinants of urbanization (because urban population grew faster in the 1980s than the 1990s), we estimate equation (2) separately for the two periods 1978–88 and 1988–98. Y is measured by real per capita GDP, which is obtained by adjusting current per capita GDP with GDP deflators in constant (1995) prices. X/GDP and FDI/GDP are computed as the ratio of nominal exports (X) and realized foreign capital (FDI) (both in US dollars) to nominal GDP (in Chinese RMB) that is converted into US dollars.

The regression for each period is run with mean values of all variables over the relevant period. Table 6.4 contains parameter estimates obtained from cross-section data for the periods 1978–88 and 1988–98. Before reporting estimating results, two issues related to the estimates that might seem problematic should be addressed. One is the possibility of heteroscedasticity in the disturbance term. The other is the feedback from the dependent variable. Based on the approach suggested by White (1980), we test at a simple level whether there are specification errors of the kinds mentioned. The White test indicates absence of both heteroscedasticity and specification errors.

The following main points emerge from the results reported in Table 6.4. First, the fit of the models is good for the two periods; with values of R^2 being 0.91 for 1978–88 and 0.88 for 1988–98. The regression F-statistics are significant at the conventional levels in practically every case, and the fit is almost equally good for both periods.

Second, the estimated coefficients of economic development (Y) and agricultural employment share (A) are significant and have expected signs in both periods. While the effects of the two explanatory variables on regional urbanization seem to be same qualitatively, the different values of coefficients may indicate structural changes from the first period (1978–88) to the second (1988–98). The impact of development levels on urban growth seems to have decreased and that of agricultural employment share seems to have increased over time.

Third, there seems no evidence that foreign trade and foreign investment would enhance regional urbanization. The coefficients of FDI/GDP in the two periods have the correct sign but are not significant even at level of 10 per cent.

Table 6.4   Estimating results of provincial urbanization with cross-section data

Independent variable	1978–88 Coefficient	1978–88 t-statistic	1988–98 Coefficient	1988–98 t-statistic
C	15.449***	2.183	30.379***	3.284
Y	0.008***	6.856	0.004***	5.123
A	−0.154*	−1.843	−0.321**	-2.733
X/GDP	−0.092	−0.350	−0.334*	−1.740
FDI/GDP	3.073	0.934	0.599	0.989
D	13.433***	5.148	14.924***	4.675
R^2	0.910		0.875	
F-statistic	48.731***		33.751***	

Notes: The sample size is 30 in each of estimations. The dependent variable is the level of urbanization (%). C is a constant. Explanatory variables include per capita GDP (Y), agricultural employment share (A), export share (X/GDP), share of FDI flows in GDP (FDI/GDP), and geographic and historical dummy (D). The asterisks ***, **, and * indicate levels of significance at 1%, 5%, and 10%, respectively.

The coefficient of exports (X/GDP) has wrong signs in both periods, and is significant in the second period. This 'anomaly' merits some attention. In the last two decades, most of the Chinese exports (88 per cent) were generated by coastal provinces and a large share of total FDI received in China (85 per cent) went to these provinces as well (Zhang and Song, 2000; and Zhang, 2001a). The higher level of exports and large amount of inflows of FDI are accelerating economic growth significantly (2001b). However, as pointed out in Section 2, the major high-income coastal provinces (Zhejiang, Fujiang, Jiangsu, Guangdong, and Shandong) had obviously low levels of urbanization, which is a statistical artifact. The nature of weak links of urbanization to exports and foreign investment thus seems to be a result of the artificial low level of urbanization in the coastal region.

Fourth, geographic and historical factors seem to be powerful in explaining regional urban growth. The estimated coefficients of dummy (D) are positive and significant at 1 per cent in both periods. This finding is reasonable since China has a vast land with a great variety of geographic conditions, and China experienced a relatively unique process of economic development.

3 Summary and Concluding Remarks

While China exhibited unmistakable signs of anti-urban bias in the Maoist era, China's urban population in the period of economic reforms grew extraordinarily in the standard of other developing countries. Studying the determinants of urbanization in China is obviously interesting, and there have been quite a few studies on the subject in recent years. This chapter seeks to advance the earlier research in several ways. Besides constructing measures of provincial urbanization on the basis of a reasonable procedure, I explore some important features of Chinese urbanization over the period 1978–98 at both national and regional levels. Then I investigate the determinants of urban growth with time-series data to judge whether increase in Chinese urbanization is a consequence of its rapid economic growth in the era of economic reforms. Further, I take a closer look at the regional patterns for 1978–88 and 1988–98 separately on the basis of cross-section data. I also conduct specification tests to see whether the assumptions of homoscedasticity and exogeneity are reasonable.

Three points summarize the study. First, the rising Chinese urbanization since 1978 is likely to have resulted from rapid economic development, and not *vice versa*. This finding suggests that the levels of urbanization should be consistent with economic growth, and excessive urbanization may damage national welfare. Second, urban growth in a province once again is determined by the province's economic development and sectoral structure of production. Geographic conditions and historical development of a province turn out to be influential in the province's urbanization, but the degree of opening-up of the provincial economy, in terms of exports and FDI inflows, seems to have a negligible impact.

References

Becker, C.M. and Morrison, A.R. (1999), 'Urbanization in Transforming Economies,' in Mills, E.S. and Cheshire, P. (eds), *Handbook of Regional and Urban Economics*, Vol. III, Amsterdam: Elsevier-North Holland.

Chang, K.-S. (1994), 'Chinese Urbanization and Development Before and After Economic Reform: A Comparative Reappraisal,' *World Development*, 22 (4), pp. 601–13.

Chen, X. and Parish, W.L. (1996), 'Urbanization in China: Reassessing an Evolving Model,' in Gugler, J. (ed.), *The Urban Transformation of the Developing World*, Oxford: Oxford University Press, pp. 61–90.

Hamer, A.M. and Linn, J.F. (1987), 'Urbanization in the Developing World: Patterns, Issues, and Policy,' in Mills, E.S. (ed.), *Handbook of Regional and Urban Economics*, Vol. II, Amsterdam: Elsevier-North Holland.

Kojima, R. (1995), 'Urbanization in China,' *The Developing Economies*, XXXIII (2), June, pp. 121–54.

Mazumdar, D. (1987), 'Rural-urban Migration in Developing Countries,' in Mills, E.S. (ed.), *Handbook of Regional and Urban Economics*, Vol. II, Amsterdam: Elsevier-North Holland.

Mills, E.S. and Becker, C.M. (1986), *Studies in Indian Urban Development*, New York: Oxford University Press.

Song, F. and Timberlake, M. (1996), 'Chinese Urbanization, State Policy, and the World Economy,' *Journal of Urban Affairs*, 18 (3), pp. 285–306.

Song, S. (2001), 'City Size and Urban Unemployment: Evidence from China,' *World Economy and China*, 9 (1), pp. 46–53.

Song, S. and Zhang, K.H. (2001), 'Urbanization and City-size Distribution in China,' a paper presented at International Conference on Urbanization in China, 2001.

State Statistical Bureau (SSB) of China (1996), *China Regional Economy: A Profile of 17 Years of Reform and Opening-Up*, Beijing: China Statistical Press.

State Statistical Bureau (SSB) of China (1999), *Comprehensive Statistical Data and Materials on 50 Years of New China*, Beijing: China Statistical Press.

State Statistical Bureau (SSB) of China (2000), *China Statistical Yearbook 2000*, Beijing: China Statistical Press.

Williamson, J.G. (1988), 'Migration and Urbanization,' in Chenery, H. and Srinivasan, T.N. (eds), *Handbook of Development Economics*, Vol. I, Amsterdam: Elsevier-North Holland.

White, H. (1980), 'A Heteroscedasticity-consistent Covariance Matrix Estimator and a Direct Test for Heteroscedasticity,' *Econometrica*, 48, pp. 817–38.

Zhang, K.H. (2001a), 'What Attracts Foreign Multinational Corporations to China?,' *Contemporary Economic Policy*, 19 (3), pp. 336–46.

Zhang, K.H. (2001b), 'Roads to Prosperity: Assessing the Impact of Foreign Direct Investment on Economic Growth in China,' *Economia Internzaional/International Economics*, 54 (1), pp. 113–25.

Zhang, K.H. (2001c), 'Exports, Human Capital, and Productivity Growth: Evidence from China,' working paper.

Zhang, K.H. and Song, S. (2000), 'Promoting Exports: The Role of Inward FDI in China,' *China Economic Review*, 11 (4), pp. 385–96.

Zhang, K.H. and Song, S. (2001), 'Rural-urban Migration and Urbanization in China: Evidence from Time-series and Cross-section Analyses,' a paper presented at International Conference on Urbanization in China, June 2001.

Zhang, L. and Zhao, S.X.B. (1998), 'Re-examining China's "Urban" Concept and the Level of Urbanization,' *China Quarterly*, 154, June, pp. 330–81.

CHAPTER 7

FLOATING POPULATION: DEFINITIONS, DATA, AND RECENT FINDINGS

DANIEL GOODKIND, PhD*
US Census Bureau

LORAINE A. WEST, PhD*
US Census Bureau

Abstract

Among recent migrants in China, one of the most difficult groups to define and measure is that referred to as the floating population (liudong renkou). This term is typically invoked to conjure up an image of unsettled persons lacking permanent residence, yet its meaning is often ambiguous and sometimes denotes distinctly different groups of people. The main aim of this chapter is to discuss these ambiguities and identify a range of important definitions. The discussion of these definitions entails a review of major sources of data (censuses, registration, surveys), the kinds of information such sources yield, and how the structure of that data affects measurements of the floating population. We also discuss factors that have influenced recent trends and that are likely to affect future trends in migration and the floating population.

Keywords: urbanization, migration, floating population, registration, *hukou*

JEL classification: J61

---

*   Correspondence: Daniel Goodkind, International Programs Center, US Census Bureau, Washington Plaza II, Room 117, Washington, DC 22203–8860. Tel: (301) 763–6240; Email: Daniel.M.Goodkind@census.gov.

This is a reprint of the original article published in *Urban Studies* (http://www.tandf.co.uk), 39 (12), 2002.

1   Introduction

Migration in China has attracted increasing attention from researchers and policy makers, and for good reason. Since major market reforms began in the late 1970s, China's population has become ever more mobile. From a demographic perspective, the rise in migration has grown in prominence because rates of other vital events (births and deaths) have declined over the course of its demographic transition. In addition, viewed from a global vantage point, population movements in China constitute an increasing proportion of the world's intra-national migratory flows. Such internal flows vastly exceed the amount of international migration. Given that China is the most populous country in the world, roughly one out of every six persons on the move today throughout the world is Chinese.

Migration takes many forms, some more permanent, others less so. Among populations on the move in China, one of the most difficult groups to measure is that referred to as the floating population (*liudong renkou*), which is largely concentrated in urban areas and whose definition, composition, and size is the focus of this paper. The proper identification of this group is important if for no other reason than knowing where China's population is actually located. Of course, that knowledge also has practical implications. For instance, good urban planning requires knowledge about the size and likely rate of growth of this group, which will place demands on local resources.

The rise of China's floating population is also relevant for signifying a major loss of government authority over rural-urban migration during its transition to a market economy. The traditional rural/urban designation embodied in the household registration system (*hukou*) was basically a means of controlling population flows into urban areas and reinforced a kind of regional apartheid. The provision of food rations and other benefits to those with an urban *hukou* reinforced the dependency of urban residents on state institutions. The denial of many of these benefits to the floating population has ironically resulted in the growing independence of such persons from state institutions (Solinger, 1999).

But what exactly is the floating population and who belongs to it? Actually, there is no official definition of this term in China (the only country we know of which routinely uses it). Nor, despite its widespread use, does such a category appear in official statistical tabulations. Rather, the term is typically invoked to conjure up an image of unsettled persons lacking permanent residence. Yet its meaning is often ambiguous and sometimes denotes distinctly different groups of people – the term is often tailored and defined more precisely depending on the interests of the observer. One goal in this chapter is to discuss these ambiguities and identify a range of important definitions. The discussion of these definitions entails a review of major sources of data (censuses, surveys, and household registration lists), the kinds of information such sources yield, and how the structure of that data affects measurements of the floating population. We also discuss factors that have influenced recent trends and that are likely to affect future trends in migration and the floating population. Along the way, we note some key empirical findings, although we do not attempt here a comprehensive review of results from all the relevant literature.

2   Definitions

The literature on migration recognizes multiple dimensions in categorizing migration, including time and space (Scharping, 1997). In addition to these two dimensions, the legal conceptualization of migration has been of key importance in China. With the introduction of the household registration system in the 1950s, migration became classified as permanent only if the household registration was formally transferred to the new location. Population movements that do not involve a change in household registration are referred to as temporary migration or the floating population. We define each of these terms in their Chinese context below.

Those who move and change their official household registration location are referred to as permanent migrants (*qianyi*). These migrants are required to change their household registration records at the local public security office at both their former residence and new residence location. China's household registration or *hukou* system registers each person at a specific place (usually the birthplace) and defines the individual's household status in terms of residence location (a specific city, town, or township) and type (either agricultural or nonagricultural). Approval must be sought to change household registration and is subject to quotas (Chan and Zhang, 1999). Rural to urban moves and urban moves up the administrative hierarchy (county-level city to prefecture-level city to province-level city) are more difficult to achieve. In the past, having ones' household registration coincide with ones' place of residency was very important. Only those with a local *hukou* had been entitled to certain jobs, housing, grain, education, medical and other services (Cheng and Selden, 1994). More generally, the distinction between agricultural and nonagricultural households was also used to determine entitlement to food rations. However, due largely to market reforms, grain has become increasingly available outside state channels and local or nonagricultural household designations carry fewer exclusive benefits.

In contrast to migrants who have permanently changed their household registration, the floating population encompasses all those residing away from the location of their official *hukou*. Duration then becomes a key factor – how long does one need to be away from one's permanent household registration location to be considered part of the floating population? Naturally, shorter durations imply a larger floating population. The standard definition of the floating population used in city surveys throughout China is based on the shortest practical duration – 24 hours – which encompasses people who are simply visiting relatives, on vacation, on overnight working trips, as well as those away for longer periods of time. For particular localities, such a comprehensive view of the floating population is important in determining the demand for electricity, transportation, hotel rooms, and other services.

Yet for those less concerned with the provision of services to tourists and business people, such a broad definition based on so short a duration seems overly inclusive. Another popular conception of the floating population encompasses those whose detachment from their official residence is presumed to be more significant or enduring. Under this conception typical sub-groups of the floating population include seasonal migrant laborers, who may move away from their official residence for weeks or months at a time. Another subgroup includes those who remain away from their *hukou* for a year or even longer, perhaps with no intention of returning. Even this more limited concept of floating population is not always well defined. Solinger (1999) highlighted such ambiguities by compiling descriptive statistics under the rubric 'floating population' as of the mid 1990s. The resulting category descriptions and counts reflected the interests of the observers, ranging from 'people who sought work in other areas' (50 million) to 'peasants away from land and home to work' (60 million) to 'migrants to other provinces or abroad' (20 million).

Yet another complicating factor is that some proportion of these sub-categories of the floating population are officially approved by the state. For instance, both seasonal migrants and longer-term migrants can, and according to regulations should, register their temporary residency with local authorities at the destination. If registered, they are then referred to by authorities as temporary residents (*linshi* or *zanzhu renkou*). Thus, characteristics commonly used to subdivide the floating population include their duration of stay at the destination, purpose of stay, whether or not they have official temporary registration, location of origin, and even the particular sectoral migration they are undertaking (e.g., rural to rural, rural to urban, extra-provincial or not, etc.). These categories often overlap in incongruent ways.

3   Data Sources and Findings

The above discussion highlighted the lack of a consistent definition of the term 'floating population' – a term commonly invoked for a variety of different purposes and which can be used to refer to various subcategories of people. In this section, we discuss major data sources themselves, showing how they structure and/or limit our measurement of migration and the floating population. We begin with the most comprehensive population counts available – national censuses. We also consider household registration records, as well as a variety of regional and city surveys. We draw on recent work by Chan and Zhang (1999), Yu (2000), Cui (2000), Chan (2001a and 2001b), and others that provides concise summaries of available data on migrants.

3.1 Population Censuses, Census Samples, and Population Surveys

In China, as in many other countries, national censuses typically provide the most complete and representative data on migration trends across the country. To be counted at a particular locality in China's 1990 census, one either had to have one's official *hukou* there, have resided there for one year or more with a *hukou* elsewhere, or have resided there for less than one year but have been away from the *hukou* location for more than a year. Otherwise people were supposed to have been counted in the area where their official *hukou* was held. The census asked where individuals resided five years prior to the census date and counted them as migrants if this was a different county or city than the place of enumeration for the census. Census results showed that 18.27 million people moved and changed their permanent household registration across county or city boundaries from 1985 to 1990 (Chan, 2001a). Another 15.82 million moved over that time interval across county or city boundaries (or city district boundaries if the city is subdivided) without changing their permanent household registration (Chan, 2001a). Thus, the total flow of migrants as measured by the census was 34.09 million from 1985 to 1990.

Another figure from the 1990 census indicated that 21.35 million people had been away from their place of permanent household registration for at least a year on 1 July 1990 (Yu, 2000). Of these people, 15.82 million were those just cited who had moved to the 1990 enumeration site between 1985 and

1990 yet did not change their *hukou*. The remainder, 5.53 million, resided on 1 July 1985 in the same place where they were enumerated on 1 July 1990 in the census and represent long term migrants living away from their permanent *hukou* area. This estimate of the floating population, 21.35 million, is clearly restricted. The required 12 month duration away from ones' local hukou excludes seasonal migrants as well as those in the process of accumulating much longer stays.

China also conducted a 1 per cent sample census in 1995. Similar to the 1990 census, people were asked in 1995 where they resided five years earlier. Although the administrative boundaries which had to be crossed in order to be considered a migrant remained the same as in 1990, the minimum required time away from one's official *hukou* was reduced from one year to six months. Over the 1990–95 period, the sample census found that 33.23 milllion people migrated across county or city boundaries, either officially changing their *hukou* or being away from that location for six months or more (State Statistical Bureau, 1997b). That number is below the over 34 million recorded in the five years prior to the 1990 census. The sample census also counted 49.7 million persons who were away from their official *hukou* residence for six months or longer (State Statistical Bureau, 1997b). Because the duration standard changed from the 1990 census to the 1995 sample census (from 12 months to six months) these measures of the floating population are not directly comparable.

We find the relatively low flow of migrants from 1990–95 hard to believe and are concerned about the completeness of migration reporting in the 1995 census sample. It seems highly unlikely that overall migration should have declined in the first half of the 1990s compared to the second half of the 1980s. Although there was likely a decline in migration following the Tian An Men incident in 1989, migration picked up following Deng Xiaoping's Southern Tour in 1992. Moreover, the minimal time period required for a migrant to be counted as resident was reduced to six months in the 1995 survey, which should have biased 1995 migration counts above those of 1990. In fact, an evaluation of the results of the 1995 1 per cent population sample survey by the State Statistical Bureau revealed underreporting and indicated that the underreported were primarily migrants who lacked a local *hukou* (Yu, 2000). We should also note in passing that the 1995 sample census was taken on 1 October, a month which should have minimized possible undercounts of migrants. If, for instance, the census had been taken on 1 July (as was the case for the 1990 census), people who made brief trips home during the Chinese lunar new year would not have been considered migrants under the six-month

Table 7.1   Measures of China's floating population (in millions)

	Stock of migrants		Implied average annual flow of migrants	
Source:	State Statistical Bureau	Ministry of Public Security	State Statistical Bureau	Ministry of Public Security
Definition:	Away from *hukou* 6 months or longer	Not specified	Away from *hukou* 6 months or longer	Not specified
Year				
1988		70		
1994		80		1.7
1995				6.7
1996	58.4			6.7
1997	60.9	100	2.5	6.7
1998	61.8		0.9	3.8
1999	63.8		2.0	3.8
2005		130		

Sources: State Statistical Bureau (2000), p. 101; (1999), p. 118; (1998), p. 112; (1997), p. 75 and Hua (2000).

standard. In fact, this was one reason the census date was changed (the 2000 census was moved one month further ahead, to November, to avoid difficulties with people traveling during the 1 October National Day holiday).

Since full population censuses in China occur only once every ten years, the State Statistical Bureau supplements those counts with an annual survey of population.[1] Starting in 1996 the annual survey of population change has collected data on those residing away from their household registration location for six months or longer. The data capture those who have crossed township, town, or even residential district (neighborhood) borders, narrower boundaries which result in a broader definition of the floating population than used in the 1990 census and the 1995 sample census. Under this definition, the floating population increased from 58.4 million in 1996 to 63.8 million in 1999 (Table 7.1).

The 2000 census used the same duration and geographic boundaries as these annual surveys to identify migrants. Yet the census questionnaire also contained a new question asking households to identify those who were away from their *hukou* for less than six months for primarily work-related purposes. In addition to asking this question about short-term migrants at their point of origin, a separate form was also created to obtain information from these same migrants at their destination. We will soon know more about how such information has been processed and tabulated, but it will almost certainly provide a more inclusive portrait China's floating population. Moreover, whatever the size of the floating population counted in this census, the true number may well be higher, because a nationwide post-enumeration check suggested an underreporting rate of 1.81 per cent (State Council Population Census Office and State Statistical Bureau, Department of Population, Social, Science and Technology Statistics, 2001), and moving populations tend to suffer disproportionate undercounts.

3.2 Public Security Registration

In addition to comprehensive counts from censuses, the department of household registration under the Ministry of Public Security is responsible for maintaining household registration records for the whole nation. Total population statistics derived from this source (Table 7.2) fall below those produced by the State Statistical Bureau utilizing population censuses and annual surveys of population change (Cui, 2000). In spite of efforts prior to

---

1   The sample size used in the annual survey of population change is 1 per 1000.

the 1990 census to rectify household registration records (e.g., register births and remove those who had died), there was a shortfall in the registers in 1990, and that gap nearly tripled by 1999 to about 30.97 million people, or nearly 2.5 per cent of China's population (1.259 vs 1.228 million). Cui (2000) attributes the widening gap to diminishing concerns about the importance of household registration.

The Ministry of Public Security also publishes annual figures of people changing their permanent household registration location (Table 7.3). These statistics reflect all official permanent moves across township, town, and residential neighborhood boundaries. The flow of these migrants has actually declined in the late 1990s. That decline does not suggest any easing of restrictions or quotas for changing one's permanent household registration locale.

Table 7.2 **Comparison of total population from population estimates and registration records (in 1000s)**

Year	State Statistical Bureau estimates	Ministry of Public Security Department of Household Registration	Difference
1990	1,143,330	1,132,740	10,590
1991	1,158,230	1,145,110	13,120
1992	1,171,710	1,155,630	16,080
1993	1,185,170	1,165,970	19,200
1994	1,198,500	1,176,740	21,760
1995	1,211,210	1,187,880	23,330
1996	1,223,890	1,198,660	25,230
1997	1,236,260	1,209,030	27,230
1998	1,248,100	1,218,180	29,920
1999	1,259,090	1,228,120	30,970

Source: Cui (2000), Table 1, p. 1.

Given their responsibilities in related functions, the Ministry of Public Security is also tasked with overseeing and managing the floating population. According to the Ministry of Public Security, China's floating population has increased steadily since the early 1980s and is projected to increase to 160 million by 2010 (Figure 7.1), or more than 10 per cent of China's entire population. The definitions and methods they used to measure the floating population are not entirely clear, but the minimum time required away from their permanent household registration location was likely to have been less than six months. For instance, the estimate of 100 million floaters as of 1997 is 64 per cent above those counted in the 1997 annual survey of population change (60.9 million) when six months away from one's official *hukou* was required (Table 7.1). Indeed, the definition used by the Ministry of Public Security may well have borrowed findings from floating population surveys in various cities, which have tended to use the minimum 24-hour duration away from ones' *hukou* (see next section). These national estimates of the floating population may reflect extrapolations from city data.

Table 7.3   Number of migrants changing permanent household registration (in millions)

Year	Migrants changing hukou
1982	17.30
1985	19.69
1988	19.92
1990	19.24
1992	18.70
1993	18.19
1994	19.49
1995	18.46
1996	17.51
1997	17.85
1998	17.13

Source: Ministry of Public Security data cited in Chan (2001), Table 1.

The estimates we have referred to so far indicate the stock of the floating population, yet it is important to distinguish between stocks and flows (Table 7.1). The annual net increase of the floating population can be determined by comparing changes in stock figures over time. Such comparisons suggest that the floating population increased by 1 to 7 million per year in the mid and late 1990s, depending on which definition one uses. Although such additions to the floating population are substantial, they are dwarfed by the 17–19 million people who officially changed their *hukou* each year in the 1990s (Table 7.3). Since official migration flows so vastly exceed unofficial flows, concerns about the floating population seem to stem more from the fact that it is, under current administrative rules, an ever accumulating stock.

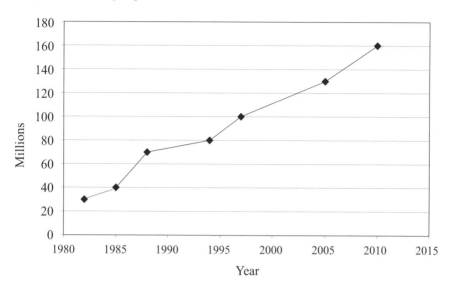

Note: 2005 and 2010 are projected figures.

Figure 7.1   China's floating population: estimates and projections of the Ministry of Public Security

Source: Hua (2000).

In order to better manage the floating population, the Ministry of Public Security issued national regulations in 1985 that required those who intended to stay in an urban area other than their place of *hukou* registration for more than three months to apply for a temporary residence certificate. In 1995 this requirement was extended to rural areas and the length of stay was reduced to one month (Chan and Zhang, 1999).[2] Efforts to register the floating population have been only moderately successful. According to Ministry of Public Security statistics, of the more than 80 million floating population in 1995, 44 million were registered as temporary residents (Chan and Zhang, 1999). By 1997, the Ministry of Public Security estimated that the floating population had grown to 100 million but only 38 million were registered as temporary residents (Chan and Zhang, 1999).

---

2   Rural to rural migration can also be understated as outside laborers arriving to work in rural township and village enterprises often do not register with local authorities. A sample of township and village enterprises in one prefecture in Guangdong found that 35 per cent of employees were from elsewhere and had not registered (US Consulate Guangzhou, 2001).

A National Floating Population Management Experience Exchange Conference, organized by the Comprehensive Public Security Commission of the Central Committee and the Public Security Management of the National Floating Population Leading Group, was held in Shenzhen in September 2000 (Xinhua, 2000a). In addition to the Minister of Public Security, representatives from the Ministry of Labor and Social Security, All-China Women's Federation, and Central Committee of the Communist Youth League of China as well as related officials from all 32 provinces and municipalities attended. Authorities attending the conference estimate that by 2005 the floating population will reach 130 million and by 2010 will reach 160 million (Hua, 2000; see Figure 7.1).

3.3 Regional and City Surveys

In part due to the limitations of data collected nationally, beginning in the 1980s a variety of survey efforts have focused specifically on the dynamics of sub-national migration in China. Although such surveys are by definition not necessarily representative of China as a whole, their focus on migration itself has produced better and more versatile data regarding population movements at regional and local levels, not to mention the characteristics of migrants themselves. One of the earliest and most significant of these efforts was the 1986 *Survey of Migration in 74 Cities and Towns of China*, sponsored by the Chinese Academy of Social Science. One analysis of the resulting data examined the differential dynamics of permanent and temporary migration (Goldstein and Goldstien, 1991). A drawback of that survey was that it was conducted only among family and collective households; the locations where temporary migrants tend to congregate (e.g., hotels, construction sites, etc.) were not represented. Even with such under-representation, however, the results showed that temporary migration (defined as living at a locality for a year or less without having a *hukou* at that locality), had by the mid-1980s become increasingly relevant compared to permanent migration.

Since the mid-1980s, a number of large cities have also undertaken surveys to try to assess the local non-registered population and its impact on their city. Such surveys typically record a snapshot in time and attempt to learn more about the characteristics and dynamics of the floating population under its broadest definition. Information gathered on these migrants often includes their reasons for coming to the city, length of stay in the city, age, education level, marital status, and place of origin. While the data from a particular city may not be representative of other cities, such data can be particularly useful in assessing and extending findings from national surveys and censuses.

Beijing has published results from its 1999 Non-native Population Dynamic Control survey (Beijing Statistical Bureau, 2000, pp. 73–7). Details on the sampling methodology are not available; however, 112,452 individuals whose permanent household registration is outside of Beijing were surveyed. Of those interviewed, 62 per cent were males and nearly 45 per cent were between the ages of 20 and 29. Just over half had been in Beijing for six months to three years. Only 8 per cent had been there less than one month and 9 per cent had resided in Beijing for five years or longer.

Beijing also conducted its latest floating population census in 1997. This census counted everyone staying in Beijing for more than 24 hours with their permanent household registration elsewhere. Those meeting this definition numbered 2.3 million, accounting for 20 per cent of Beijing's total population (Beijing Statistical Bureau, 1998). Naturally, this percentage of floaters exceeds that for China as a whole because floaters tend to concentrate in urban areas (in 1997, the 100 million estimate by the Ministry of Public Security would constitute just over 8 per cent of China's total population (1.24 billion as of 1997). Yet, as mentioned earlier, the percentages calculated from city surveys have likely been used by the Ministry of Public Security and other observers as a guide in extrapolating the floating population for all of China. For instance, if 20 per cent of China's *urban* population (e.g., about 370 million in 1997) consisted of floaters away from their *hukou* for a day or more, that would imply a national floating population of 74 million. Of course, since there are also floaters in China's rural areas, the estimate for China would have to be further inflated beyond that extrapolation.

3.4 Summary of Data Sources and Implications for Definitions

The preceding review of data sources reiterates the earlier discussion of ambiguities in definitions. The floating population is a flexible concept, the definition of which can change depending on the interest of observers and the available data. For instance, the primary purpose of a census is to provide a comprehensive view of the whole population, to locate it spatially under current administrative rules, and to understand general trends in population movements. For such purposes, a *de jure* approach to identifying the typical location of citizens is paramount, and short term movements away from that location are less important. In contrast, the Ministry of Public Security is primarily concerned with a *de facto* approach – that is, to identify, locate and monitor citizens residing at their *hukou* location or away from it at specific points in time. Similarly, local governments need to adopt such an approach in order to determine the demand for local services. Despite inherent ambiguities in definitions, over time efforts have evolved to collect more complete, detailed, and flexible data on the floating population.

4   Factors Affecting Recent and Future Trends

The transfer of rural labor out of farming and into other activities was very rapid following Deng Xiaoping's 1992 tour of southern China (to promote economic development) and continued through 1996. The Asian financial crisis led to a slow down in China's economic growth in 1996–97 and reduced opportunities for migrant laborers. Starting in 1998 the central government instituted fiscal stimulus programs, such as major infrastructure projects, in the hopes of accelerating economic growth. This spending created demand for unskilled laborers and contributed to the recent rise in floating population totals. Recently the government reported that economic growth rates have resumed their higher levels.

China's succession to the World Trade Organization (WTO) in December 2001 will further the integration of China's economy with the world economy, including the agricultural sector, and potentially accelerate the exodus of labor out of agriculture and increase the floating population. China has a high agricultural share of employment (47 per cent in 1999 according to State Statistical Bureau) and a low ratio of land per farm worker. China's 1997 Agricultural Census reported 425 million persons primarily employed in agriculture, forestry, and fisheries. Another 136 million rural persons were employed in nonagricultural endeavors, of whom 57 million worked primarily in urban areas (Gale, Somwaru, and Diao, 2002). Estimates of surplus or underemployed rural labor vary but commonly are upwards of 200 million. Growth in labor intensive sectors and low skilled jobs will be critical if workers shifting out of agriculture are to be absorbed. While some workers will find new employment in rural areas, cities are likely to continue to attract many rural laborers.

Several other factors, however, are working against continued increases in the floating population. First, a number of cities are experiencing sizeable layoffs of workers from state-owned enterprises and are reacting by limiting migrant access to jobs. In some cases specific categories of jobs are identified and earmarked exclusively for permanent residents of the city. Nevertheless, state owned enterprise workers are resistant to taking on the more physically demanding jobs and these job opportunities remain for migrants. Cities also may restrict the number of migrants by limiting temporary residence certificates and rounding up and expelling migrants. Layoffs from state-owned enterprises are expected to remain high for the next five years or so as restructuring of the state sector continues. Some cities are further along (and had a smaller problem to begin with) in restructuring state-owned enterprises and will pass the peak of layoffs sooner than other cities.

Second, technological change and the progressive development of the economy may reduce the demand for unskilled labor, especially in the coastal cities. For example, by the mid 1990s, ten million Sichuan farmers had left their farms for employment elsewhere, with about half going to other provinces (US Consulate Chengdu, 2001). By the end of the 1990s, the number away from home had declined slightly (at most by 20 per cent). Officials cited the industrial transformation of coastal areas which requires fewer unskilled laborers as one reason for the decline. They also pointed out that faster economic growth in Sichuan drew some of the migrants home.

Characteristics of migrants in the late 1990s and their reasons for migrating remained relatively unchanged compared to prior years (Mallee, 2000; Du, 2000; Knight and Song, 1997). Migrants tend to be younger than the general population, are concentrated between the ages of 20 and 35, and have average or above average income compared to others in their hometown (Cai, 1999). The flow of interprovincial migration is basically from rural areas to cities, with rural laborers moving from central and western regions to east coast regions for work in township and village enterprises and unskilled urban jobs. A small percentage of labor also migrates from very poor regions of China to agriculture jobs in developed regions.

A comparison of two similar nationally representative surveys focused on rural migrant laborers in 1993 and 1998 reveals a few new trends (Chan, 2001a).[3] The total number of rural labor migrants was nearly the same in the two years (51.3 million in 1993 and 49.3 million in 1998) as was the share finding outside work within their home county (about 35.5 per cent). One difference is that more are traveling further for work leaving not only their home province but also their region (rising from 9 per cent in 1993 to 15.4 per cent in 1998). In addition, a larger share of interprovincial rural labor migrants came from the western region of China in 1998 than was the case in 1993. The east region was the main destination of these rural labor migrants in both years but more so in 1998.

---

3   The earlier survey was conducted by the Agricultural Bank of China and covered labor migrants from rural areas working away from home for at least part of 1993. The more recent 1998 survey also focused on rural migrant laborers although its definition was not exactly the same (Chan, 2001a).

While economics drives the flow of migrant laborers, other factors play a role in determining how long the migrant will stay in the destination and whether the migrant will be accompanied by non-working family members. Migrants' status in the destination is often quite low and their privileges few. Even if they register as temporary residents they have no rights to the services provided to other city residents with permanent registration status. One important issue is access to education for children. In 1998 the Ministry of Education and Ministry of Public Security jointly issued a regulation requiring local governments to guarantee education for migrants' children between the ages of 6 and 14 if they had lived in the area for more than six months (Xinhua, 1999a). Most cities are handling this by opening separate schools for migrant children rather than allowing them to attend the same schools as the children of permanent residents. The number of children at risk of not receiving an education or an inferior one at best is growing. In 1998 Hefei (the capital of Anhui) had 6,000 children to whom the new regulation applied, Shanghai had 14,000, and Shenzhen 110,000. Guangdong province is more progressive than a number of other regions and adopted regulations in 1998 which state that children of migrants who reside in the same location for at least five consecutive years enjoy the same education rights as permanent residents (Xinhua, 1999b).

Obtaining permanent household registration status in the destination would place migrants on par with native residents; however, this is rarely an option. Instead, since the late 1980s, new 'categories' of *hukou* have emerged. Typically these intermediate *hukou* categories are valid only locally and have served as revenue generating propositions for urban areas. The privileges extended to the holders of these *hukou* are limited. One such category which has received attention in the press and literature is the blue stamp urban *hukou*. Applicants for this *hukou* must pay an entry fee, which varies depending on the administrative status of the urban area. For example, one source lists the fee for cities and towns below the county-level as under 5,000 yuan, while Shanghai charged 40,000 yuan for the city proper, 20,000 yuan for a suburban district, and 10,000 yuan for a suburban county (Chan and Zhang, 1999). If they choose to leave the location of their blue stamp residency, migrants must return to the site of their original permanent household registration. Blue stamp *hukou* holders are not given the same political and economic rights as holders of permanent household registration but they are sometimes offered the prospect of being granted permanent household registration status if they meet some further criteria (Chan and Zhang, 1999).

In 1997, the central government launched a pilot program in towns and small cities allowing them to grant urban *hukou* to qualified rural *hukou* holders (Chan and Zhang, 1999). The required qualifications are a stable nonagricultural job or source of support, regular accommodations, and two years of residency. No fee is to be charged and they are to enjoy the same rights as other residents, including access to employment, education, social security programs, and medical services.

Some cities, anxious to offload vast stocks of unsold and overpriced housing, offer migrants the chance to get a residency permit if they have capital to invest. In Ningbo migrants can get an urban residence permit (*hukou*) if they buy a house of at least 100 square meters (average cost 250,000 yuan), have a steady job and have lived in Ningbo for at least three years. Wenzhou will grant a *hukou* to those who have two years residency, a steady job, and a place to live. Guangdong's regulations state that migrants who reside in the same location for seven consecutive years and have permanent housing can apply for permanent residence status (Xinhua, 1999b).

The Custody and Repatriation Act allows the police to detain migrants and send them back to the countryside. Migrant workers can be expelled from a city and summarily sent back to their home village if they do not have legal residence permits, a permanent or long term job, or proper identification papers. Beijing is notorious for ejecting migrant workers, especially just before major holidays. In the first eight months of 1999, 16,000 laborers were expelled from the capital. In the first half of 2000, Beijing's police expelled some 180,000 floating population who had no legal ID cards, no long-term contract jobs, or no regular place to stay (Xinhua, 2000b). Any resident or establishment that might provide lodging to 'illegal' migrants is also threatened with judicial action (Hong Kong Agence France Presse, 1999).

Major cities are concerned with controlling both the natural population growth rate and immigration. Beijing, for example, has a goal of controlling permanent residents to within 12.3 million by 2010 and the total population to within 14.6 million by 2010 (Liu, 1999). That is, its nonresident population who stay more than six months should not exceed 2.3 million. By 2000 the non-resident population meeting this six-month definition had reached 1.7 million. In the next ten years, the non-resident population can grow by only 60,000 per year to not exceed the target. However, between 1998 and 2000 Beijing's temporary resident population increased by more than 100,000 per year. In order to not exceed its target, Beijing will need to continue active measures to control the flow of immigrants.

Although migrant workers contribute to the local economy and often work side by side with permanent resident workers, their rights in the work place are very limited (Tan, 2000). Even if rights exist on paper, migrants often are unaware of them or are unsuccessful in having them enforced. There are numerous reports of migrant workers being cheated out of their pay. In one recent example a large state-owned enterprise hired a group of rural migrants to construct facilities on a ten-year contract. Workers were promised an extra month's salary for each year worked. At the completion of the project, the enterprise paid the bonus based only on the basic salary, a fraction of total salary. The workers complained and their representative ended up in jail (US Consulate Shanghai, 2001).

In spite of their inferior treatment, millions of migrants still choose to leave their homes for work elsewhere. A primary motivation continues to be the opportunity to earn more money. Studies indicate that the average migrant worker sends between 2000 (Cai, 1999) and 3000 (Chan, 2001b) yuan annually back to their families. Using an estimate of 50 million migrant laborers nationally, this translates into 100–150 billion yuan in remittances, which ranges well above the government's entire budget for agriculture in 1998 (State Statistical Bureau, 2000).[4]

5   Concluding Summary

This chapter began with a review of various definitions of China's floating population, an inherently ambiguous term, and one that reflects China's unique administrative *hukou* system specifying the local area in which citizens are supposed to reside. The broadest practical definition of the floating population includes all peoeple who are away from their official *hukou* location for 24 hours or more. Yet, given whatever issue observers are most concerned about, the term can, and often is, applied to more limited subcategories under that broadest definition. This chapter then reviewed various sources of data that can be used to assess the size of the floating population – censuses, surveys, and various types of household registration systems – and reviewed some findings from these sources at the national and sub-national level. For instance, according to the most recent statistics from the Ministry of Public Security, the floating population was about 100 million persons as of 1997, which constitutes roughly a quarter of China's urban population, and nearly 8 per cent of China's total population. The Ministry expects those numbers to grow substantially in

---

4   In 1998 the government spent 115 billion yuan on supporting agricultural production and operating expenses, capital construction for agriculture, science and technology promotion, and rural relief (State Statistical Bureau, 2000).

the future. Although the exact definition being used by the Ministry remains murky, and even if their estimates and projections prove to be incorrect, this is the number likely being used by urban planners in China. The chapter also discussed some recent factors expected to impact the floating population and future trends, including national and local legislation. Among some notable legislative changes was a shortening of the intended duration of stay that would require a newly arrived migrant to register with local authorities (shortening in 1995 from three months to one month).

Despite inherent ambiguities in definitions, there have been attempts to collect more complete, detailed, and flexible data on the floating population. For instance, following the 1990 census, the period required away from one's *hukou* in order to be considered a migrant was reduced from one year to six months. After 1995 the boundary crossing required was narrowed from counties to townships, which resulted in higher migrant counts in the State Statistical Bureau's annual survey of population change. The month in which the 2000 census was taken was switched to November in order to avoid undercounts of migrants who might be excluded under the six-month rule if they made short trips to their ancestral homes for the lunar new year or around October holidays. The 2000 census added a question asking households to identify the number of people who primarily for work purposes were away from their *hukou* location for less than six months. A separate form was also created to query these same migrants at their point of destination. It remains unclear how such data will be tabulated, but they will almost certainly provide even more inclusive measures of the floating population in China.

References

Beijing Statistical Bureau (2000), *Beijing Statistical Yearbook 2000*, Beijing: China Statistical Publishing House.

Beijing Statistical Bureau (2000), *Beijing Statistical Yearbook 1998*, Beijing: China Statistical Publishing House.

Cai, F. (1999), 'Population Shifts and the Reassignment of Resources,' *Jingji ribao*, 4 August, C1, translated in Foreign Broadcast Information Services Document No. FTS19990901000388.

Chan, K. (2001a), 'Migration in China: Definitions, Data and Trends,' paper presented at the Population Association of America annual meeting, 28–30 March, Washington, DC.

Chan, K. (2001b), 'Recent Migration in China: Patterns, Trends, and Policies,' *Asian Perspective*, 25 (4), pp. 127–55.

Chan, K. and Li, Z. (1999), 'The *Hukou* System and Rural-Urban Migration in China: Processes and Changes,' *The China Quarterly*, 160, pp. 818–55.

Cheng, T. and Selden, M. (1994), 'The Origins and Social Consequences of China's *Hukou* System,' *The China Quarterly*, 139, pp. 644–68.

Cui, H. (2000), 'On China's Total Population,' paper presented at the 19th Population Census Conference, 26–28 April, Beijing.

Du, Y. (2000), 'Rural Labor Migration in Contemporary China: An Analysis of Its Features and the Macro Context,' in West, L.A. and Zhao, Y. (eds), *Rural Labor Flows in China*, Berkeley, CA: Institute of East Asian Studies, pp. 67–100.

Gale, F., Somwaaru, A. and Diao, X. (2002), 'Agricultural Labor: Where Are the Jobs?,' in *China's Food and Agriculture Issues for the 21st Century*, USDA ERS, Agriculture Information Bulletin Number 775, pp. 44–46.

Goldstein, S. and Goldstein, A. (1991), 'Permanent and Temporary Migration Differentials in China,' papers of the East-West Population Institute, No. 117, February.

Hong Kong Agence France Presse (1999), 'AFP: Beijing Expels Migrant Workers Prior to Anniversary,' 8 September, translated in Foreign Broadcast Information Service Document No. FTS19990908000227.

Hua, S. (2000), 'China's Floating Population Will Increase by Five Million Each Year,' *Shanghai Jiefang Ribao*, internet version 28 September, translated in FBIS Document No. CPP20000928000018.

Knight, J.B. and Song, L. (1997), 'Chinese Peasant Choices: Farming, Rural Industry, or Migration,' Institute of Economics and Statistics, University of Oxford, Applied Economics Discussion Paper, Series, no. 188.

Liang, Z. and Chen, Y. (2001), 'Urbanization in China: Historical Overview and Emerging Patterns in the 1990s,' paper presented at the Annual Meeting of the Population Association of America, 29–31 March, Washington DC.

Liu, G. (1999), 'The Floating Population in Beijing and Its Management,' *Qian Xian*, No. 2, February, pp. 31–34, translated in FBIS Document No. FTS199902240224001085.

Mallee, H. (2000), 'Agricultural Labor and Rural Population Mobility: Some Observations,' in West, L.A. and Zhao, Y. (eds), *Rural Labor Flows in China*, Berkeley, CA: Institute of East Asian Studies, pp. 34–66.

Scharping, T. (1997), 'Studying Migration in Contemporary China: Models and Methods, Issues and Evidence,' in Scharping, T. (ed.), *Floating Population and Migration in China. The Impact of Economic Reforms*, Hamburg: Institut Fuer Asienkunde, pp. 9–55.

Solinger, D.J. (1999), *Contesting Citizenship in Urban China*, Berkeley, CA: University of California Press.

State Council Population Census Office and State Statistical Bureau, Department of Population, Social, Science and Technology Statistics (2001), *Major Figures on 2000 Population Census of China*, Beijing: China Statistics Press.

State Statistical Bureau (1997a), *China Statistical Yearbook 1997*. Beijing: China Statistical Publishing House.

State Statistical Bureau (1997b), *1995 National 1% Population Sample Survey Materials*, Beijing: China Statistical Publishing House.

State Statistical Bureau (1998), *China Statistical Yearbook 1998*, Beijing: China Statistical Publishing House.

State Statistical Bureau (1999), *China Statistical Yearbook 1999*, Beijing: China Statistics Press.

State Statistical Bureau (2000), *China Statistical Yearbook 2000*, Beijing: China Statistics Press.

Tan, S. (2000), 'The Relationship between Foreign Enterprises, Local Governments, and Women Migrant Workers in the Pearl River Delta,' in West, L.A. and Zhao, Y. (eds), *Rural Labor Flows in China*, Berkeley, CA: Institute of East Asian Studies, pp. 292–309.

US Consulate Chengdu (2001), 'Transforming Sichuan's Countryside: Mission Impossible?,' Cable P 121730Z MAR 01.

US Consulate Guangzhou (2001), 'Township and Village Enterprises in Guangdong: Challenges for a New Decade,' Cable R 090849Z JAN 01.

US Consulate Shanghai (2001), 'Migrant Labor Advocacy in Shanghai–Risky Business,' Cable R 260234Z MAR 01.

West, L. and Banister, J. (1996), 'Demographic Trends in China's Eastern Provinces,' US Census Bureau: International Programs Center (mimeo).

Wu, W. (2001), 'Migrant Housing in Urban China: Choices and Constraints,' paper presented at the Population Association of America annual meeting, 29–31 March, Washington, DC.

Xinhua (1999a), 'Obligatory Schooling Provided for Migrant Children,' Foreign Broadcast Information Service Document No. FTS19990107001548.

Xinhua (1999b)'Guangdong Strengthens Control Over "Floating Population",' Foreign Broadcast Information Service Document No. FTS199990104001327.

Xinhua (2000a), 'Public Security Minister on Strengthening Floating Population Management,' Foreign Broadcast Information Service Document No. CPP20000926000070.

Xinhua (2000b), 'Crimes by 'Floating Population' fall in Beijing,' 2000b, 2 August, translated in Foreign Broadcast Information Service Document No. CPP20000802000124.

Yu, H. (2000), 'The Enumeration of Floating Population During the 2000 Population Census of China,' paper presented at the 19th Population Census Conference, 26–28 April, Beijing.

CHAPTER 8

HUKOU SYSTEMS AND MIGRATION CONTROLS

FEI-LING WANG*

Georgia Institute of Technology

Abstract

Domestic migration has been a major source of economic efficiency, development and urbanization. The often socially, politically, economically, and environmentally shattering effects of urbanization have made control of domestic migration imperative. This chapter discusses the unique nature of China's urbanization. It examines one of the most important fabrics of China's political economy, the hukou *(household registration) system, as a highly institutionalized and deeply legitimized way of controlling the pace and size of China's urbanization. After two decades of comprehensive economic reform, the* hukou *system has adopted several important changes of its own and has thus become fairly accommodating to the needs of labor mobility, yet at the same time provides a strong support for China's political and social stability. China's urbanization, as a consequence, has been highly controlled, orderly, and slow.*

Keywords: urbanization, China's *hukou* system

JEL classification: O14, R11, R14

1   Introduction

Domestic migration has been a major source of economic efficiency and development as well as affecting urbanization. Developing nations have

---

*   Correspondence: Fei-Ling Wang, Associate Professor, The Sam Nunn School of International Affairs, Georgia Institute of Technology, Atlanta, GA 30332–0610, USA. Tel: 404–894–1904; Fax: 404–894–1900; Email: fei-ling.wang@inta.gatech.edu.

URBAN TRANSFORMATION IN CHINA, edited by Aimin Chen, Gordon G. Liu and Kevin H. Zhang

inevitably faced this issue yet nevertheless have devised varied strategies to address the process and its consequences. The often socially, politically, economically, and environmentally shattering effects of urbanization have made control of domestic migration imperative. The various patterns of domestic migration control in different countries, however, have produced very different impacts on their economic marketization, political changes, and nation-building efforts.

This chapter discusses one unique aspect of the People's Republic of China's urbanization. It examines one of the most important parts of China's political economy, the *hukou* (household or residential) registration system (*hukou* system for short), as a highly institutionalized and deeply legitimized way of controlling the pace and size of China's urbanization. After two decades of comprehensive economic reform, the *hukou* system has adopted several important changes of its own and has thus become fairly accommodating to the need of labor mobility yet at the same time provides a strong support for China's political and social stability. The basic structure, mechanism, and roles of this keystone of the PRC institutional framework remain largely intact.

2   An Overview of the *Hukou* System

Officially, the *hukou* system is defined as a system to administratively collect and manage the information of the citizens' personal identification, kinship, and legal residence as 'the necessary foundation of the overall population management and social administrations.'[1] In addition to those administrative tasks that are invariably found in other countries, the PRC *hukou* system has its own three 'unique missions': the administrative control of domestic migration and urbanization; the management of temporary residents/visitors mainly in the urban areas; and a tiered management of focal (key or special) segments of the population, also primarily in the cities.[2]

---

1   X. Jiang and L. Feng (eds) (1996), *Jingca yewu shiyong quanshu* (*Complete Guide of Police Works*), Beijing: Quinzhong Press, p. 218; BPT-MPS (Bureau of Personnel and Training-Ministry of Public Security) (2000), *Huzheng guanli jiaocheng* (*Textbook on Hukou Management*), Beijing: Qunzhong Press, p. 5.

2   X. Jiang and L. Feng (eds) (1996), *Jingca yewu shiyong quanshu* (*Complete Guide of Police Works*), Beijing: Quinzhong Press, p. 220; BPT-MPS (Bureau of Personnel and Training-Ministry of Public Security) (2000), *Huzheng guanli jiaocheng* (*Textbook on Hukou Management*), Beijing: Qunzhong Press, pp. 161–73.

The basic law governing the operation of the PRC *hukou* system has been the 'Regulation on Hukou Registration of the People's Republic of China' promulgated on 9 January 1958. Twenty-seven years later, on 6 September 1985, Beijing adopted its 'Regulation on Resident's Personal Identification Card in the People's Republic of China.' These two regulations and their implementational procedures are the 'main legal basis' for the *hukou* system. The State Council and its ministries and bureaus, especially the Ministry of Public Security, have issued numerous regulations, provisional regulations, directives, decrees, and documents that have substantiated and fine-tuned the *hukou* system. The majority of those 'State Documents,' estimated to be over 200 from 1958 to 1996, have been on the ever-changing criteria and the various mechanisms of domestic migration control or *hukou* relocation.[3] Local public security bureaus, police stations and substations are the administrators of the *hukou* system, while many other ministries are involved in its operation. For example, the State Planning Commission sets the quota for and monitors the cross-region and especially rural to urban migrations.

Archival research reveals that the Ministry of Public Security has been the most active maker of policies governing the operation of the *hukou* system. With the authorization of the central government, provincial and municipal governments have made certain marginal changes and experimental policies to the *hukou* system in their respective jurisdictions. Despite the fact that the *hukou* system has been so comprehensive and lasting, admits an official police handbook, 'our legal framework of the *hukou* management is still very insufficient.'[4] Namely, the *hukou* system is largely an administrative system based on very sketchy legal foundation.

By the beginning of the twenty-first century, under China's *hukou* system, every PRC citizen is legally required to register with the *hukou* authorities and acquire a *hukou* certification. A police substation in the cities or a rural township (*xiangzheng*) constitutes a '*hukou* management zone.' Full time specialized *hukou* police are in charge of the system, under the supervision of the superior public security bureaus and the local CCP committees. One can only have one permanent *hukou* at one of those *hukou* zones where he is a permanent resident. The unit of the registration is the household which may be a family (nuclear or extended), a single resident, or a 'collective household' such as a *danwei* (work unit) or a dormitory. By late 1980s, more than 30 million people (fewer than 3

---

3   BPT-MPS (Bureau of Personnel and Training-Ministry of Public Security) (2000), *Huzheng guanli jiaocheng* (*Textbook on* Hukou *Management*), Beijing: Qunzhong Press, p. 122.

4   X. Jiang and L. Feng (eds) (1996), *Jingca yewu shiyong quanshu* (*Complete Guide of Police Works*), Beijing: Quinzhong Press, p. 225.

per cent of the total population) registered in over one million such 'collective' households (about 0.5 per cent of total households).[5]

A family household, other than related, must primarily be living together and sharing a same family budget. Every household shall have a household head who is responsible for the registration. Family members or collective household members can acquire their 'independent' *hukou* status as a new unit of household. Merged households, as a result of marriage/divorce or adoption, can form a new household and re-register accordingly. A new-born or adopted must register with the *hukou* authority within one month and acquire his/her parents' primarily mother's *hukou* location and status.[6] The household-head, family members, or neighbors of the deceased must inform the *hukou* police before the burial (in the urban area) or within one month of the burial (in the rural areas) and thus cancel the *hukou* record of the deceased. Each urban household is given a *Hukou* Booklet as a legal copy of the *Hukou* Registration Form maintained in the public security bureaus. The *Hukou* Booklet and the later adopted personal identification card serve as the legal proof of one's *hukou* location, status, and other personal information, kinship, and family relationships. Except for some cities that have computerized their record-keeping, the *hukou* files are generally stored at police substations or township governments with a copy filed to the superior public security bureau.

Everyone who moves out of his/her *hukou* zone must apply for a 'Migrating *Hukou* Certificate' from the *hukou* police and then cancel the old *hukou* record and register at the new *hukou* zone. For the rural residents moving to urban areas, one of the following special documentation is required for the application of the Migrating *Hukou* Certificate: An employment notice from an urban labor bureau above the county level or an admission from a urban school (must be state accredited professional schools, colleges or graduate schools); or a special immigration permit called *Hukou* Relocating Permit from an urban *hukou* authority. Any migration to the border region must be approved by the public security bureaus at or above the county level.

Military personnel register in the collective household of their military units. Draftees cancel their old *hukou* and restore it upon discharge.

---

5   BPT-MPS (Bureau of Personnel and Training-Ministry of Public Security) (2000), *Huzheng guanli jiaocheng* (*Textbook on* Hukou *Management*), Beijing: Qunzhong Press, p. 46.

6   Until 1998, Chinese children could only acquire their mother's *hukou* status at birth. A new regulation allowed the parents to choose either the mother's or the father's *hukou* for the new born. State Council (1998), 'Approval of Public Security Ministry's Notice on Solving Several Pressing Issues in the Current Management of the *Hukou* System,' Beijing, 22 July.

Demobilized or retired officers generally are all given an urban *hukou*. The *hukou* police cancel automatically the *hukou* of the convicts and re-register them with the *hukou* police at the location of incarceration. Upon release, a former convict may or may not restore his previous *hukou*. As a very frequent anti-crime practice by the government, many urban convicts especially the repeat offenders are reassigned a new *hukou* in generally remote and even rural areas to prevent them from moving back to the cities upon release. Travelers to overseas for more than one year must cancel their *hukou* during the process of passport application and may restore the previous *hukou* upon returning permanently.

Anyone who is living outside his/her *hukou* zone (excluding within the same city or county) for more than three days must register with the local *hukou* police for a temporary *hukou* certificate. Temporary *hukou* is issued for three months and must be renewed by the local *hukou* police for proper reasons. Travelers must register with the innkeepers for the inspection by the local police. Other than being dictated by the planned state hires and transfers, all domestic migration is controlled by *hukou* police according to certain nationally set and regionally adjusted principles. There are four overall principles governing *hukou* relocation and domestic migration: 1) 'To strictly control any migration' that leads to changes from agricultural or rural *hukou* to non-agricultural or urban *hukou*, from town *hukou* to city *hukou*, and from city *hukou* to *hukou* of three metropolitan cities (Beijing, Shanghai, and Tianjin); 2) 'To properly control migration' from countryside to the suburban areas, from suburban areas to the cities, and from small cities to large cities; 3) 'To not control parallel or swapping migration' between *hukou* zones in similar villages, between comparable towns, or between similarly ranked cities; and 4) 'To encourage dispersing type migration' from cities to towns, from large cities to small cities, and from urban areas to the countryside.[7]

Ordinary Chinese need their *hukou* documentation for education, marriage, passport, traveling, employment, and business activities. Before 1990s, many important economic benefits such as food rations, subsidized heavily by the state, were only allocated to the urban residents – the so-called 'non-agricultural *hukou*' holders. Subsidized housing, schooling, and healthcare were generally not available to non-local *hukou* holders. This changed after 1985 when the PRC started to reform the *tonggou tongxiao* (state monopoly of the procurement and

---

7   Yu Ju (1991), 'Qiantang hukou shengpi quanxian de xiafang' ('Preliminary Discussion on the Decentralization of *Hukou* Authorities'), *Zhongguo renmin jingguang daxue xuebao* (*Journal of the University of Chinese People's Police Officers*), Beijing, 1, p. 55; BPT-MPS (2000), p. 121.

sales of) grain policy. By 1992/93, nearly 500 cities/counties have abandoned the grain ration system, although some major cities restored it in 1994 to guarantee a low price of food for the urban residents. The market allocation of grain has become the main avenue of food distribution in today's PRC.[8]

Ten years later, by 2001, the urban *hukou* holders, however, still clearly enjoy significant state subsidies in housing, transportation, education and healthcare. The market alternative of urban housing to the *hukou*-based allocation has been generally exorbitant. The redistribution of income, in the forms of welfare and poverty relief as well as unemployment insurance and community cultural activities, by the local government, is generally conducted strictly benefiting the local *hukou* holders only. Non-local *hukou*-holders can send their children to local schools only after paying substantially for the available slots. Their children, however, must still return to their permanent *hukou* to take the college and professional school entrance exams which are usually much more competitive outside the major cities. To many, the regional differential in college entrance examination and admission remains perhaps the most significant state subsidy to the selected urban population especially in the major metropolitan areas such as Beijing and Shanghai.[9]

Upon graduation from colleges, the students are generally sent back to the urban sector of the province, prefecture, and even county where their original *hukou* were located. This much cursed policy is now considerably compromised in a number of ways by various urban governments interested in attracting and/or keeping 'the talents.' By 2001, college graduates, especially those with highly demanded skills and training, have achieved substantial but only *de facto* nation-wide mobility through various temporary and expedient arrangements such as the blue stamp *hukou* scheme and the increased employment opportunities generated by the non-state sectors. One of the most important aspects of the *hukou*-based institutional exclusion, however, still perpetuates in the area of employment. All employers must record the *hukou* information of the employees. Without proper authorization from the local

---

8   Gao Shangquan et al. (eds) (1993), *Zhongguo jingji gaige kaifang dashidian* (*Book of Chinese Economic Events on Reforming and Opening*), Beijing: Beijing Gongye University Press, p. 92.

9   Chinese universities have different admission standards in different *hukou* zones. For example, a high school graduate with Beijing urban *hukou* could get into the top Beijing University with a college entrance exam score 20–50 per cent lower than an rejected applicant who has a rural *hukou* from Hubei or Anhui provinces. The main reason was that all the universities were ordered by the state to have disproportionally large quota for applicants from major cities where they are usually located. The details of such disproportional quota are classified and vary across the region. Author's field notes, 1996–2002.

labor bureaus, all employers are generally prohibited from hiring anyone with a non-local *hukou*. Private employers and foreign investors, however, have in practice been able to hire non-locals since the mid-1990s.[10] They either pay substantially for a permit to hire non-locals or run the risk of heavy fines and even forfeiting of license if they are caught for violating the *hukou* system.

3   To Control Urbanization through the *Hukou* System

Perhaps the most distinctive and most significant feature of the Chinese *hukou* system has been its rural-urban dual structure and the related control of domestic migration. Some have explored this institutional peculiarity in the PRC from the analytical angles of citizenship, labor mobility, and urbanization.[11] In a very 'Chinese' way, this significant and lasting institutional exclusion and control of urbanization are based on only two sentences of the basic law of the PRC *hukou* system, the 'Regulation on Household Registration of the People's Republic of China' of 1958. Article 10 of that Regulation simply states:

> Citizen migrates out of a *hukou* zone: the citizen or household head applies for an emigration registration to the *hukou* agencies and claims migration documents, the original *hukou* is canceled.
>   Citizen migrates from countryside to the cities must have employment proof from urban labor agencies, admission proof from schools, or proof of immigration permission from urban *hukou* registration agencies. ...[12]

This additional requirement for the rural-urban migration later developed into a legal Great Wall separating the majority of the Chinese in the countryside from the minority in the cities, institutionally creating the most striking community-based, family-defined, and geographic location-centered legal exclusion in modern times. Chinese citizens have thus become two segments:

---

10 F.-L. Wang (1998), *From Family to Market: Labor Allocation in Contemporary China.* Lanham, Boulder, New York, and Oxford: Rowman and Littlefield, pp. 262–4.

11 For example, D.J. Solinger (1999), *Contesting Citizenship in Urban China: Peasant Migrants, the State, and the Logic of the Market*, Berkeley, CA: University of California Press; F.-L. Wang (1998), *Institutions and Institutional Change in China: Premodernity and Modernization*, London and New York: Macmillian Press; D. Davin (1999), *Internal Migration in Contemporary China*, New York: Palgrave.

12 Wang Huaian et al. (eds) (1989), *Zhonghua renmin gongheguo fali quanshu (Complete Collections of the Laws of the People's Republic of China)*, Changchun: Jilin Renmin Press, p. 1502.

agricultural and non-agricultural *hukou* holders.[13] To perhaps a lesser extent, there is also a legal separation between the metropolitan centers and smaller cities and between cities and townships.

The PRC had a short period of 'free migration' in 1949–57 when the early versions of the *hukou* system were mainly designed for the government's social control purposes. In 1950, Beijing set its *hukou* system to 'guarantee the freedom of migration.' By 1951 and later in 1954, the various registrations under the *hukou* system were codified; yet there were no specific conditions on migrating from the rural to the urban areas.[14] Even though the chronic shortage of supplies start to appear almost immediately after the completion of 'socialization of the urban economy' and the rural collectivization in 1956–57, the CCP did not fully realize that its planned economy just simply could not handle the increase of urban population. Nonetheless, to 'persuade' the peasants to migrate into the cities was mentioned almost annually in the CCP Central documents after 1953.[15] The 1958 Regulation gave the *hukou* system its urban vs. rural duality but this legal separation was not actively enforced until the disastrous years of the early 1960s. The need for controlling domestic migration and especially the migration from the rural to the urban became painfully clear as Mao's 'Great Leap Forward' (1958–61) led to an economic crash with the magnitude rarely seen in human history.

Since the beginning of the 1960s, Beijing has always restricted the migration from the countryside to the cities through controlling the change of agricultural *hukou* to non-agricultural *hukou*. The motivation for such a role of the *hukou* system was political and economic necessities. Politically, the CCP felt its inability in developing China's largely agrarian economy and fulfilling its burning political ambitions. A search for a solution in the past thus was only

---

13   The PRC currently has a *hukou*-based categorization of the population: non-agricultural *hukou* holders versus agricultural *hukou* holders. It also has a statistical categorization of urban population (those who live in the 'cities or townships') and rural population. In the later case, urban population may include some agricultural *hukou* holders who live inside the boundaries of a city or a township. Namely, the 'urban population' is likely to be larger than 'non-agricultural population' while the later is the legally meaningful term in the *hukou* system. See Tables 7 to 13 of T. Xueyuan (ed.) (1995), *1995 Zhongguo renkou nianjian* (*1995 Annual Book of the Chinese Population*), Beijing: Jingji Gunagli Press, pp. 291–7. For a rather problematic interpretation of these two sets of categorization, see H.X. Wu (1994), 'Rural to Urban Migration in the People's Republic of China,' *The China Quarterly*, pp. 674–5.

14   BPT-MPS (Bureau of Personnel and Training-Ministry of Public Security) (2000), *Huzheng guanli jiaocheng* (*Textbook on* Hukou *Management*), Beijing: Qunzhong Press, p. 118.

15   T. Wang (1997), *Huzheng yu renkou guanli lilun yanjiu zhongshu* (*Summary of the Theoretical Study on* Hukou *System and Personnel Managment*), Beijing: Qunzhong Press, p. 233.

natural. The century old *hukou* system hence became a new lifeline to the CCP's political regime, social control, and economic planning.[16] Economically, the dire need for capital smashed the hopes of the rural population for a better life associated with urbanization. Inefficient, stagnant, and mismanaged, Beijing simply could not sustain the politically crucial ration system in the cities if the urban population kept growing, powered by the inevitably emigrating rural population that was more than 80 per cent of the nation.[17]

From 1960 to the 1980s, the Chinese population was legally divided into two, with the minority in the cities vs the majority in the rural. The only narrow bridge between them was the state's approval of changing one's *hukou* status. Within each of the two Chinas, the cities as well as the villages (communes until 1978) were also kept apart from one another by the *hukou* relocation control. Domestic migration in this period was primarily a state administrative behavior with over 43 million urban residents forcefully 'sent down' to the countryside, while several million peasants were allowed to become non-agriculture *hukou* holders through state employment, military services, and college admission.[18] The control role of the *hukou* system was so resilient that even the chaotic 'Culture Revolution' (1966–76) did no more than barely scratch it.[19] The previously stipulation on 'citizens' right of freedom of migration,' however nominal it might had been to begin with, was finally removed from the PRC Constitution in 1975.

Since the mid-1980s, the reform has dislodged many formerly affixed rural laborers and created the possibility for many rural *hukou* holders to work and even live in the cities especially the small towns. But their *hukou* status are still strictly controlled to be agricultural so the rural-urban institutional exclusion continues despite that many of the excluded have now lived in

---

16 An imperial version of the *hukou* system was in place in China for the most part of its imperial history since the Warring States Era. The Republic of China also implemented an ROC version of the *hukou* system in the 1930s and it still exists in today's Taiwan. For a discussion on Mao's 'leaping forward to the past,' see F.-L. Wang (1998), *Institutions and Institutional Change in China*, pp. 93–104.

17 More in-depth analysis on the rationale of the *hukou* system is presented in the author's forthcoming book on China's *hukou* system.

18 BPT-MPS (Bureau of Personnel and Training-Ministry of Public Security) (2000), *Huzheng guanli jiaocheng* (*Textbook on* Hukou *Management*), Beijing: Qunzhong Press, p. 119. For an examination of such state allocation, see F.-L. Wang (1998), *From Family to Market: Labor Allocation in Contemporary China*. Lanham, Boulder, New York, and Oxford: Rowman and Littlefield, pp. 87–162.

19 T. Wang (1997), *Huzheng yu renkou guanli lilun yanjiu zhongshu* (*Summary of the Theoretical Study on* Hukou *System and Personnel Managment*), Beijing: Qunzhong Press, p. 234.

the same urban location for years. They are on temporary *hukou* or Lodging Residential Permits thus can not fully enjoy the rights and benefits of the urban *hukou* holders. Those new urban residents with agricultural *hukou*, just like those still living in the villages, can still not access the exclusively urban benefits such as subsidized housing, education, and health care. Jobs in the state sector including the government itself, and state subsidized training and unemployment insurance are off-limit to those urban-residing agricultural *hukou* holders.[20]

4   The Quota and The Rules of Control

Each year, the PRC state allows for only a very small number of agricultural *hukou* holders to change to non-agricultural *hukou* status.[21] Ever since 1980, that limit has been set at two-tenths of a percentage point (0.2 per cent) to half of a percentage point (0.5 per cent) of the total agricultural population. Based on that, each locality then develop an annual quota of '*nongzhuanfei*' (agricultural to non-agricultural *hukou* changes) to be observed by the *hukou* police. 'Other than allowed for by the state planning and migration policies, no rural resident can move into the urban areas especially the big cities without approval.'[22]

The State Council approved on 14 August 1964 and reaffirmed on 8 November 1977 the Public Security Ministry's 'Rules on Handling *Hukou* Relocation.' Those 'internal rules' have been the foundation of the rural-urban institutional exclusion. Various agencies of the PRC Central Government from 1958 to 1988 issued as many as 207 policies and decrees (mostly internal only) concerning domestic migration especially the rural-urban migration.[23]

---

20   In the open city of Shanghai, all agricultural *hukou* holders as well as all non-Shanghai urban *hukou* holders were clearly excluded from the housing benefits, public schools, much higher chances of college education, newly socialized pension and health care plans. Author's field notes, 1996–2001.

21   The most talked about official reasons have been 'maintaining an orderly construction of the urban economy,' 'to avoid overburdening the urban infrastructure,' and 'ensuring enough grain producing manpower in the countryside.' Sun Yao (1994), *Hukou guanlixue jiaocheng* (*Textbook on* Hukou *Management*), Beijing: Qunzhong Press, for circulation in the MPS only, pp. 139–47.

22   Sun Yao (1994), *Hukou guanlixue jiaocheng* (*Textbook on* Hukou *Management*), Beijing: Qunzhong Press, for circulation in the MPS only, p. 141.

23   Sun Yao (1994), *Hukou guanlixue jiaocheng* (*Textbook on* Hukou *Management*), Beijing: Qunzhong Press, for circulation in the MPS only, pp. 147–50.

Several dozen new policies have been put into effect by late 1990s.[24] By the new millennium, Beijing has devised a four-part new guideline dealing with *hukou* changes and domestic migration:

> *Hukou* relocation from the rural to urban areas (including mining zone and forestry); or from other cities to Beijing, Shanghai, Tianjin, and Chongqing (municipalities directly under the central government) must be controlled as restrictedly as possible – *chongyan kongzhi* (strict control).
>
> *Hukou* relocation from township to city; from small city to large city; from ordinary village to outskirts of city/township, state-run farm, village specialized in vegetable-growing, or cash crop-growing area should be controlled appropriately – *shidang kongzhi* (appropriate control).
>
> *Hukou* relocation from city/township to village; from city to township; from large city to small city; and between similar cities, between similar townships, or between similar villages, with proper reasons (such as marriage), should be approved – *buyu kongzhi* (no control).
>
> *Hukou* relocation by college graduates and professionals from city/township to village, from interior to border regions, from area or unit that has plenty technical talents to place where there is shortage of such talents should be encouraged with various means – *guli liudong* (encourage migration).[25]

And the purpose of hukou relocation control is:

> (We) should encourage the dispersal of the population. (We should) make it harder to migrate to major cities, easier to small cities; harder to migrate to cities/townships, easier to villages; harder to migrate to Southeastern regions, easier to the Northwest; harder to migrate to the economically developed areas, easier to the old revolutionary bases [usually in remote and mountainous areas-author added], (ethnic) minority regions, border regions, and the poor areas. ... (We) should make it easier for the people with high qualities to relocate, harder for the low quality people; easier for the professionals to relocate, harder for the general labor; ... (We should) especially work to *prevent a national 'blind floating' of low quality population* [emphasis added].[26]

Beyond these principles, there are over two dozen government and military agencies in Beijing and numerous local government agencies that regulate

---

24 Wang Zhongfang et al. (eds) (1996), *1995 Zhongguo Fali Nainjan* (*Legal Yearbook of China, 1995*), Beijing: Zhongguo Fali Nianjan Press.

25 BPT-MPS (Bureau of Personnel and Training-Ministry of Public Security) (2000), *Huzheng guanli jiaocheng* (*Textbook on* Hukou *Management*), Beijing: Qunzhong Press, pp. 235

26 BPT-MPS (Bureau of Personnel and Training-Ministry of Public Security) (2000), *Huzheng guanli jiaocheng* (*Textbook on* Hukou *Management*), Beijing: Qunzhong Press, pp. 139.

hukou relocation. Such a decentralization of policy-making regarding *hukou* relocation has provided the *hukou* system with a much needed flexibility and room for experiment; but has also created problems of equality and uniformity of law as well as much 'chaos' to the *hukou* system.[27] As a consequence, China's urbanization has been slow and small, especially compared to the rapid economic development and industrialization. By the early 2000s, China's urbanization is far below the world average, whereas its economic growth and industrialization level are at or above the world average.

5   The Reform of the *Hukou* System

During the two-decade long economic reform and opening-to-the-outside, the *hukou* system's functions have experienced some adaptations. Measures were devised to allow for a varied degree of *de facto* mobility for the powerful, the rich, the educated and talented, as well as for the needed manual laborers. In 2001–2002, the migration quota in the small cities and towns was largely replaced by the locally set 'entry conditions' that still nonetheless function as effective tools for the Chinese government to regulate and restrict internal migration, with perhaps increased local control and variations.

Two major rationales have been driving criticisms against the *hukou* system in the reform years. First, there is a strong economic logic for reform, as the *hukou* system and the related population immobility are considered to be creating economic irrationalities such as low labor efficiency, market segmentation, and market retardation since the massive rural population is still significantly excluded from the new market economy and the Chinese urbanization is still small and slow.[28] Hence, the *hukou* system is commonly believed to have restricted China's economic growth.[29] Secondly, there is an increasingly powerful ethical concern over the incomplete citizenship of the excluded rural residents and the uneven regional development and horizontal

---

27   According to an internal assessment, the 'chaotic' operation of *hukou* relocation is a major problem that needs to be addressed nationwide. T. Wang (1997), *Huzheng yu renkou guanli lilun yanjiu zhongshu* (*Summary of the Theoretical Study on* Hukou *System and Personnel Managment*), Beijing: Qunzhong Press, p. 243.

28   Wu Pengsen (2001), 'Mingongchao dui zhongguo xibu diqu fazhan chaju de fumian yingxiang' ('The Negative Impact of the Tide of Migrant Peasant Workers on the Economic Backwardness in the Western Regions'), *Shehui* (*Society*), Shanghai, 7, pp. 4–6.

29   'Yiwei zhe shenfen butong? tequan? jiedu hukou zhenshi yiyi' ('Does it Mean Different Identity? Privileges? To Understand the Real Meaning of *Hukou*'), *Zhongguo qingnian bao* (*Chinese Youth Daily*), Beijing, 12 August 2001.

stratification in the PRC. External factors, such as China's accession into the WTO and the required 'conformity to international standards,' especially the call for 'national citizen [equal] treatment of foreign investors and businessmen,' have highlighted and energized these two rationales.

The previously all-important role of resource allocation has decreased noticeably in the past decade. In mid-2001, Beijing authorized further relaxation of the migration control in the small cities and towns. Now a rural resident could easily obtain an urban *hukou* in a small city or a township where he has a legitimate job and residence.[30] Many localities (such as Shijiazhuang in Hebei Province and Ningbo in Zhejiang Province) are indeed currently experimenting with deeper reforms or even *de facto* abolishment of the *hukou* relocation quotas, replaced by certain locally set 'conditions.' This is likely to speed up China's urbanization significantly, at least at the levels of small cities and townships. Yet, the *hukou* system still enjoys a high degree of legitimacy. Given its obvious and proven political values, Beijing is unlikely to abolish this system in the near future.

6   The Future of *Hukou*-based Urbanization Control

The *hukou* relocation control has affected China's urbanization process fundamentally. In general, the *hukou* relocation control appears to be much less subject to the erosion forces of corruption and local corporatist resistance (*duice*) to Beijing than in many other areas such as the PRC's industrial policies or even the taxation system. The reasons for that relatively high effectiveness and stability of the *hukou* relocation control may lie in the strong political and social legitimacy the *hukou* system still enjoys, the relatively simple and uniform mechanisms of the system, the newly devised and localized accommodating measures such as the blue stamp *hukou,* and the strictly enforced quotas by the public security agencies.

There are still almost daily occurrences of harassment, arrests, and deportation of the unregistered or unauthorized migrants in many Chinese cities in 2001. Field observations reveal that the police often physically mistreat those *hukou*-less floating people and confiscate their personal belongings. A somewhat surprising finding has been that, despite the clear rise of individualism and sense of human rights in the PRC in the past

---

30   *Renmin Ribao (People's Daily)*, Beijing, 24 September 2001, p. 9; *South China Morning Post*, 29 September 2001.

decade, most people (including those excluded rural residents) seem to take the *hukou* relocation control as a necessary and legitimate way to ensure order and stability. There is still no visible public discourse on the discriminatory aspects of the *hukou* system or the abuses of human rights associated with its implementation (except for some overseas Chinese electronic bulletin boards and web postings). Most people interviewed in private tend to believe that the *hukou* relocation control is something of a 'necessary evil.' Even studies by the police itself have found that there is only a small minority questioning the whole *hukou* relocation control and suggesting an eventual 'restoration of the freedom of migration.'[31]

Passive and individual resistance and challenges to the *hukou* relocation control, however, are clearly widespread. The repatriation of the floating people from those 'hot spots' (highly attractive places) such as the special economic zones like Shezhen has appeared to be a losing battle as the repatriated often simply float back right away. As a consequence of such spontaneous acts and the political decentralization, *nongzhuanfei* (from *agriculture* hukou to non-agriculture *hukou)* or legal urbanization developed rapidly in the two decades of reform. Over 40 million agricultural *hukou* holders became urban *hukou* holders in the 1980s, in addition to the state plans, and created heavy burdens on the state. The State Council responded by issuing a 'Notice on Strictly Controlling the Overgrowth of *nongzhuanfei*' on 31 October 1989. Numerous other decrees for the controlling of *nonzhuanfei* were issued by the State Council, the Public Security Ministry, and other ministries in the 1990s (including one on 2 August 1994 to reaffirm the 1988 prohibition of the 'sales' of urban *hukou* to rural *hukou* holders). Consequently, *nonzhuanfei* appeared to have experienced some slow down in the first half of the 1990s. It is officially estimated that there were about one million less cases of *nongzhuanfei* in 1992, compared to 1989.[32]

Serving as a cornerstone of China's institutional arrangement that conditions the Chines economy development and determines much of China's sociopolitical stability, the *hukou* system has shaped China's urbanization process: its nature, pace, extent, regional variations, and

---

31 T. Wang (1997), *Huzheng yu renkou guanli lilun yanjiu zhongshu (Summary of the Theoretical Study on* Hukou *System and Personnel Managment)*, Beijing: Qunzhong Press, pp. 237–57.

32 Gao Shangquan et al. (1993), p. 675. For the 1988 prohibition, see the State Council notice dated on 29 October 1988, in Supreme People's Court of the PRC (ed.) (1990), *Xinzheng shengpang shouce (Handbook of Administrative Trials)*, vol. 3, Beijing: Renmin Fayuang Press, pp. 23–4.

consequences. In China, despite the tremendous development and opening of the economy and very deep social and cultural changes in the past two decades, urbanization remains relatively orderly and thus slow. The majority of China's huge population still lives in the countryside and is still categorized as agricultural population even though many of them are already employed in various industrial enterprises. The relatively low domestic mobility of the general masses has created a host of political and economic as well as social consequences. The impressive stability of the CCP (Chinese Communist Party) authoritarian government is directly linked to the *hukou* system. Controlled and administratively divided domestic migration has provided a constant supply of willing and cheap labor while avoiding overburdening the infrastructure in the cities. The massive rural population continues to be a major source of China's capital accumulation under the powerful institutional exclusion generated by the *hukou* system. China, is perhaps the only major developing nation that has so far effectively avoided the large existence of urban slum populations that existed so prominently and so destructively in countries such as India, Brazil, and Mexico. But for the rural population, the slow and controlled urbanization has been maintained at their expenses.

The system's high degree of legitimacy appears to have benefited from its history that allows for a deep root in the Chinese tradition of culture and society. The regionalized and secretive operation of the system may have also minimized criticisms and resistance. Finally, the newly developed adaptive measures of the *hukou* system have produced some flexibility for the system and greatly extended its effectiveness and life span. Functionally speaking, the *hukou* may have significantly contributed to the Chinese style economic development, regional experimentation, social stability, and crime fighting.

The strains and forces generated by the economic reform have impacted the *hukou* system in the past two decades. The *hukou* system has hence changed in some significant ways. First, we have seen that the system, especially its implementation, has become less rigid and less exclusive as it now strives to accommodate the needs of the labor market and population mobility. The *hukou*-based resource allocation diminished and internal mobility of selected groups (primarily the powerful, the rich, and the educated). Second, the sociopolitical control aspects of the *hukou* system have become less political and less *ad hoc*, as legal norms and awareness of individual rights are both on the rise. Third, the *hukou* system has reduced its discriminatory impact in the areas of economy and income distribution as its long time role as the basis for urban rations is now significantly reduced and minimized.

From 1997 to 2002, a national effort of reforming the *hukou* system was launched in the PRC.[33] This new round of reform has the promise to significantly transform the *hukou* system. Beijing appears to have now acknowledged some of the irrational and unethical consequences of the *hukou* system and attempted to accommodate the millions of 'unauthorized' migrants in the country. The control of internal migration, especially the rural-to-urban migration, is relaxed as the previously strictly enforced quota of urbanization is being replaced with locally-defined 'entry conditions' in the small cities and towns. Some large cities and even whole provinces have followed the suite. Additional measures were adopted to address some of the needs of the millions 'temporary' migrants in the urban sector and to polish the public image of the *hukou* system.

Nevertheless, the *hukou* system is still expected to execute on daily basis much of China's institutionalized social injustice and unfairness especially institutionally excludes the rural population. The *hukou*-based geographic exclusion has succeeded in controlling a segmented nation and implementing targeted development plans. Besides the much talked about rural-urban division, a community/city based regional differentiation or regionalism have also grown out of the *hukou* system to become a very important institutional feature of today's PRC. The powerful force of accelerated urbanization driven by the rapid development of the market economy is likely to produce lasting pressure on the *hukou* system. The ethically troubling questions about the citizen's freedom of migration, about equal treatment under the law, and about the fate of political democracy and national unity are likely to prompt the Chinese to retool, reform, and even restructure the *hukou* system, beyond the new yet localized relaxation, in the years ahead.

---

33 E. Rosenthal, 'China Eases Rules Binding People to Birth Regions,' *The New York Times*, 23 October 2001.

PART III: URBAN SPATIAL STRUCTURES

CHAPTER 9

SPATIAL DYNAMICS OF CITY-SIZE DISTRIBUTION

SHUNFENG SONG*
University of Nevada, Reno

KEVIN H. ZHANG
Illinois State University

Abstract

This chapter investigates the spatial dynamics of China's city system by applying the Pareto law of city-size distribution. Based on 1985 and 1999 city-level data, it finds that Chinese cities are quite evenly distributed and the intercity concentration declined in the 1980s and 1990s. The chapter also finds that the Pareto law fits the Chinese data quite well. Several factors have contributed to the rapid urban growth and changes in urban systems in the past two decades. The recent industrialization of China's economy has created many job opportunities in cities and attracted many rural workers to migrate into urban areas. The urban sector reform has relaxed many rural-urban migration restrictions and resulted in a huge influx of rural workers in cities. The open-door policy and foreign direct investment have also helped China to become more urbanized, especially in the coastal areas. The government's urban policy and the inclusion of many new cities have affected Chinese city-size distributions.

Keywords: city-size distribution, urbanization, and urban system

JEL classification: R12

---

*   Correspondence: Shunfeng Song, Professor of Economics, University of Nevada, Reno, NV 89557–0207. Tel: (775) 784–6860; Email: song@unr.nevada.edu.

URBAN TRANSFORMATION IN CHINA, edited by Aimin Chen, Gordon G. Liu and Kevin H. Zhang

1   Introduction

China has been experiencing a rapid urbanization since the economic reform started in 1978. Non-agricultural population in urban areas increased from 171.45 million in 1978 to 388.92 million in 1999 (NBS, 1994, 2000), a 125.5 per cent growth. This growth rate is much greater than the national population growth rate of 30.8 per cent between 1980 and 1999. In consequence, China has become more urbanized, with an urban population share increased from 17.9 per cent in 1978 to 30.9 per cent in 1999. Rapid urbanization in China can be also observed by the increase of the number of cities. In 1980, China had 223 cities, with 15 cities having a population size over 1 million. In 1999, China had 667 cities, with 37 cities having a population size over 1 million (NBS, 2000). Naturally, urbanization in China and China's city system have formed an important area for Chinese research.

However, few studies have investigated the size, growth, and distribution of Chinese cities (Fan, 1988, 1999). This research has three purposes. First, it examines China's urbanization and evolution of city system. We show that urbanization in China has experienced three phrases since the PRC was founded in 1949 and the number of cities has increased greatly, especially during the past two decades. Second, we use 1985 and 1999 city-level data and apply the Pareto law to investigate the spatial dynamics of city-size distribution in China. We find that the Pareto law fits the Chinese data well and the size distribution of Chinese cities became more even in the past 15 years. Third, we discuss how economic and institutional factors affect the patterns of city growth and urban system. We argue that both economic and institutional factors are important in explaining China's dynamic city system.

This chapter is organized as follows. Section 2 summarizes facts of urbanization in China and the dynamics of China's city system. Section 3 applies the Pareto law to 1985 and 1999 city-level data to examine Pareto behavior of Chinese cities and changes of city systems during these fifteen years. In section 4, the chapter argues that in China both the market and the government play active roles in the spatial dynamics of China's city system. Section 5 provides conclusions.

2   Urbanization and Dynamics of City System in China

Urbanization in China has experienced three phrases since the PRC was founded in 1949. In the first phase (1952–65), China emphasized the growth of heavy industries. With this development strategy, many rural workers were recruited in state-owned enterprises and industrial cities were developed, especially in inland areas. During this period, urban population increased faster than the national population. The former grew at an annual average rate of 4.6 per cent, while the latter grew at an annual average rate of 1.8 per cent. Table 9.1 shows that urban population increased from 71.63 million in 1952 to 130.45 million in 1965, an 82.1 per cent growth. During the same period, the pace of national population growth was slower, from 574.82 million to 725.38 million, a 26.2 per cent growth. As a result, urban population share increased from 12.5 per cent in 1952 to 15.4 per cent in 1957 and 18.0 per cent in 1965 (NBS, 1994). It is worth mentioning that China completed its ownership transition in 1957 and experienced the 'Great Leap Forward' movement in the period 1958–60, both providing favorable conditions for the growth of Chinese cities. However, the readjustment in the early 1960s led to a Huixiang (return to village) movement, in which many workers were transferred back to the countryside. The urban population share decreased in 1961–63 (NBS, 1998).

The second phase was during the Cultural Revolution (1966–77). In this period, the pace of urban growth was either negative or static. A major reason was the policy that required millions of urban youth to go to rural areas in order to 'undergo peasants' education', which Mao thought important to prevent the younger generation from accepting capitalist influences and to channel and cultivate new revolutionary successors. In 1966–77, 17 million urban people were resettled in the countryside because of the political situation and worsening housing shortages, job opportunities, and the infrastructure in the cities (Song and Timberlake, 1996). As shown in Table 9.1, the growth rate of the national population was higher than that of urban population between 1965 and 1975. In consequence, the urban population share stagnated and even decreased, being 18.0 per cent in 1965, 17.4 per cent in 1970, 17.3 per cent in 1975, and 17.9 per cent in 1978 (NBS, 1994).

The third phase is a rapid urbanization in the reform era (1978–present). Since 1978, China has not only promoted an open-door policy and a 'socialist market economy' but also encouraged urbanization. Many county towns (*xian-zhen*) have been upgraded and classified as cities. The number of cities increased dramatically from 191 in 1978 to 667 in 1999, and the urban population share increased from 17.9 per cent to 30.9 per cent, respectively (NBS, 2000, pp. 95 and 347). As shown in Table 9.1, it took 26 years (1952–78) to have a 5.5 per cent increase in urbanization, while it took 21 years (1978–99) to have a 13.0 per cent increase in urbanization. Without question, China has experienced faster urbanization in the past two decades.

Table 9.1   China's population and urbanization

Year	Total population (m.)	Growth rate[a] (%)	Urban population (m.)	Growth rate[a] (%)	Urbanization (%)
1952	574.82	–	71.63	–	12.46
1957	646.53	2.495	99.49	7.779	15.388
1962	672.95	0.817	116.59	3.438	17.325
1965	725.38	2.597	130.45	3.963	17.984
1970	829.92	2.882	144.24	2.114	17.380
1975	924.20	2.272	160.30	2.227	17.345
1978	962.59	1.385	172.45	2.527	17.915
1980	987.05	1.271	191.40	5.494	19.391
1983	1030.08	1.453	222.74	5.458	21.624
1984	1043.57	1.310	240.17	7.825	23.014
1985	1058.51	1.432	250.94	4.484	23.707
1986	1075.07	1.564	263.66	5.069	24.525
1987	1093.00	1.668	276.74	4.961	25.319
1988	1110.26	1.579	286.61	3.567	25.815
1989	1127.04	1.511	295.40	3.067	26.210
1990	1143.33	1.445	301.91	2.204	26.406
1991	1158.23	1.303	305.43	1.166	26.370
1992	1171.71	1.164	323.72	5.988	27.628
1993	1185.17	1.149	333.51	3.024	28.140
1994	1198.50	1.125	343.01	2.848	28.620
1995	1211.21	1.060	351.74	2.545	29.040
1996	1223.89	1.047	359.50	2.206	29.373
1997	1236.26	1.011	369.89	2.890	29.920
1998	1248.10	0.958	379.42	2.576	30.400
1999	1259.09	0.881	388.92	2.504	30.889

Note: a = growth rates before 1984 are average annual growth rates.

Source: NBS (1994, 2000) and authors' calculations.

In China, cities are classified into three levels according to their administrative status: county-level cities, prefecture-level cities, and central municipalities. In 1993, for example, China had 371 county-level cities, 196 prefecture-level cities, and 3 central municipalities. These numbers changed to 437, 227, and 4, respectively in 1998.[1] Chongqing became the fourth central

1   The 227 prefecture-level cities in 1998 include 15 quasi-province-level cities (NBS, 1999). Quasi-province-level, newly designated, has an administrative status higher than the prefecture-level but lower than the central-level.

municipality in July 1997. Cities at different status are given different levels of authority such as investment decision-making and foreign-funded project approvals. The higher the level, the more directly the city reports to Beijing and the greater is its autonomy and influence. Usually, larger cities have higher administrative status. But there are some exceptions. For example, Xiamen in Fujian province is a quasi-province-level city but has a nonagricultural population (0.59 million in 1998) only about half of Fuzhou's population (1.06 million in 1998). The latter is only a prefecture-level city even though it is the capital of the province and has a much larger population (NBS, 1999).

The definition of city in China is not straightforward. Chinese cities are administrative entities and must be officially designated, with designation criteria being a function of political-administrative status, economic development, openness, and total population of an urban place. Since upgrading status in the administrative hierarchy is usually accompanied by greater autonomy, political power, and access to resources, local authorities are eager to pursue upgrading of their settlements to higher statuses (Fan, 1999). Such efforts, together with relaxation of designation criteria, have brought a significant growth in China's urban sector in the past two decades. Many county towns (*xian cheng*) were reclassified as cities (*shi*), resulting in a sharp increase in the total number of cities, from 223 in 1980 to 667 in 1999. Some county towns earned city status even though their population may be small. During the past two decades, many existing cities were upgraded by expanding their territories or merging two adjacent cities or combining a city with its surrounding county.

China also classifies its cities into five categories according to their sizes. Table 9.2 shows the definitions and the number of cities in each category in 1980 and 1999. In 1980, China had seven super-large cities, eight very large cities, 30 large cities, 72 medium cities, and 106 small cities. These numbers increased to 13, 24, 49, 216, and 365 in 1999, respectively. These changes indicate a rapid urban growth in the past two decades. Table 9.2 also shows that most are small cities. In fact, the primacy and intercity concentration is relative low in China. For example, the primacy measured by the share of the largest city's population to the total urban population was only 4.87 per cent in 1991 and 4.08 per cent in 1998, compared with the primacy of 10.14 per cent for the USA in 1990 based on urbanized area data. The urban population share of the top ten largest cities for China was 23.76 per cent in 1991 and 19.37 per cent in 1998, compared with 36.66 per cent for the USA in 1990 based on urbanized area data.

Table 9.2   Number of cities by size of nonagricultural population

Size	1949	1965	1980	1991	1994	1999
Total	132	168	223	479	622	667
Super-large (over 2 million)	1	5	7	9	10	13
Very large (1–2 million)	4	8	8	22	22	24
Large (0.5–1 million)	7	18	30	30	41	49
Medium (0.2–0.5 million)	18	42	72	121	175	216
Small (less than 0.2 million)	102	95	106	297	374	365

Sources: NBS (various issues).

3   The Spatial Dynamics of City-Size Distribution in China

To examine the spatial dynamics of China's city-size distributions, this chapter applies the Pareto law that can be written as

$$G_i = A P_i^{-\alpha} \tag{1}$$

where G_i is the number of cities with population P_i or more, P_i is the population of the *i*th largest city, A is a constant, and α is the Pareto exponent. When $\alpha=1$, the Pareto law becomes the so-called rank-size rule. In this case, the product of a city's rank and population is a constant equal to the population of the largest city, also indicating that the third-largest city is one-third the size of the largest, and so on. When $\alpha>1$ ($\alpha<1$), populations of cities far down in the size distribution are greater (less) than is predicted by the rank-size rule, indicating a more (less) even distribution of city sizes. For example, the rank-size rule ($\alpha=1$) predicts that the population of the second largest city would have half of that of the largest city, while when $\alpha = 1.5$ the Pareto law predicts that the population of the second largest city would have 63 per cent of that of the largest city. Thus, the Pareto exponent measures the overall intercity concentration.

Data come from the *Urban Statistical Yearbook of China* compiled by the National Bureau of Statistics of the PRC (NBS, 1986, 2000). This chapter uses data on nonagricultural population in urban areas (*shi-qu*). Table 9.3 presents the results that are obtained by estimating a double-log model of equation 1 with the OLS method. Table 9.3 also shows that the lowest R^2 value is 0.8569. Judging from the R^2 values, it appears that the Pareto law explains Chinese city-size distributions well.

Table 9.3 Regression results on pareto distributions: Chinese cities (dependent variable: log G)

Year	Variable	Coefficient	SD	Sample size	Adj. R^2-value
1985	Constant	15.2239	0.2380	324	0.8569
	LogP	0.8557	0.0195		
1999	Constant	18.6348	0.1428	667	0.9273
	LogP	1.0750	0.0117		
1985[a]	Constant	15.4911	0.2270	307	0.8807
	LogP	0.8796	0.0185		
1999[a]	Constant	17.2584	0.2504	307	0.8914
	LogP	0.9846	0.0196		

Note: a = regressions are on common cities of 1985 and 1999.

Two interesting findings are observed. First, for the 1985 data, the estimated Pareto exponent is 0.8557 with a standard deviation of 0.0195, suggesting that the rank-size rule ($\alpha = 1$) is statistically rejected. The estimated Pareto coefficient indicates that size distribution of Chinese cities in 1985 is less even than that implied by the rank-size rule. For 1999 data, however, the estimated coefficient (1.0750, with a standard deviation of 0.0117) is statistically greater than 1, indicating that the city-size distribution became more even than that predicted by the rank-size rule.

Second, the results show a significant increase in the Pareto exponent, from 0.8557 in 1985 to 1.0750 in 1999. Since the exponent measures the overall intercity concentration, an increase in it implies that the overall intercity concentration in China decreased between 1985 and 1999. The question here is what caused this change. Was it caused by the inclusion of many new cities in 1999 or by the dynamic changes among 1985 cities? To answer this question, we ran regressions by using data on common cities in both 1985 and 1999. As Table 9.3 shows, the estimated exponents based on the common sample become 0.8796 for 1985 and 0.9846 for 1999. Considering their standard deviations (0.0185 and 0.0196, respectively), we conclude that the latter is statistically greater than the former, suggesting that cities in the common sample became more evenly distributed between 1985 and 1999. We further notice that the estimated coefficient with full 1999 sample (1.0750) is statistically greater than that obtained by using the common sample (0.9846). This finding suggests that the change in the overall intercity concentration have been also caused by the inclusion of new cities in 1999.

Some previous studies have shown that estimates of the Pareto exponent are sensitive to sample thresholds and size (Rosen and Resnick, 1980; Guerin-Pace, 1995). To examine whether it is also the case for China's cities, we use various thresholds of low-end cutoffs in the 1998 city-size distribution. Table 9.4 presents the results. Clearly, the estimated Pareto exponent is sensitive to sample thresholds. In China's case, it increases with higher cutoff thresholds, at least within the range reported in Table 9.4. This finding suggests that the intercity concentration decrease if we focus on large Chinese cities. Another interesting finding revealed in Table 9.4 is related to the fit of the Pareto law for different sample thresholds. As the last column shows, R^2 value increases until it reaches a maximum of 0.9974 at the threshold of 185 thousands. This result indicates that explaining power of the Pareto law is also sensitive to sample thresholds. For 'right' sample thresholds, the law could appear superior in explaining Chinese city-size distributions.

Table 9.4   Sensitivity of the Pareto exponent to the size of city sample, 1999

Threshold	Sample size	Pareto exponent	Adj. R^2-value
Full sample	667	1.0750	0.9273
50,000	644	1.1719	0.9696
100,000	550	1.2740	0.9904
150,000	400	1.3541	0.9969
185,000	325	1.3760	0.9974
200,000	302	1.3798	0.9973

4   Factors of China's Urbanization and City System

In section 2, this chapter showed that China experienced a rapid urbanization in the past two decades. Between 1979 and 1999, the number of cities increased from 191 to 667 and the urban population share increased from 17.9 per cent to 30.9 per cent. A number of factors promote the growth of China's cities and urbanization. First of all, there is a relationship between industrialization and urbanization, as well demonstrated by the literature of urban growth (e.g., Henderson, 1988). Cities with concentration of economic activities enjoy scale and agglomeration economies and continue to grow, primarily through rural-urban migration, until diseconomies become dominant. Since the economic reform started in the late 1970s, China has greatly upgraded its economic structure. In 1978, 70.5 per cent of employed person were in the agricultural (primary) sector, which contributed 28.1 per cent to the national GDP (NBS, 2000, pp. 54, 116). In 1999, these proportions decreased to 50.1 per cent and 17.7 per cent, respectively. Industrialization and upgrading China's economic structure have created a great number of job opportunities in urban areas and absorbed a large amount of rural surplus workers, thus promoting China's urbanization.

Rural-urban migration in recent years is another important factor of city growth in China. Before urban reforms started in 1984, China had a long policy that strictly restricted rural-urban migration through a static urban household registration system. Under this system, rural people were not entitled for urban employment and state subsidies in housing, food, fuel, medical care, and school. Without employment and state subsidies, rural workers could not survive in urban areas. The urban reforms since 1984 have relaxed restrictions on rural-urban migration in many ways. For example, enterprises in urban areas have become autonomous in hiring and firing their workers, and the former 'iron-bowl' employment system has been replaced by a labor contract system. Hence, many enterprises prefer to hire rural workers because of their lower labor costs. Other institutional changes have also facilitated rural-urban migration. For instance, housing has been delinked with employment, rationing of food and fuel has been abandoned, and the urban household registration system is being gradually phrased out. In short, most economic and institutional deterrents of rural-urban migration have been removed. As a result, China has been experiencing a huge influx of rural workers into urban areas. In 1998, 44.24 million rural workers left their homeland to seek jobs somewhere else (NBS, 1999). According to Liu (2000), between 2.3 to 2.7 million rural workers migrated to cities each year. Chen and Parish (1996) found that about one-fifth of the entrants in the urban labor force came from rural areas.[2]

China's open door policy has also promoted China's urbanization. Specifically, foreign direct investment (FDI) has been a key force driving the recent coastal city growth and urbanization in east China. In the period of 1986–98, China attracted over 260 billion dollars of FDI, with 87.7 per cent locating in the coastal region. The role of FDI in urban economic development and thus

---

2 Generally, there are three types of rural migrants. The first are those who are officially permitted to move to cities. The second involves peasants who engage in industrial, commercial, and service activities in cities (the floating population). The third are the daily commuters who live in villages and go to nearby cities to work on a daily basis (the pendulum population).

urbanization can be observed in several aspects. First, FDI directly promotes exports. According to Zhang and Song (2001), the share of foreign-invested enterprises' (FIEs) exports in China's total exports increased from a negligible proportion (0.05 per cent) in 1980 to 12.58 per cent in 1990 and to 45.50 per cent in 1999. Second, FDI indirectly affect exports because local domestic firms may increases their exports by observing the export activities of FIEs and FIEs improve the linkage between local and foreign firms. Third, FDI creates jobs. Song (2000) found that FDI has become a more important contributor of creating urban employment. In 1985, FIEs employed 0.13 million workers, accounting for only 0.1 per cent of the total urban employment. In 1998, FIEs' employment reached 5.9 million workers, accounting for 3.8 per cent of the total urban employment. Finally, FDI affects urban growth through technology spillover, information diffusion, and management expertise. The experience of Shenzhen, the first special economic zone in China, is a good demonstration of FDI's role in promoting China's urbanization. In eight years between 1991 and 1998, the population of Shenzhen increased 165.2 per cent, from 432.1 to 1146.0 thousand. Each year during this period, data used in this chapter show that per capita FDI for Shenzhen was far greater than the average per capita FDI for all Chinese cities. It is quite evident that FDI has indeed promoted China's city growth and urbanization.

In section 3 of this chapter it was found that cities in China are relatively more evenly distributed and city-size distribution became even more dispersed between 1985 and 1999. This finding is consistent with the conclusion made by Rosen and Resnick (1980). In their study, Rosen and Resnick argued that in populous countries, intermediate-sized cities are likely to develop since the major cities may reach a size where negative externalities discourage growth. Therefore, the Pareto exponent tends to be higher for populous countries, suggesting that populous countries tend to have more evenly distributed cities.

China's city system exhibits profound impacts of institutional factors. One important institutional factor is the government development strategy. As several previous studies argued, Chinese leaders have always attempted to control the growth of the large cities and to limit severely rural-urban migration (Ma and Fan, 1994; Hsu, 1996; Fan, 1999). Before the economic reform, Chinese urban policy emphasized the growth of heavy industries. Cities were narrowly viewed as potential sites of industrial plants, and favored cities were assigned a number of large state-owned heavy industrial enterprises. Such urban development strategy discouraged the growth of light and service industries in most cities, thus unnecessarily restricting their economic base and limiting employment growth. In addition, the Chinese government was very concerned with coastal security. Because of this concern, China carried out the 'three-front' project in the 1950s and 1960s. Many strategic manufacturing plants were moved from the coastal region to inland. New industrial cities were built far from the coastal line and the government sent many workers and technical personnel to these new cities. Hsu (1996) analyzed city development in Luoyang and Guiyang and found a lasting impact of early government decision on city growth. Hsu showed that government economic policies and urban directives of the 1950s have been critical determinants of the development of Chinese cities, not just in that decade but also for many years beyond that period.

China's current urban policy still favors the development of small cities. The official urban policy is to 'control large cities, develop medium-sized cities rationally, and actively develop small cities.' This urban policy, however, has been challenged by scholars. For example, Zhao and Zhang (1995) showed a high positive correlation between city efficiency and city size, not only in economic but also in social and environmental measures. Wang and Xia (1999) argued that small cities are not efficient because of smaller scale economies but larger government burden (as measured by the ratio of government spending to city's GDP). Using cross-sectional and panel city-level data, they found an optimal city size of about 2 million and concluded that a good size range for Chinese cities to be is 1–4 million. Hong and Chen (2000) studied cities in Jiangsu Province and found that small cities are at a disadvantage in providing urban infrastructure. They argued that certain consumption scale and population size are necessary conditions for promoting service industry and markets. Song (2001) used 1997 city-level data and showed a negative relationship between city size and urban unemployment rate. As far as employment is concerned, job creation is associated with urban size. Varieties in production and consumption are related to urban size. Varieties, in turn, demand labor specialization, thus creating jobs (Abdel-Rahman and Fujita, 1990; Ogawa, 1998).

China's city system has also been affected by China's migration policy. To maintain low urban consumption and to increase industrial investment, China has implemented anti-migration policy since the 1950s. Through a static urban household registration system (*chengshi hukou*), the government has not only monitored where people live but also strictly limited rural-urban migration, especially to large cities. Thus, the anti-migration policy has slowed the pace of China's urbanization. It has also affected the structure of China's city system because China limits migration to larger cities more strictly than to smaller cities.

Another unique characteristic of China's city system is the dramatic increase in the number of cities during the past two decades. As stated earlier in this chapter, Chinese cities are administrative entities and must be officially designated, with designation criteria being a function of political-administrative status, economic development, openness, and total population of an urban place. The higher status in the administrative hierarchy, the greater autonomy and political power the city has. Hence, local authorities have strong incentives to pursue upgrading of their settlements to higher statuses. Such efforts, together with relaxation of designation criteria, have upgraded many county towns (*xian cheng*) to cities (*shi*), resulting in a sharp increase in the total number of cities, from 223 in 1980 to 667 in 1999. Many existing cities have also upgraded to a higher status by expanding their territories or merging two adjacent cities or combining a city with its surrounding county. The inclusion of many new cities, in term, has changed the structure of China's city system. Our regression results (Table 9.3) suggest that Chinese cities have become more evenly distributed by the inclusion of these new cities.

5   Conclusions

China's urbanization has experienced three phrases: 1952–65, 1965–77, and 1978 to present. The pace of urban growth during the first period was fast. The urban population share increased from 12.5 per cent in 1952 to 18.0 per cent in 1965. Anti-urbanization, however, prevailed during the Cultural Revolution and resulted in millions of urban youth being sent to the countryside. The urban population share stagnated, at 18.0 per cent in 1965 and 17.9 per cent in 1978. Rapid urbanization started with the economic reform in 1978 and has continued since then. As a result, urban population share has steadily increased, from 17.9 per cent in 1978 to 30.9 per cent in 1999.

The chapter has investigated the spatial dynamics of China's city system by applying the Pareto law of city-size distribution. Based on 1985 and 1999 city-level data, we concluded that Chinese cities are quite evenly distributed and the intercity concentration declined in the 1980s and 1990s. We also found that the Pareto law fits the Chinese data quite well. The empirical results on Pareto exponent are consistent with early findings that populous countries tend to have more evenly distributed cities.

Several major economic and institutional factors have contributed to the rapid urban growth and changes of urban systems in the past two decades. The recent industrialization of China's economy has created many job opportunities in cities and attracted many rural workers to migrate into urban areas. The urban sector reform has relaxed many rural-urban migration restrictions and resulted in a huge influx of rural workers in cities. The open-door policy and foreign direct investment have also helped China to become more urbanized, especially in the coastal areas. Government's urban policy and the inclusion of many new cities have affected Chinese city-size distributions.

References

Abdel-Raham, H.M. and Fujita, M. (1990), 'Product Varieties, Marshallian Externalities, and City Size,' *Journal of Regional Science*, 30, pp. 165–83.

Alperovich, G. (1982), 'The Size Distribution of Cities: On the Empirical Validity of the Rank-size Rule,' *Journal of Urban Economics*, 16, pp. 232–9.

Chen, X. and Parish, W.L. (1996), 'Urbanization in China: Reassessing an Evolving Model,' in Gugler, J. (ed.), *The Urban Transformation of the Developing World*, New York: Oxford University Press, pp. 60–90.

Fan, C.C. (1988), 'The Temporal and Spatial Dynamics of City-size Distribution in China,' *Population Research and Policy Review*, 7, pp. 123–57.

Fan, C.C. (1999), 'The Vertical and Horizontal Expansions of China's City System,' *Urban Geography*, 20, pp. 493–515.

Guerin-Pace, F. (1995), 'Rank-size Distribution and the Process of Urban Growth,' *Urban Studies*, 32 (3), pp. 551–62.

Henderson, J.V. (1988), *Urban Development: Theory, Fact, and Illusion*, New York: Oxford University Press.

Hong, Y. and Chen, W. (2000), 'The New Development of Urbanization Pattern,' *Economic Research Journal*, 392, pp. 66–71.

Hsu, M.L. (1996), 'China's Urban Development: A Case Study of Luoyang and Guiyang,' *Urban Studies*, 33, pp. 895–910.

Liu, S. (2000), 'The Current Conditions and Policies of China's Employment,' in Wang, Y. and Chen, A. (eds), *China's Labour Market and Problems of Employment*, Southwestern University of Finance and Economics Press, Chengdu, Sichuan, pp. 22–9.

Ma, L.J. and Fan, M. (1994), 'Urbanisation from Below: The Growth of Towns in Jiangsu, China,' *Urban Studies*, 31 (10), pp. 1625–45.

National Bureau of Statistics of the PRC (NBS) (1986), *Urban Statistical Yearbook of China*, Beijing: China Statistics Press, 1992–2000.

National Bureau of Statistics of the PRC (NBS) (1994), *China Statistical Yearbook*, Beijing: China Statistics Press, 2000.

National Bureau of Statistics of the PRC (NBS) (1998), *China Population Statistics Yearbook*, Beijing: China Statistics Press.

National Bureau of Statistics of the PRC (NBS) (1999), *China Labor Statistical Yearbook*, Beijing: China Statistics Press.

Ogawa, H. (1998), 'Preference for Product Variety and City Size,' *Urban Studies*, 35, pp. 45–51.

Rosen, K.T. and Resnick, M. (1980), 'The Size Distribution of Cities: An Examination of the Pareto Law and Primacy,' *Journal of Urban Economics*, 8, pp. 165–86.

Song, F. and Timberlake, M. (1996), 'Chinese Urbanization, State Policy, and the World Economy,' *Journal of Urban Affairs*, 18 (3), pp. 285–306.

Song, S. (2000), 'Policy Issues of China's Urban Unemployment', EAI Working Paper No. 49, The National University of Singapore.

Song, S. (2001), 'City Size and Urban Unemployment: Evidence from China,' *World Economy and China*, 9 (1), pp. 46–53.

Wang, X. and Xia, X. (1999), 'Promoting the Economic Growth by Optimizing Urban Size,' *Economic Research Journal*, 377, pp. 22–9.

Zhang, K. and Song, S. (2000), 'Promoting Exports: The Role of Inward FDI in China,' *China Economic Review*, 11, pp. 385–96.

Zhao, X. and Zhang, L. (1995), 'Urban Performance and the Control of Urban Size in China,' *Urban Studies*, 32 (4–5), pp. 813–45.

CHAPTER 10

SPATIAL DISTRIBUTION OF INDUSTRIES AND CITIES:
COORDINATION BETWEEN INDUSTRIAL AND URBAN
DEVELOPMENT

MEI WEN*
Australian National University

Abstract

This chapter studies the spatial distribution of China's industry and cities. It investigates the coordination issue between China's industry and urban development. Historical comparisons on location of two-digit manufacturing industries and location of cities suggest there has been agglomeration of industries and cities in the same regions following the economic reform. However, empirical evidence indicates that development of rural industry may have stunted China's urban development. To further coordinate urban and industry development, the development of large and medium sized cities for promoting the formation of new special-large and super-large cities seems desirable. In addition, the development of satellite cities and transportation hubs would be helpful for the economic development of middle and western China.

Keywords: Urbanization, agglomeration, rural industry, regional development

JEL classification: R12, R30, R50

*   Correspondence: Mei Wen, Division of Economics, RSPAS, Australia National University, Canberra, ACT0200, Australia. Email: rosemei.wen@anu.edu.au.

I am grateful to the participants of CES 2001 annual conference in Xiamen for helpful comments. Any remaining errors are my own.

1   Introduction

The economic functions of cities have long been recognized in urban studies. Cities are deciphered by von Thünen (1826) as central trading places which can reduce the transportation costs of individual trading activities. During the past decade, the political economy of city size and city formation has developed rapidly. Among the large literature, it is worth noting that many papers link industrialization with urbanization through endogenizing the formation and size of cities via individuals' and firms' rational choices over their economic activities.[1]

Geographical agglomeration of industries is one driving force behind urban development and the agglomeration of cities. In addition to savings in transportation costs, industrial agglomeration can exist due to increasing returns of scale based on the large scope for division of labour, which comes from a variety of consumption goods, an increased number of intermediate goods and increased individual levels of specialization. Close proximity of trading partners provides ample population size for urban development. Cities, with governmental planning, can efficiently provide infrastructure, such as a legal system, transportation and communication networks, and other public services, such as schools and public libraries. Improved infrastructure can facilitate trade and reduce transportation costs. Public schools and libraries provide opportunities for people to learn from each other and to accumulate knowledge, thus enlarging the scope for the evolution of the division of labour. In addition, governmental planning on land use and urban housing can reduce the pressure on rent increases due to industrial and population agglomeration. Owing to geographical differences, cities with close proximity to international ports and geographical convenience in collecting local products can emerge endogenously as transportation hubs with a population agglomeration due to labour demand for shipping and handling commodities. The hierarchical structure of cities, transportation systems and communication networks can be used to increase transaction efficiency and central planning efficiency in order to fully explore the benefits of industrial agglomeration.

However, industrial agglomeration can not only push up rents, wages and general prices, but can also generate negative externality such as crowding and air pollution. With firms' decisions on minimizing production costs, dispersion of industrial firms can occur when the increase in production costs outweighs the benefit of savings on transportation and transaction costs.

---

1   See Fujita and Krugman (1995), Hochman (1997), and Konishi (2000), for example.

With individuals' choice for ample living space and fresh air, the hierarchical structure of an urban system can evolve with the development of satellite cities and transportation hubs.

Historically, although the economic functions of urban systems were strengthened in certain periods, such as the Five Dynasties, Song dynasty, Yuan dynasty, and the period from 1840–1949, since the Qing and Han dynasties, the political and administrative functions of an urban system based on the hierarchical structure of cities had been the main driving forces in China's urbanization process prior to economic reform. Amiti and Wen (2001) and Wen (2001) have found that industrial agglomeration in China has followed economic reform. Has this industrial agglomeration changed the regional distribution of China's cities? Strikingly, a large thread of literature[2] has paid special attention to the contribution of TVEs to China's industrial and economic growth. With theirs rural locations, Chinese TVEs have developed into a major industrial sector during the past two decades, producing 58 per cent of gross industrial output value and 46 per cent of industrial gross domestic product in 1998.[3] Would the fast development of TVEs create an imbalance between industrial and urban development? In this chapter, the author addresses these questions by providing empirical evidence.

The chapter is organized as follows. Section 2 provides a historical comparison of China's industrial concentration in order to see how manufacturing industries have been re-localizing and concentrating following economic reform. Section 3 makes a historical comparison on the spatial location of cities and examines whether industrial agglomeration promotes agglomeration of cities. The effect of rapid rural industrial development on China's urbanization will be investigated in Section 4. Section 5 analyses urbanization approaches for further coordination between industrial and urban development. Concluding remarks follow.

2   Industrial Agglomeration

When the People's Republic of China was established in 1949, Chinese industry was highly geographically concentrated (DRCSC, 1992). Due to the impact of Japanese occupation of the Eastern Liaoning Peninsula and the

---

2   See Weitzman and Xu (1994), Chang and Wang (1995), Li (1996) and Tian (2000), for example.

3   The data are calculated from *China Statistical Yearbook* 1999 and *China Statistical Yearbook of Township and Village Owned Enterprises* 1999.

effect of leasing territories to foreigners in Shanghai, 70 per cent of industry was localized in China's eastern coastal belt which occupied less than 12 per cent of national land. Among all these industries, heavy industries were concentrated in the middle part of Liaoning province, while light industries such as textiles and repair of machinery, were localized in Shanghai, Wuxi, Tianjing, and Qingdao cities. However, from 1953 to 1978, the location of Chinese industrial firms was not determined by economic concerns. Instead, concern about destruction from potential military conflicts led to the strategic location of industrial firms towards inland China. From 1965 to 1978 in particular, large industrial firms were located according to the following three principles: close proximity to mountains, dispersion, and concealment. These inland development policies balanced regional development and substantially changed the spatial distribution of China's industry. By 1980, many two-digit manufacturing industries were distributed among Shanghai, Jiangsu, Liaoning, Shandong, Heilongjiang, Beijing, Hubei, Henan, Sichuan and Shanxi provinces.

Due to the fact that there was no railway in western China up to 1949,[4] the development of a transportation system in inland China could not keep pace with the development of industry in inland China from 1949 to 1978. The three stated principles guiding industrial firms' location caused an inefficient allocation of resources and products owing to the poor transportation conditions in inland China, especially those in mountainous regions. As Amiti and Wen (2001) observed an agglomeration of three-digit manufacturing industries in coastal regions, especially in Guangdong and Jiangshu provinces, it would be expected that there was industrial re-location and concentration following the economic reforms. In order to see how industries were re-located and concentrated, the author adopts industrial locational Gini as the measure of industrial concentration and calculates the Gini coefficients from the gross industrial output value of 25 two-digit industries in 1980, 1985 and 1995.[5] Increase in an industrial locational Gini indicates that the industry becomes more geographically concentrated. Provinces are used as regional units in the calculation. The data for 1980 and 1985 are drawn from the second national industrial census (LBNICSC, 1986) and the data for 1995 are drawn from the third national industrial census (TNICO, 1997). The calculated Gini coefficients with the provices of the highest or second highest share in each industry are reported in Table 10.1.

---

4   See Lu (1983) for detailed description of construction of China's railways before 1949.
5   See Amiti and Wen (2001) for the formulae of calculating Gini-coefficient and an explanation
     of why industrial locational Gini can be used to measure industrial concentration.

In Table 10.1, GINI95, GINI85, GINI80 are the locational Gini coefficients of 1995, 1985 and 1980, respectively. RHSH95, RHSH85 and RHSH80 label the regions with the highest share and the second highest share in order in the gross industrial output value of the years 1995, 1985, and 1980, respectively. From Table 10.1, the following observations are obtained.

First, from 1980 to 1995, 22 of the 25 industries became more geographically concentrated. The Gini coefficients of these 22 industries increased on average by 21 per cent with the highest increase in industry 19 – leather, fur, feather and manufacturing of leather, fur and feather products, which recorded a 64 per cent increase. In 1995, most industries were highly concentrated in Guangdong and Jiangsu provinces. Second, two manufacturing industries – smelting and pressing of ferrous metal and smelting and pressing of nonferrous metal – became geographically dispersed.

The locational Gini of these two industries declined by 9 per cent and 19 per cent, respectively. One industry – the chemical fiber industry – was less concentrated in 1995 than in 1980. Its locational Gini decreased from 0.72 in 1980 to 0.67 in 1985, then rose back to only 0.68 by 1995. Third, among those twenty-two more geographically concentrated industries, nine became more concentrated consecutively from 1980 to 1985, and from 1985 to 1995. However, the other thirteen industries experienced dispersion to different extents from 1980 to 1985, then concentration to a higher degree from 1985 to 1995. Some of these 13 industries involved re-localization in the dispersion-concentration process. Fourth, except for industry 12 – logging and transport of wood and bamboo, the other eight two-digit industries that experienced consecutive concentrations were industries producing mainly final consumption goods, and had many new products produced with new technologies. Fifth, from the results shown in RHSH95, RHSH85 and RHSH80, it can immediately be seen that by 1995 Guangdong Province replaced Shanghai City as the core location for manufacturing industries, although some manufacturing industries were still highly localized in Shanghai. Furthermore, more industries were concentrated in fewer and geographically closer regions in 1995, indicating industrial agglomeration.

The industrial concentration and agglomeration may have had significant impact on the development of China's hierarchical urban system. In the next section, a historical development of cities will be reviewed and a historical comparison on spatial distribution of different sizes of cities will be provided to see whether industrial agglomeration was accompanied with agglomeration of cities following the economic reform.

Table 10.1 Historical comparison of industrial concentration (gini) and regions with the highest and the second highest industrial shares

Industry	GINI95	RHSH95	GINI85	RHSH85	GINI80	RHSH80
Logging and transport of wood and bamboo	0.793	HLJ, JL	0.777	HLJ, JL	0.750	HLJ, JL
Food manufacturing	0.472	SD, GD	0.376	JS, SC	0.362	JS, GD
Beverage manufacturing	0.475	GD, SD	0.423	SC, ZJ	0.429	ZJ, SD
Tobacco processing	0.542	YN, HUN	0.485	HEN, YN	0.483	HEN, SD
Textile	0.641	JS, ZJ	0.554	JS, SH	0.555	SH, JS
Garments and other fiber products	0.692	GD, JS	0.473	SH, JS	0.446	SH, JS
Leather, fur, feather and manufacturing of leather, fur and feather products	0.666	GD, ZJ	0.405	JS, SH	0.405	SD, SH
Processing of wood and manufacturing of bamboo, cane, palm and straw products	0.495	GD, JS	0.461	HLJ, SH	0.485	HLJ, SH
Furniture	0.547	GD, SD	0.414	GD, JS	0.388	GD, SD
Paper milling and manufacturing of paper products	0.493	GD, SD	0.407	LN, SH	0.411	LN, SH
Printing and record media reproduction	0.490	GD, JS	0.413	BJ, SH	0.393	BJ, SH
Cultural, educational and sports goods	0.756	GD, JS	0.696	SH, GD	0.712	SH, BJ
Raw chemical material and chemical products	0.492	JS, GD	0.451	JS, SH	0.459	SH, JS
Medical and pharmaceutical products	0.485	JS, GD	0.448	SH, JS	0.461	SH, JS
Chemical fiber	0.684	JS, SH	0.667	SH, JS	0.720	SH, JS
Rubber products	0.536	SD, SH	0.447	SH, SD	0.469	SH, SD
Plastic products	0.630	GD, JS	0.526	JS, ZJ	0.513	JS, SH
Non-metal mineral products	0.513	JS, GD	0.413	JS, LN	0.415	JS, LN
Smelting and pressing of ferrous metal	0.525	SH, LN	0.557	LN, SH	0.579	LN, SH
Smelting and pressing of nonferrous metal	0.433	JS, GD	0.476	SH, LN	0.532	SH, LN
Metal products	0.596	JS, GD	0.479	SH, JS	0.477	SH, JS

Table 10.1 cont'd

Industry	GINI95	RHSH95	GINI85	RHSH85	GINI80	RHSH80
Transport equipment	0.534	SH, JS	0.473	HUB, LN	0.477	LN, HUB
Electric equipmentand machinery	0.644	GD, JS	0.525	SH, JS	0.509	SH, LN
Electronic and Communications equipment	0.701	GD, JS	0.584	JS, SH	0.593	SH, JS
Instruments, meters, cultural and office machinery	0.629	GD, SH	0.549	SH, JS	0.554	SH, JS

Note: The names of the 30 regions are abbreviated in this table as follows: Anhui – AH, Beijing – BJ, Fujian – FJ, Gansu – GS, Guangdong – GD, Guangxi – GX, Guizhou – GZ, Hainan–HAIN, Hebei – HEB, Heilongjiang – HLJ, Henan – HEN, Hubei – HUB, Hunan – HUN, Inner Mongolia – IM, Jiangsu – JS, Jiangxi – JX, Jilin – JL, Liaoning – LN, Ningxia – NX, Qinghai – QH, Shandong – SD, Shanghai – SH, Shaanxi – SAX, Shanxi – SX, Sichuan – SC, Tianjin – TJ, Tibet – TB, Xinjiang – XJ, Yunnan – YN, Zhejiang – ZJ.

3   Agglomeration of Cities?

Owing to regional development in coastal and port areas during the semi-colonial and semi-feudal period, more than 53 per cent of China's cities were established in the eastern region in 1949. With inland development policies from 1952 to 1976, growth in the number of cities in middle and western China was much faster than the growth in eastern China. By 1976, the share of the eastern region in total number of cities decreased to 42 per cent while the shares of the middle and western regions increased from 37.8 per cent and 9.1 per cent in 1949 to 39.7 per cent and 18.2 per cent, respectively, even though the number and density of cities in the eastern region remained the highest among the three regions in 1976 as shown in Table 10.2.

The high density of cities in the eastern region indicates better infrastructure than the other regions at the beginning of economic reform. Close proximity to export ports, better infrastructure and preferential regional development policies made China's industries re-locate and concentrate in the eastern coast region. As discussed in the last section, some two-digit manufacturing industries experienced dispersion, then concentration to a higher degree. During the dispersion process, the two-digit industrial share of some middle and western provinces, such as Hubei, Sichuan, and Yunnan, increased from 1980 to 1985 in those industries where they had a comparative advantage. In addition, the investment made in inland China in the 1970s still exerted an effect onto the economy during the early period of economic reform. Hence, in Table 10.2, it is observed that the share in number of cities of the middle region increased to 41.2 per cent and the number of cities in the middle region surpassed the number of cities in the eastern region in 1985. To see whether the industrial agglomeration affected the formation of Chinese cities, two figures are drawn to show the historical regional number and density of cities.

From Figure 10.1, it can be seen that the eastern region experienced the greatest increase in the number of cities from 1985 to 1995 while the increase in the western region was the slowest. From 1995 to 1999, the increase in the number of cities was minor nationwide.

However, from Figure 10.2, it can be clearly seen that since 1949 the eastern region has had the highest density of cities. The density in the eastern region in 1999 was more than two and half times the density in 1985. The density in the middle region in 1999 was just about the level of the eastern region in 1985. Yet, the western region still had a very low density of cities. Hence, in terms of both number of cities and density of cities, there is geographical concentration in the eastern region.

Table 10.2   Distribution of cities among three regions and change in the regional density of cities

Region	National	Eastern	Middle	Western
1949 No. of cities	143	76	54	13
%		53.1	37.8	9.1
Density of cities	0.15	0.57	0.2	0.02
1957 No. of cities	186	85	69	32
%		45.7	37.1	17.2
Density of cities	0.20	0.64	0.26	0.05
Growth in no. of cities	30.0	11.8	27.8	146.2
1965 No. of cities	181	79	72	30
%		43.6	39.8	16.6
Density of cities	0.19	0.59	0.27	0.05
Growth in no.of cities	-2.7	−7.1	4.3	−6.3
1976 No. of cities	209	88	83	38
%		42.1	39.7	18.2
Density of cities	0.22	0.66	0.31	0.06
Growth in no.of cities	15.5	11.4	15.3	26.7
1985 No. of cities	324	113	133	78
%		34.9	41.2	24.1
Density of cities	0.34	0.85	0.49	0.12
Growth in no. of cities	55.0	28.4	60.2	105.3
1995 No. of cities	640	290	234	116
%		45.3	36.6	18.1
Density of cities	0.67	2.18	0.87	0.18
Growth in no.of cities	97.5	156.6	75.9	48.7
1999 No. of cities	667	300	247	120
%		45.0	37.0	18.0
Density of cities	0.70	2.25	0.91	0.18
Growth in no.of cities	4.2	3.4	5.6	3.4

Notes: (1) Eastern region includes Liaoning, Beijing, Tianjing, Shanghai, Hebei, Shandong, Jiangshu, Zhejiang, Fujian, Guangdong, Hainan, and Guangxi; Middle region includes Heilongjiang, Jilin, Shanxi, Inner Mongolia, Anhui, Jiangxi, Henan, Hunan and Hubei. Western region includes Sichun, Chongqing, Yunnan, Guizhou, Tibet, Shaanxi, Gansu, Qinghai, Ningxia and Xingjiang. (2) The unit of density of cities in a region is number of cities per 10,000 square kilometres.

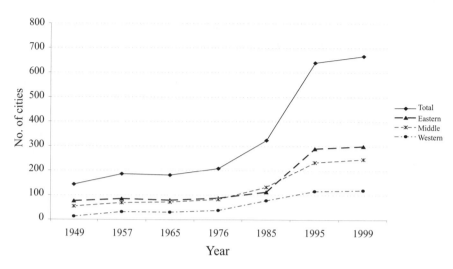

Figure 10.1   Regional number of cities

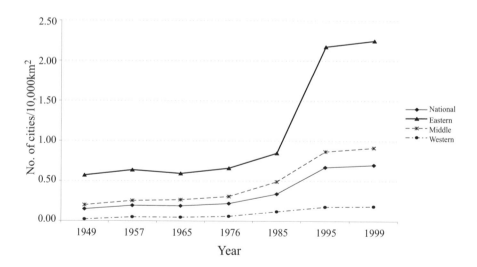

Figure 10.2   Regional density of cities

In section 2, it was observed that many two-digit manufacturing industries were concentrated in Guangdong and Jiangsu provinces in 1995. According to SSB (1986 and 1996), from 1985 to 1995, Guangdong and Jiangsu provinces had the greatest and second greatest increase in number of cities. Guangdong had 36 new cities while Jiangsu had 30. The next three regions in terms of increase in number of cities, in descending order, are Shandong, Zhejiang and Hebei. This regional pattern of city formation seems consistent with the pattern of regional shares in industries. In other words, from 1985 to 1995, a province with a higher industrial share might have experienced a higher increase in number of cities. However, the most significant changes in city patterns was the increase in small cities with a population size of under 0.2 million and a population size of between 0.2 and 0.5 million. Wang (1999) studies the positive and negative externalities of cities with a different size and concludes that cities with a population size of between 1 to 4 million people had the highest net returns to scale. Wen (2001) observes that China's industrial agglomeration is based on both transaction agglomeration and production agglomeration with increasing returns to scale. Therefore, although the regional pattern of city formation seems consistent with the pattern of regional shares in industry, the question is whether the pattern of formation of cities of different sizes represents the optimal urbanization pattern, which would coordinate urban development with long-term industrial development and GDP growth.

4   Development of TVEs and China's Urbanization

During the past two decades, one of the most remarkable phenomena in China's economy has been the fast growth of TVEs. This has been seen by many economists as an unexpected success in China's economic reform, because by 1997, TVEs occupied 27 per cent of GDP and contributed 41 per cent to gross domestic product in secondary industry.[6] Although TVEs were not centrally planned, there were many factors promoting the development of TVEs. Among former studies, sociological factors (Weitzman and Xu, 1994), conflict of interests between central and local governments (Chang and Wang, 1995), risk-sharing behavior between nominal owners and local government in an imperfect market environment (Li, 1996), degrees of economic freedom,

---

6   The data are calculated by the author according to the data of total GDP and GDP of secondary industry from SSB (1998) and the data of GDP and GDP of secondary industry produced by TVEs from EOYCTVE (1998).

decentralization, and market perfection (Tian, 2000) are all used to explain the success of TVEs.

In addition to the above reasons, institutional constraints, such as the household registration system, state ownership of urban land, and slow development of urban system, also played a major role in the development of rural industries. With the success of agricultural reform, a large amount of surplus labour was released from agricultural production. Under the existing household registration system and state ownership of urban land, it was unlikely for all of the labour force released from the agriculture sector to shift to industry through urban employment. After fiscal decentralization in the 1980s, local governments had an incentive to set up TVEs to absorb surplus labour, capitalize on the collectively owned rural land and increase the income of rural citizens, as they were able to raise more taxes from the development of TVEs.

In fact, since economic reform, TVEs have been the major channel for absorbing surplus labour released from the agricultural sector. From 1978 to 1998, the shift of surplus labour from agriculture into industry was mainly through self-employment, employment in private or individual businesses, employment in TVEs, and temporary employment in SOEs. In 1998, among these employment channels, 0.88 million of 492.8 million employed rural citizens worked as employers of private business, 19.4 million were self-employed, 25.6 million were employees in private business or individuals, 125.4 million were employees in TVEs, and 321.5 million were the labour force in the agricultural sector. In 1996, about 80 million rural citizens worked in the industrial sector under employment in TVEs alone.[7] Hence, TVEs are viewed as an important industrial organization in China's industrialization process.

Nevertheless, the potential negative effect of the fast development of TVEs on China's urbanization and, hence, the long-term effect on economic growth has not been paid enough attention. Due to the fact that TVEs' locations are not economic choices and are usually limited to affiliated towns or villages, their development may have stunted China's urbanization process. Therefore, it may have slowed down the infrastructure development essential for sustainable economic growth.

To support the above arguments, the relationships between rural industrial share and the urbanization rate are to be investigated. Provincial data for 1978, 1980, 1990, 1991, and 1992 will be used in the investigation. It would

---

7   The data are from *Yearbook of Chinese Township and Village Owned Enterprises 1997 and 1999*.

be expected that a province with a low urbanization rate is more likely to develop its rural industry in order to absorb surplus labour, and hence would have a higher rural share in industrial output value. If rural industry is able to develop very fast in a province so that it occupies a large share in total industrial output value, it can be expected that the higher rural share will have a negative effect on the urbanization rate in the following years. As discussed in the last section, the density of cities varies across the three regions in China. This may indicate that the urbanization process would be faster in the eastern region and slower in the western region than in the middle region. As firms in better geographical locations (in terms of transportation) would be more competent than firms in poor geographical locations, it can be expected that better infrastructure in the eastern region would be helpful to the development of rural industry while poor infrastructure in the western region would be detrimental to rural industry. Therefore, panel data of 1978, 1980, 1990 and 1992 are used to estimate the following relationships.

$$RSI = \alpha_0 + \alpha_1 UR + \alpha_2 ED + \alpha_3 WD + t \qquad (1)$$
$$UR = \beta_0 + \beta_1 RSI_{-2} + \beta_2 ED + \beta_3 WD + t \qquad (2)$$

where *RSI* is the rural share in industrial output value of each province; *UR* is the urbanization rate of each province, which is equal to the ratio of non-agricultural population in cities and towns to total population; *ED* and *WD* are locational dummies for the eastern and western regions, respectively; subscript $_{-2}$ denotes a two-year lagged variable; *t* equals 0 for 1980, and 1 for 1992.

The estimated results are shown in the regressions [1] and [2] in Table 10.3, where instrumental variable approach is adopted for the regression [1] and all exogenous variables are used as instruments. Although the adjusted R-squared are not very high, all the variables in the two relationships are highly significant. The explanatory variables are significant at 0.01 level except that the western region dummy variable is significant at 0.05 level in the regression [1]. The low R-squared means both *RSI* and *UR* are not fully explained by the explanatory variables in (1) and (2). This might be because that using two regional dummies to catch the infrastructure differences among provinces would be too rough as even in the same region, different provinces can have quite different speeds in the formation of cities for historical, geographical and economic reasons. Fortunately, in the *Yearbook of Chinese Township and Village Owned Enterprises 1993*, a name list of developed towns, less developed towns and undeveloped towns of each province has been provided. This enables the author to calculate the share of developed towns in total number of towns in

Table 10.3   Relationship between rural share in industrial output and urbanization rate

Dependent variables	Rural share in industrial output value (*RSI*)		Urbanization rate (*UR*)	
Explanatory variables	Regression [1]	Regression [3]	Regression [2]	Regression [4]
Constant	30.374	31.304	0.235	0.263
	(0.000)	(0.000)	(0.000)	(0.000)
UR	−128.96		−117.24	
	(0.000)	(0.000)		
RSI_{-2}			−0.008	−0.010
			(0.000)	(0.000)
Eastern region dummy (*ED*)	15.157		0.113	
	(0.008)		(0.006)	
Western region dummy (*WD*)	−12.757		-0.089	
	(0.025)		(0.049)	
Share of developed town in total number of towns (SDT_{-1})		63.080 (0.000)		0.553 (0.000)
Share of less developed town in total number of towns ($SLDT_{-1}$)		18.795 (0.004)		0.145 (0.006)
Time dummy (*t*)	25.126		0.182	
	(0.000)		(0.000)	
Adjusted R2	0.36	0.866	0.302	0.935

Note: The numbers in brackets are p-values.

each province as well as the share of less developed towns. As these two shares are actually endogenized in the urbanization process, e.g., the ratio of developed towns would be affected by the density of cities in the province, it is expected that the two ratios can better capture regional infrastructure differences than the rough distinction among the three regions. Hence, the 1990, 1991, and 1992 data are used to estimate the following relationships.

$$RSI = \gamma_0 + \gamma_1 UR + \gamma_2 SDT_{-1} + \gamma_3 SLDT_{-1} \tag{3}$$
$$UR = \delta_0 + \delta_1 RSI_{-2} + \delta_2 SDT_{-1} + \delta_3 SLDT_{-1} \tag{4}$$

where SDT_{-1} and $SLDT_{-1}$ are share of developed towns, and less developed towns in total number of towns, respectively. The results are shown in the regressions [3] and [4] in Table 10.3. Similarly, the instrumental variable approach is adopted and all exogenous variables are used as instruments for estimating the regression [3]. It can be seen that adjusted R-squared increased significantly when SDT_{-1} and $SLDT_{-1}$ are used to capture regional differences.

Both regression [1] and [3] strongly suggest that a high rural share in industry of a province would be due to a low urbanization rate of the region. Both regressions [2] and [4] confirm that development of rural industry like TVEs would retard the urbanization process as a high rural share in industry would keep more labor force in rural area and hence have a significantly negative effect on the urbanization rate in the following years. Therefore, although it was observed that industrial agglomeration and city agglomeration were consistent in regions from the last section, China's industrial and urban development may not have coordinated well due to institutional constraints, such as unfavourable policies towards domestic private ownership up to the middle of 1990s, the household registration system, state ownership of urban land, and the resulting fast development of rural industries during the past two decades.

5   Acceleration of Urbanization Process for Further Coordination between Industrial and Urban Development

Unlike its well-recognized rapid economic and industrial growth, China's urbanization has been relatively slow. Table 10.4 gives the urbanization rate for 1970, 1980, 1990 and 1998, and the change in urbanization rate of each province in the 1970s, 1980s, and 1990s. From the Table, it can be observed that, except for Beijing, Tianjing and Shanghai which are metropolises, up to 1998, the urbanization rate of other regions was lower than 0.5. Although the three heavy industry provinces, Liaoning, Jilin and Heilongjiang, reached urbanization rates higher than 0.4, the urbanization rate of most other provinces was lower than 0.3. As the major homes of manufacturing industries, Guangdong had an urbanization rate of just over 0.3 while Jiangsu had an urbanization rate of 0.25. Even though that urbanization rate calculated from official data might underestimate the true urbanization rate due to illegal migration from rural to urban areas, China's urbanization process need to be speeded up in the following directions.

5.1 Development of Large and Medium Sized Cities and Formation of Super-large and Special-large Cities

As discussed in Section 3, before economic reform, the growth of cities in the middle region was the fastest. According to Gu (1992), from 1949 to 1957,

Table 10.4 Urbanization rate and change in urbanization rate

Region	1970	1980	1990	1998	1970-80	1980-90	1990-98
National total	*0.13*	*0.14*	*0.19*	*0.24*	*0.01*	*0.05*	*0.05*
Beijing	0.50	0.55	0.60	0.65	0.05	0.05	0.06
Tianjin	0.72	0.52	0.55	0.57	-0.21	0.03	0.02
Hebei	0.07	0.09	0.13	0.18	0.02	0.04	0.05
Shanxi	0.12	0.14	0.21	0.25	0.02	0.07	0.04
Inner Mongolia	0.23	0.23	0.29	0.32	0.00	0.06	0.03
Liaoning	0.28	0.33	0.41	0.45	0.05	0.08	0.04
Jilin	0.24	0.29	0.38	0.43	0.05	0.09	0.05
Heilongjiang	0.32	0.31	0.39	0.42	-0.01	0.08	0.03
Shanghai	0.54	0.57	0.63	0.76	0.03	0.06	0.13
Jiangsu	0.10	0.12	0.19	0.25	0.02	0.07	0.07
Zhejiang	0.09	0.10	0.16	0.20	0.01	0.06	0.05
Anhui	0.08	0.09	0.13	0.18	0.01	0.04	0.05
Fujian	0.12	0.12	0.15	0.19	0.00	0.03	0.04
Jiangxi	0.10	0.12	0.16	0.20	0.02	0.04	0.04
Shandong	0.06	0.07	0.16	0.23	0.01	0.08	0.08
Henan	0.06	0.08	0.11	0.16	0.01	0.04	0.05
Hubei	0.10	0.13	0.21	0.26	0.03	0.08	0.06
Hunan	0.08	0.09	0.14	0.18	0.02	0.04	0.05
Guangdong	0.11	0.13	0.23	0.31	0.01	0.10	0.08
Guangxi	0.07	0.08	0.11	0.16	0.01	0.03	0.05
Hainan			0.18	0.24		0.18	0.06
Chongqing				0.20			0.20
Sichuan	0.08	0.09	0.13	0.17	0.01	0.04	0.04
Guizhou	0.09	0.09	0.11	0.14	0.00	0.02	0.03
Yunnan	0.09	0.08	0.10	0.13	0.00	0.02	0.02
Tibet	0.04	0.10	0.09	0.10	0.06	-0.01	0.01
Shaanxi	0.12	0.12	0.17	0.21	0.01	0.05	0.04
Gansu	0.10	0.11	0.15	0.18	0.01	0.04	0.02
Qinghai	0.19	0.17	0.24	0.24	-0.02	0.07	0.01
Ningxia	0.16	0.15	0.22	0.27	-0.01	0.07	0.05
Xinjiang	0.15	0.22	0.28	0.31	0.07	0.06	0.03

Source: Calculated from *China Statistical Yearbook of Population 1999*.

there were 71 newly established cities. The urbanization rate increased from 10.6 per cent to 15.4 per cent. Most of these 71 cities were in Hunan, Sichuan, Henan, Yunnan, Gansu, Heilongjiang, Inner Mongolia, Shanxi, Hebei, Anhui and Fujian provinces. From 1958 to 1965, urban development fluctuated in both number of cities and urbanization rate. During the Great Leap Forward movement from 1958 to 1960, 44 new cities were set up with an increase in the urbanization rate from 15.4 to 19.7 per cent. Due to the fiscal burden as a result of the fast increase in urbanization rate, the government decided to revoke some cities and reduce urban population. Subsequently, 52 cities were revoked and about 30 million people sent back to rural areas. By 1965, the total number of cities was 7 less than in 1957. During the period of the Cultural Revolution (1966-1976), the formation of cities was slow. The average annual increase in number of cities was 1.7.

Since economic reform, both the formation of cities and the increase in urban population have been accelerating. From 1977 to 1985, the average annual increase in number of cities was 15.1. The urbanization rate increased to 18 per cent in 1985. From 1985 to 1999, the average increase in number of cities reached 22.9, indicating an average annual growth rate of 5.29 as shown in Table 10.5.

Table 10.5   Average annual growth rate of cities of different size: 1985–99

Year	1985	1999	Average annual growth rate 1985–99
Total number of cities	324	667	5.29
No. of cities with 2 million people or over	8	13	3.53
No. of cities with 1–2 million people	13	24	4.48
No. of cities with 0.5–1 million people	31	49	3.32
No. of cities with 0.2–0.5 million people	94	216	6.12
No. of cities with 0.2 million people or less	178	365	5.26

Source: Calculated from SSB (1986 and 2000).

There are two dimensions to increase urban non-agricultural population: formation of cities of different size and an increase in the population of cities in certain categories. To view changes in one dimension with ignorance of another would provide incomplete or misleading information on the development of cities of different sizes. In China's urban hierarchy structure, cities are divided into five categories. Cities with a population of not less than 2 million people are classified as super-large. Cities with a population of between 1 and 2 million people are classified as special-large. Cities with a population of between 0.5 and 1 million people, between 0.2 and 0.5 million people, and under 0.2 million people are classified as large, medium and small cities, respectively.[8] In Table 10.5, the growth rate in the number of different cities is different from 1985 to 1999, with the fastest growth in medium and small sized cities and the slowest in large cities. However, from Table 10.6, it can be seen that the non-agricultural population in the small sized cities decreased during the same period. And super large cities had the highest increase in non-agricultural population.

To view the development of different layers of the urban hierarchical system for raising the urbanization rate, a ranking of cities of different sizes according to their contribution to the absorption of increased non-agricultural urban population is presented in Table 10.6. From Table 10.6, it can be observed that, except during the Cultural Revolution period, super-large and special-large cities contributed most to the increase in the urban non-agricultural population. Interestingly, large cities made smallest (greatest) contribution in the period from 1957 to 1965 and from 1975 to 1985 (from 1965 to 1975). Due to the fast growth in their numbers and the rapid increase in their average size, medium-sized cities, as a whole, significantly contributed to the increase in the urban population. Although small cities grew rapidly in number, their contribution to the urbanization process varied from time to time. In particular, although there was the most rapid increase in the number of small cities during the reform period, the contribution of small cities to urban population increase seemed to be negative due to the decline in their average size. This might be related to the development of TVEs during the same period, considering that the development of TVEs promoted the formation of small-sized cities with a non-agricultural population of less than 100,000 people.

In the current urban hierarchical system, the formation of cities of size-1, 2, 3, and 4 are usually based on upgrading cities of size-2, 3, 4, and 5, respectively. This upgrading can be either through natural population growth within the city or through migration. Among the 13 super-large cities in 1998, three of them, Shanghai, Beijing, and Tianjing, had a population of more than 4 million people. The other nine cities had a population of between 2 and 4

8   These five categories of cities are called size-1, size-2, size-3, size-4 and size-5 cities in descending order of population size in Table 10.6.

Table 10.6 Development of cities of different size in absorption of non-agricultural urban population

Period	1957–65	1965–75	1975–85	1985–98
Increase in non-agricultural urban population	1076	321	3610.76	4389.32
Increase in non-agricultural population in size-1 cities	476	–141	1472.96	2006.41
Increase in non-agricultural population in size-2 cities				1614.75
Increase in non-agricultural population in size-3 cities	–131	626	527.11	822.99
Increase in non-agricultural population in size-4 cities	326	243	903.2	1315.56
Increase in non-agricultural population in size-5 cities	411	–413	707.49	–1370.4
	Ranking of different size of cities in terms of contribution to increase in non-agricultural urban population			
Size-1 cities	1	3	1	1
Size-2 cities				2
Size-3 cities	4	1	4	4
Size-4 cities	3	2	2	3
Size-5 cities	2	4	3	5

Note: Size-1, size-2, size-3, size-4 and size-5 cities, in this table, refer to cities with a non-agricultural population not less than 2 million people, between 1 and 2 million people, between 0.5 and 1 million people, between 0.2 and 0.5 million people and under 0.2 million people, respectively.

Sources: Original data before 1985 are drawn from Gu (1992). Original data for 1985 and 1998 are drawn from USEST (1986 and 1999). Data in the table are from the author's calculation based on the original data.

million people. There were 24 special-large cities. From Table 10.6, it can be observed that size-1 and size-2 cities contributed most to the increase in urban population. In addition, according to Wang (1999), cities of population size between 1 to 4 million people (size-1 and size-2 cities) have had the highest net returns of scale. Hence, further formation of super-large and special-large cities will be very important in China's urbanization process. Nevertheless, the formation of super-large and special-large cities will be based on the development of large cities, which will be based on the development of medium-sized cities.

In 1999, there were 49 large cities, 216 medium cities and 365 small cities. Small and medium cities usually have a disadvantage in obtaining or adopting advanced technology due to the immature capital market in China. Their low GDP means financial constraint. In addition, a small population can hardly exert the functions of public facilities and infrastructure. Hence, investment in public facilities (such as libraries and schools) and infrastructure (such as transportation and communication networks) are usually low, resulting in both the slow accumulation of human capital and slow evolution in the division of labour. Compared with medium and small cities, size-3 cities may have the capability of adopting advanced technology. However, the population size may still not be large enough to fully explore the increasing net returns of scale. This might be one reason why there seemed to be an imbalance (not proportionate) in the number of large-sized cities between the number of size-2 cities and the number of size-4 cities. Size-3 cities seem to be transitional in the hierarchical structure. Therefore, to promote the formation of new size-1 and size-2 cities, further development of medium and large cities is needed.

5.2 Development of Satellite Cities and Formation of Transportation Hubs[9]

During the past 24 years, several satellite city groups have formed accompanying the economic reform. These satellite city groups include those in the Pearl River triangle, the Yangtzi River triangle, the Shenyang-Dalian region, and the Beijing-Tianjing-Tangshan region. There is also one satellite city group in Henan province and one in Sichuan province. Satellite cities in the Pearl River triangle include the triangle formed by Hong Kong, Shenzhen, Macau, Zhuhai, and Guangzhou, and cities within the triangle and close to the triangle, such as Dongwan, Zhongshan, Foshan, Zhaoqing, Jiangmen and Huizhou. The satellite cities in the Yangtzi River golden triangle include Shanghai, Nanjing, Zhenjiang, Changzhou, Wuxi, Suzhou, Changshu, Hangzhou, Jiaxing, Huzhou, Wuhu, Maanshan and Tongling. The satellite cities in Henan province are centred at Zhenzhou and distributed along the railway across the Beijing-Guangzhou line and Lanzhou-Lianyungang line. The satellite cities in Sichuan province are along the Chengdu-Chongqing railway. Although these six satellite city groups are exerting their economic functions with different characteristics, the agglomeration of cities in the Pearl

---

9   Data used in this section are all calculated from USEST (1999).

River triangle and in the Yangtzi River golden triangle are consistent with the industrial agglomeration in these two regions.

As the leading region of economic reform and the current home of many manufacturing industries, the satellite cities in the Pearl River triangle (excluding Hong Kong and Macau) have more than 60 per cent of the non-agricultural urban population of Guangdong province and contribute more than 9.5 per cent to domestic GDP of all cities not under Diqi level. Their share in commodity and passenger transport is higher than 0.057 and 0.059, respectively. In addition, this satellite city group has Hong Kong as a big export port, three international airports in Hong Kong and Guangzhou, and a big port in Zhongshan. The highway system in Guangdong Province is the most developed in China. Taking into account these geographical and transport advantages, this satellite city group has become not only home to many manufacturing industries, but also the centre of industries of import processing for exporting, international trade, and information exchange.

With Shanghai as its centre, the satellite cities in the Yangtzi River golden triangle contributed to more than 15 per cent of domestic GDP of all cities not under Diqi level. These satellite cities are home to many light industries. Transport systems connecting these satellite cities include the shipping system along the Yangtzi river and along the Beijing-Hangzhou canal, as well as railway and highway systems. In the passenger transport and commodity transport of all cities at or above Diqi level, these satellite cities have a share of 0.128 and 0.095, respectively. Recent development of Pudong district as an international financial centre and high technology district will further increase the importance of these satellite cities. Although there are two international airports in Shanghai and sea transport in several cities, the lack of a deep-sea port will be a main obstacle preventing these satellite cities from fully exerting their function in international trade.

Surrounding China's capital city Beijing, Tianjing, Tangshan, Qinghuangdao, and Langfang form another satellite city group. These five cities contributed more than 9.1 per cent to the GDP of all cities at or above Diqi level. This satellite city group sits at a high level in the urban hierarchical system as it includes two super-large cities, one special-large city, one large city and one medium city. It maintains and stretches the administrative, cultural and economic functions of the capital, Beijing.

Compared with the above three groups, the other three satellite city groups need further development to exert more significant economic functions. Although the satellite cities in the Shenyang-Dalian region have a good size structure: two size-1 cities (Shenyang and Dalian), two size-2 cities

(Anshan and Fushun), three size-3 cities (Benxi, Dandong and Laioyang), one size-4 city (Yingkou) and two size-5 cities (Haicheng and Wufangdian), further improvement in infrastructure seems to be required for maintaining and strengthening their role in heavy industry and commodity transport for north-eastern China. As to the satellite cities in Henan province, consisting of 13 cities within the rhombus formed by Anyang, Kaifeng, Zhumadian and Shanmenxia, their economic functions can be further reinforced through development of national highways to connected regions and the upgrading of some of the cities in the urban hierarchical structure. Although they are located along the Beijing-Guangzhou and Lanzhou-Lianyungang railway, national investment in the railway system was far less than investment in the highway system during the reform period. Furthermore, the highway system facilitates commodity transport by reducing costs through faster door-to-door specialized transport. Regarding the satellite cities in Sichuan Province, despite their location in a mountainous region, they occupy a high share in GDP and commodity transport with a comparative advantage in food production, motorcycle production, electronic measures and satellite communications. Under government advocacy to develop western China, this satellite city group will play a more and more significant role in the economic development of central and western China through further development of the highway system and the shipping system along the Yangtzi River. Development of transport systems connecting to these cities would make Chongqing and Chengdu form a transportation hub and promote the upgrading of the other cities in this group.

In the current regional development pattern, the formation of transportation hubs in central China seems important in accelerating the development of western China. But which cities are suitable to becoming transportation hubs? Up to 1998, only three super-large cities, Shanghai, Tianjing and Guangzhou, had a share higher than 0.03 in Shiqi passenger transport (Their shares are 0.076, 0.03 and 0.036, respectively). Only two super-large cities, Chongqing and Chengdu, occupied a share higher than 0.03 in Shiqi domestic commodity transportation while Guangzhou had a share of 0.028. In other words, Guangzhou played a very important role in both passenger and commodity transport. Shanghai was the pivot for passenger transport while Chongqing and Chengdu were the pivot for commodity transport. As both Guangzhou and Shanghai are in the coastal region, further formation of transport hubs in inland China will be necessary for accelerating development of the middle and western regions. Potential new transportation hubs would be Wuhan, which was a transport pivot before the 1980s, Xian, which connects the middle and western regions, and the satellite cities centred at Zhenzhou, which connect the eastern and middle regions.

6   Concluding Remarks

The empirical evidence in the foregoing sections suggests there were both industrial agglomeration and city agglomeration in several coastal provinces following economic reform. However, development of rural industry seems to retard the urbanization process, although it contributes to industrial growth in a certain period of time. To further coordinate the industrialization and urbanization process, development of medium and large cities for the formation of new super-large and special-large cities is desirable as they can accelerate the urbanization rate, take advantage of advanced technology, and generate economies of scale. In addition, further urban development along the lines of development of satellite cities and transport hubs will be helpful to the economic development of middle and western China.

References

Amiti, M. and Wen, M. (2001), 'Spatial Distribution of Manufacturing in China', in Lloyd, P. and Zhang, X. (eds), *Modeling the Chinese Economy*, Cheltenham: Edward Elgar.

Chang, C. and Wang, Y. (1994), 'The Nature of the Township-Village Enterprises,' *Journal of Comparative Economics*, 19 (3), pp. 434–52.

Department of Population, Social, Science and Technology Statistics of State Statistical Bureau of China (DPSSTS) (1999), *China Population Statistics Yearbook*, Beijing: China Statistics Press.

Development Research Center of the State Council (DRCSC) (1992), *China: Urban Development Towards the Year 2000*, Shenyang: the People's Publishing House of Laioning (in Chinese).

Editorial Office of Yearbook of Chinese TVEs (EOYCTVE) (1988–99), *Yearbook of Chinese Township and Village Owned Enterprises*, Beijing: Chinese Agricultural Publishing House (in Chinese).

Fujita, M. and Krugman, P. (1995), 'When is the Economy Monocentric?: Von Thünen and Chamberlin Unified,' *Regional Science and Urban Economics*, 25, pp. 505–28.

Gu, Z. (1992), *China's Urban System – History, Status Quo, and Perspective*, Beijing: Shang Wu Press (in Chinese).

Hochman, O. (1997), 'More on Scale Economies and Cities', *Regional Science and Urban Economics*, 27, pp. 373–97.

Konishi, H. (2000), 'Formation of Hub Cities: Transportation Cost Advantage and Population Agglomeration', *Journal of Urban Economics*, 48, pp. 1–28.

Leading Body of National Industrial Census of the State Council (LBNICSC) (1986), *The Data of the 1985 Industrial Census of the People's Republic of China, Volume 4 (regional Volume)*, Beijing: China Statistical Publishing House.

Li, D. (1996), 'A Theory of Ambiguous Property Rights in Transition Economies: The Case of the Chinese Non-state Sector,' *Journal of Comparative Economics*, 23 (1), pp. 1–19.

Lu, Y. (1983), *Almanac of China's Railway Construction 1881-1981*, Beijing: Chinese Railway Publishing House (in Chinese).

The State Statistical Bureau of China (SSB for abbreviation) (various years), *China Statistical Yearbook*, Beijing: China Statistics Press.

Tian, G. (2000), 'Property Rights and the Nature of Chinese Collective Enterprises,' *Journal of Comparative Economics*, 28, pp. 247–68.

Third National Industrial Census Office (TNICO) (1996), *The Organization and Implementation of the Third National Industrial Census*, Beijing: China Statistical Publishing House.

Urban Social and Economic Survey Team of State Statistical Bureau of China (USEST) (various years), *Urban Statistical Yearbook of China*, Beijing: China Statistics Press.

von Thünen, J.H. (1826), *Der Isolierte Staat in Bezieehung auf landwrirtschaft and Nationalekonomie*, Hamburg.

Wang, X. (1999), 'Optimal City Size and Economic Growth', *Economic Research*, 1999, 9, pp. 22–9 (in Chinese).

Weitzman, M. and Xu, C. (1994), 'Chinese Township-Village Enterprises as Vaguely Defined Cooperateives,' *Journal of Comparative of Economics*, 18, pp. 121–45.

Wen, M. (2001), 'Relocation and Agglomeration of Chinese Industry', Working Paper #2001/07, Division of Economics, RSPAS, The Australian National University, Canberra, Australia.

CHAPTER 11

How Do Industrialization and Urbanization Affect Land Use?

XIAOBO ZHANG, PhD*
International Food Policy Research Institute (IFPRI)

Abstract

Rapid industrial development and urbanization transfer more and more land away from agricultural production and affect the patterns of land use intensity. This chapter analyzes the determinants of land use by modeling arable land and sown area separately. An inverse U-shaped relationship between land use intensity and industrialization is explored both theoretically and empirically. The findings highlight the conflict between the two policy goals of industrialization and grain self-sufficiency. Several policy recommendations are offered to reconcile the conflict.

Keywords: land use, industrialization, urbanization, China

JEL classification: O14, R11, R14

1   Introduction

Land scarcity has become an increasingly important issue in China. Because of rapid industrial development, urbanization, and population growth, the land base for agricultural production has been shrinking steadily. Since 1952,

---

*   Correspondence: Xiaobo Zhang, IFPRI, 2033 K Street, NW, Washington, DC 20006. Tel: (202) 862–8149; Email: x.zhang@cgiar.org.

URBAN TRANSFORMATION IN CHINA, edited by Aimin Chen, Gordon G. Liu and Kevin H. Zhang

more than 13 million hectares of arable land have been lost.[1] In contrast to the decline of arable land, the sown area, a product of arable land area and the multiple-cropping index, has increased by more than 13 million hectares since 1952. Understanding the driving forces behind the change in multiple-cropping index (land use intensity) is crucial for analyzing China's future grain production and trade situation.

Accompanying industrialization, land use intensity usually undergoes dramatic change as shown in the newly industrialization Asian (NIA) countries. In the case of Taiwan, the multiple-cropping index rose from 1.2 in 1921 to around 1.6 in the sixties and seventies, when the rapid industrialization took place. However, it declined to 1.4 in the nineties when the opportunity cost of labor in farming significantly increased (Mao and Schive, 1995). How do agricultural land use patterns evolve in the process of industrialization and urbanization? Is China's land use intensity going to follow the same patterns of the NIA counties and start declining? The rapid economic growth and large regional variations in China provide us with an opportunity to quantitatively examine these issues.

We develop an analytical framework based on policy and historical details. Compared with previous studies on China's land use, this study has at least two unique features. First, land intensity is modeled separately from arable land area. Most previous studies (Heilig, 1997; Li and Sun, 1997; Fischer, Chen, and Sun, 1998) have just focused on arable land area, thus understating China's grain production capacity. In China, local governments have much authority to procure land for non-agriculture use, whereas the central government responds to the overall food situation by setting policy guidelines for local governments and farmers. Since land is nominally owned by the collective, individual farm households are not allowed to convert their land to non-agriculture use, but they do have the right to cultivate their land and use multiple cropping. Therefore, it is sensible to model the different decision processes separately.

---

1   Arable land area and cultivated area are often used interchangeably. Sown area or cropping area is equal to the multiplication of arable land area and multiple-cropping index. It has been noted that the official arable land area might be under-reported (SSB, 1997, p. 368; Ash and Edmonds, 1998; Smil, 1999). In spite of the shortcomings of the official statistics, they are the only source for land stock at the provincial level readily available and consistently compiled. The trends of land use may not be severely affected by this problem considering that most under-reporting of arable land occurred in hilly and mountainous regions (Ash and Edmonds, 1998). In addition, by taking advantage of the availability of a panel data set, we can use regional dummies to largely reduce possible systematic measurement errors in our econometric analysis.

Second, using a 33 year (1965–97) panel data set at the provincial level, we can quantify the driving forces behind the changes in arable land and land use intensity. This is an improvement over previous studies on land use, which generally are qualitative or just based on time series data (Brown, 1995; Heilig, 1997; Zhang et al., 1997; Ash and Edmonds, 1998).

2   An Historical Review of China's Agricultural Land Use

Arable land area per capita in China is now less than 0.08 hectare (SSB, 1998), which ranks among the lowest in the world. Figure 11.1 plots the time paths of land use (arable land and sown area), industrialization, urbanization, and grain trade balance. Three features are apparent from Figure 11.1. First, it appears that there is a negative relationship between arable land area and industrialization and urbanization. During the period 1952–97, the arable land area declined by 12 per cent, from 108 million hectares to 95 million hectares, while population more than doubled, from less than 0.6 billion to more than 1.2 billion. The ratio of non-agricultural GDP to agricultural GDP, an indicator of industrialization, increased four fold and the share of urban population rose from 14 per cent to about 26 per cent. It appears that industrialization and urbanization are among the most important factors explaining the decline of China's agricultural land use.

Second, land has been increasingly cultivated. Figure 11.1 shows that the sown area increased by about 9 per cent from 1952 to 1997. The multiple-cropping index (calculated by the authors using the sown and arable areas) increased from 1.3 in 1952 to 1.6 in 1997, indicating that land is being more intensively cultivated. Clearly, the increase in grain production stems largely from the rise in multiple-cropping practices as well as higher yields. Third, it seems that the cycles in the grain trade balance are related to fluctuations in the sown area. Tang (1984) observed that Chinese agriculture had been marked by persistent cycles in response to the central government's policies. To gain a better understanding of the observed trends, it is necessary to review the history of China's development and agricultural policies.

2.1 Land Reforms (1949–55)

Following the establishment of the People's Republic of China in 1949, the state confiscated land from landlords and distributed it equally to peasants in order to improve both equity and efficiency. At that time, China faced a hostile

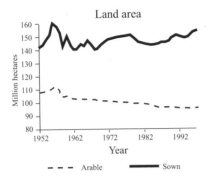

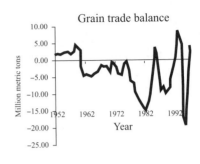

**Figure 11.1   Land use, grain trade, industrialization, and
urbanization**

international environment with political isolation and economic embargos.
The political leaders adopted two important development strategies – the
prioritization of heavy industrial development to catch up with developed
western countries and a grain self-sufficiency policy to lessen its reliance on
international markets (Lin et al., 1996). However, these two policies were not
complementary over time.

2.2 Great Leap Forward and the Great Famine (1956–61)

With net grain exports continuing to rise during this period, the focus of
national policy shifted from agricultural to industrial development. The
'Great Leap Forward' was called to boost steel and other heavy industry
output at the expense of agricultural production in order to catch up with

other industrialized nations. The ratio of industrial GDP to agricultural GDP rose threefold in four years, from 0.6 in 1956 to 1.9 in 1960. There was an accompanying sharp decline in arable land and sown area as land and labor were diverted away from agricultural production. The sharp decline in the agricultural land base together with the collectivization movement resulted in a serious food shortage, triggering the greatest famine in human history. During the early 1960s, China had to import as much as four million metric tons of grain, although it hesitated to do so initially.

2.3 Pre-reform (1962–78)

In reaction to the Great Famine and the increasing reliance on international grain markets, the central government was forced to reconsider its industrialization policy. Grain self-sufficiency emerged as a priority theme of governmental policy. The slogan, 'Yi Liang Wei Gang, Gang Ju Mu Zhang' (Grain must be taken as a core; once it is grasped, everything falls into place) reflected the spirit of this policy. One way to reconcile the conflict between the two policies was to reduce the urban population and increase the rural population through the existing household registration system. The share of the urban population kept dwindling until the late 1970s, which kept the demand for land for non-agricultural purposes under control.

By the early 1970s, the potential for boosting sown area through reductions of the urban population was almost exhausted. Therefore, from the early 1970s, all collectives were mobilized to learn from Da Zhai (a model village in Shanxi Province) how to claim more land from marginal areas such as hillsides and lakes. During the 1960s and 1970s, grain self-sufficiency was barely achieved, primarily through keeping a large base of rural population and by cultivating more marginal land. The share of grain imports relative to total grain production was controlled at a level of less than 4 per cent during this pre-reform period.

2.4 Rural Reform and Afterwards (1979–present)

With the end of the Cultural Revolution, the Chinese economy was on the verge of collapse. The potential for increasing grain production through developing more marginal land and increasing land utilization under the old collective system was nearly exhausted. By the late 1970s, China had to import as much as 10 million metric tons of grain from the world market. In response to the agricultural crisis, the government started to give more flexibility in decision making to individual household producers by officially promoting the household responsibility system nationwide. Thanks to the success of rural reform, agricultural output and grain production (measured at constant prices) grew 7.4 per cent and 4.8 per cent annually from 1978 to 1984, respectively (SSB, 1998). Because of the rapid agricultural growth, the share of agricultural GDP in total GDP increased from 0.28 to 0.32 during this period. Although there was little change in sown area during this period, a spectacular growth in agricultural output was generated.

The rural reforms released a large amount of labor and provided a base for industrial development. Since the mid-1980s, the town and village enterprises (TVEs) in rural areas have experienced a phenomenal growth, making it possible to absorb much of the surplus labor in rural areas. However, the development of the TVEs has not been distributed evenly. The TVEs developed much more rapidly in coastal provinces than in inland provinces. Meanwhile, localized migration from rural areas to nearby towns was much easier although many institutional barriers still existed for cross-regional migration (Kanbur and Zhang, 1999). As a result, the industrialization level in coastal provinces was of a different magnitude from that in inland provinces. In many of the industrialized coastal provinces, farmers faced more opportunities for higher pay from non-farm work. Thus, farmers had less incentive to continue intensive cropping. Accordingly, the multiple-cropping index for many coastal provinces, such as Jiangsu Province, began to decrease from their historical highs of the late 1980s.

However, for inland provinces, the dual economy, characterized by lower levels of industrial development and large surpluses of rural labor, was still dominant. Most farmers had to stick to their land because of limited local non-farm opportunities and the potential cost on migration across regions. Thanks to cheaper fertilizer and other land saving technologies resulting from industrialization throughout China, farmers were able to intensify cropping on their land. As a result, many inland provinces, such as Sichuan Province, experienced an increase in the multiple-cropping index over this period. For China as a whole, there appears an inversed U-shape relationship between cultivation intensity and industrialization as shown in Figure 11.2.

Our review of the history of China's agricultural policy reveals that balancing industrial development, urbanization, and food security has been a persistent challenge for the central government. From time to time, the government had to adopt mandatory administrative means to manage the problem. Urbanization and industrialization are important driving forces behind the conversion of farmland. Nevertheless, the relationship between

Lowess smoother, bandwidth = .8

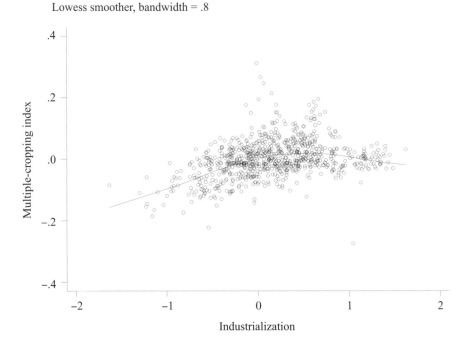

**Figure 11.2   Land use intensity and industrialization for all the
provinces**

industrialization and land intensification is more complicated. Total grain
production depends on total sown area, which in turn, is determined by the
availability of arable land area and the extent of land use intensity.

3   Conceptual Framework

Since arable land area and land use intensity are determined by different actors,
we need to model them separately. In the first step, we present a model of
arable land use for a local government because it has the authority to convert
farmland for non-agricultural use. For simplicity, we assume that the total
arable land area is fixed, and the land can be used for either agriculture or
non-agriculture.

As discussed in the previous section, the demand for agricultural land is likely
to be associated with industrialization, urbanization, land use decisions in
neighboring regions, and national policy. Therefore, the arable land function
can be expressed as follows:

$$A_t = F(ind_{t-1}, urb_{t-1}, pop_{t-1}, p_{t-1}, \theta_{t-1}), \tag{1}$$

where is the arable land area in time t; ind_{t-1} refers to the industrialization level at time t−1, defined as the ratio of industrial GDP to agricultural GDP; urb_{t-1} is the share of urban population; pop_{t-1} refers to population growth rate at year t-1; p_{t-1} represents terms of trade, the relative price of agricultural products to the price of non-agricultural products; and θ_{t-1} is the national grain trade deficit, which we use as a proxy for the overall national policy for land use in year t−1.

Generally, the demand for non-agricultural land use is positively related to industrialization and urbanization. Because the total endowment of land is fixed, if more land is used for industrial and urban development, then less land is left for agricultural use. Therefore, we expect a negative relationship between agricultural land use and industrialization and urbanization. Since the demand for arable land cannot exceed a region's natural limit, it is sensible to model the share of arable land as a logit model so that a prediction based on the model will not exceed its natural endowment. The model can be written explicitly as:

$$\frac{A_t}{\bar{A}} = \underset{(-)}{f(ind_{t-1}}, \underset{(-)}{urb_{t-1}}, \underset{(-)}{pop_{t-1}}, \underset{(+)}{p_{t-1}}, \underset{(+)}{\theta_{t-1})}, \tag{2}$$

where f is a logit function of the form

$$\frac{1}{1 + \exp(\beta X)}$$

and all the independent variables in $X = \{ind_{t-1}, urb_{t-1}, pop_{t-1}, p_{t-1}, \theta_{t-1}\}$ are in logarithmic form and β is a vector of corresponding coefficients. The hypothesized signs of the coefficients in β are shown in the parentheses under expression (2). A negative sign for industrialization suggests a conflict between the objectives of the industrialization and grain self-sufficiency policies. Since the total land area $\bar{A}$ and land allocations for non-agricultural uses are generally unknown, we cannot estimate (2) directly. By multiplying through by $\bar{A}$ and taking the logarithm of both sides, the following equation is obtained for estimation:

$$\ln(A_t) = \ln(\bar{A}) - \ln(1 + \exp(-\beta X)). \tag{3}$$

Since $\ln\bar{A}$ is fixed for each province, a dummy variable for each province is an appropriate proxy. The dummy variable also helps eliminate some systematic measurement errors of arable land. Accordingly, (3) can be estimated by a nonlinear regression procedure.

The next step is to model land use intensity. In a dual economy with plentiful surplus labors, an increase in nonfarm wage rate due to urbanization and industrialization may not lead to a change in wage rate in the rural sector, therefore having little effect on the intensity of labor input in a given piece of land. However, industrialization usually provides better and cheaper technologies for agricultural production, such as fertilizer and machinery. Therefore, we expect that land use intensity may increase as a result of industrialization in the initial stage of economic development. However, when industrialization develops to a certain stage, the tighter labor market will put upward pressure on the agricultural wage rate, therefore reducing the intensity of labor input per unit of land. We hypothesize that there exists an inverse-U shape relationship between land intensity and industrialization.[2]

4   Results

To test the above two hypotheses empirically, we use a panel data set for the period 1965 to 1997 for 24 provinces that includes land use, industrialization, and urbanization. 1965 is the earliest year for which systematic sown area data for each province are available. After taking a one-year lag for all the independent variables, we have 768 observations in total. A detailed description of the data is provided in Zhang, Mount and Boisvert (2000).

Table 11.1 reports the estimated model for the arable land area (3). Provincial dummies are used as a proxy for total land $\bar{A}$ for all the regressions. To capture the effect of regime changes, we create regime dummies by dividing the whole period of 1966–97 into three periods: pre-reform (1966–78), reform (1979–85), and post-reform (1986–97). The first regression (R1) does not include any regime dummies. In the second regression (R2), we add a dummy variable for the pre-reform period to check whether there is a systemic difference between the pre-reform period and the rest years. The third regression (R3) includes not only the dummy variable for the pre-reform period but also the dummy variable for post-reform period.

In general, the results are similar across the three specifications. The negative and statistically significant coefficients for industrialization, urbanization, and population growth suggest that these variables are indeed

---

2   A detailed proof can be found in Zhang, Mount, and Boisvert (2000).

driving forces behind the conversion of farmland to non-farm use. The coefficients on these variables are robust across the three specifications. The relatively large values of the coefficients for the urbanization and population illustrate the economic rationale behind the government's strict migration and one-child policies. The coefficients for the grain deficit price ratio have the expected positive signs, but they are poorly determined.

Table 11.1 Estimation results for arable area

	R1	R2	R3
Industrialization	−0.106**	−0.104**	−0.115**
	(0.032)	(0.036)	(0.037)
Urbanization	−0.621**	−0.615**	−0.702**
	(0.103)	(0.107)	(0.115)
Grain trade deficit	0.169	0.194	0.608*
	(0.334)	(0.338)	(0.364)
Population growth	−0.424**	−0.432**	−0.485**
	(0.174)	(0.175)	(0.176)
Price ratio	0.010	0.011	0.022
	(0.053)	(0.053)	(0.052)
Pre-reform		0.003	−0.031
(1965–78)		(0.018)	(0.020)
Reform			
(1979–85)			−0.047
			(0.028)
Log likelihood	1648.15	1648.17	1650.21

Notes:

1 This is the logit equation (3). The dependent variable is the logarithm of arable land. All the independent variables have a one-year lag. One and two asterisks indicate that estimates are at the 10% and 5% significance levels, respectively.
2 The industrialization variable is defined as the ratio of non-agricultural GDP to agricultural GDP; the urbanization variable is represented as the share of urban population in total population; the peer pressure variable refers to the logarithm of the total arable land area in a neighboring province, which has the highest GDP per capita.
3 Figures in parentheses are standard errors.

Next, we model land use intensity and test the curvature of the land use intensity with respect to industrialization. Specifically, we want to show that the second derivative is negative. Thus, the model needs to include both a linear and quadratic term for industrialization.[3] In addition, we use a quadratic function of urbanization to partly capture the effect of the agricultural wage rate and technical progress. The multiple-cropping index can be estimated as a function of the following variables:

$$\hat{a}_t = \hat{a}\,(ind^2_{t-1},\, urb_{t-1},\, urb^2_{t-1},\, pop_{t-1},\, p_{t-1},\, irrigation_{t-1},\, R\&D_{t-1}), \quad (4)$$

where *ind* measures industrialization, expressed as the ratio of non-agricultural GDP to agricultural GDP; *urb* is the share of urban in total population; *pop* represents population growth rate; *p* is defined as the ratio of grain procurement price index relative to consumer price index; *irrigation* is the share of irrigated area relative to total arable area; and *R&D* is the logarithm of total expenditure on agricultural research. To account for possible endogeneity problems, all the variables have a one-year lag.

Table 11.2 presents the estimated results for four different specifications. In all the four specifications, we include provincial dummies to capture the difference in land use intensity due to regional-specific factors, such as weather conditions and soil quality. The first regression R1 does not includes regime or year dummies. The second regression (R2) includes two dummies in the intercept, one for the pre-reform period and one for the reform period, to capture the possible effect of policy changes. In the third specification (R3), we replace regime dummies with year dummies, which can capture more year-specific effects. The fourth specification allows for coefficients to vary across the three periods by including interaction terms of the independent variables with the regime dummies. The corresponding coefficients for the three different periods are presented in columns 5, 6, and 7.

The positive coefficients for IND and the significant negative sign on IND^2 across all the specifications confirm our model's prediction of an inverse-U shape relationship between land use intensity and industrialization. The coefficients for urbanization are significantly negative, implying that urbanization may absorb labor from the farming sector and reduce land use intensity. The two public inputs – irrigation and R&D – have significant positive effects on land use intensity, which is consistent with the theoretical prediction. In contrast to the model for arable land, the coefficient for the reform period is highly significant confirming the importance of institutional change on cropping intensity.

---

3   Other functional forms, such as an inverse function, were also tried and the results are similar.

Table 11.2 Estimated results for land use intensity

	R1	R2	R3	R4 Pre-reform	R4 Reform	R4 Post-reform
IND	0.224**	0.224**	0.165*	0.206**	0.307**	0.515**
	(0.022)	(0.021)	(0.023)	(0.025)	(0.065)	(0.073)
IND^2	−0.092**	−0.108**	−0.122**	−0.132**	−0.144**	−0.234**
	(0.012)	(0.011)	(0.011)	(0.019)	(0.039)	(0.032)
URB	−0.250**	−0.391**	−0.706**	−0.487**	−0.058	−0.521**
	(0.114)	(0.113)	(0.108)	(0.194)	(0.234)	(0.251)
URB^2	−0.064	−0.094**	−0.158**	−0.108**	0.001	−0.118**
	(0.028)	(0.027)	(0.025)	(0.047)	(0.063)	(0.075)
Irrigation	0.072**	0.083**	0.031*	0.069**	0.131**	0.092**
	(0.018)	(0.017)	(0.018)	(0.020)	(0.025)	(0.025)
R&D	0.008	0.050**	0.037**	0.075**	0.016	0.048**
	(0.011)	(0.012)	(0.016)	(0.015)	(0.019)	(0.013)
Population growth	0.069	−0.098	−0.087	−0.117	−3.140**	0.132
	(0.163)	(0.154)	(0.145)	(0.162)	(1.374)	(0.424)
Price ratio	−0.098**	−0.028	−0.047	−0.024	0.016	−0.140*
	(0.032)	(0.030)	(0.041)	(0.042)	(0.051)	(0.078)
Pre-reform (1965–78)		0.038		−0.057		
		(0.015)		(0.222)		
Reform (1979–85)		−0.059**			0.874*	
		(0.010)			(0.283)	
Year dummies	No	No	Yes**			
Log likelihood	764.6	810.0	803.6		806.2	
AIC	763.6	809.0	802.6		805.2	

Notes:

1 One and two asterisks indicate that estimates are at the 10% and 5% significance levels, respectively.
2 The dependent variable is the multiple-cropping index. IND (Industrialization) is represented by the ratio of non-agricultural GDP to agricultural GDP; URB (Urbanization) is measured as the share of urban population in total population; the learning variable denotes the multiple-cropping index by the richest neighboring province.
3 Intercept and province dummies are not reported here. All the independent variables, except the regime and provincial dummies, are lagged by one year.
4 Figures in parentheses are standard errors.

The results in Table 11.2 can be used to calculate the turning points of land intensity in terms of industrialization. Using the most recent 1997 data and the R4 model in the post-reform period, we find that the multiple-cropping index reaches a maximum when the ratio of agricultural GDP relative to total GDP reaches to 24.9 per cent. In 1997, all the coastal provinces, except Guangxi Province, surpassed the turning point, while ten inland provinces did not. Clearly, the potential for future growth in grain output exists primarily in the inland provinces. It may take a long time for all provinces to reach or exceed the turning point. However, as provinces become more industrialized, the growth of land use intensity will decrease and be insufficiently large to offset the loss of total arable land due to industrialization. There are at least two other ways to increase grain production. One way is to slow population growth further and reduce the demand for land and food. In this respect, China has been rather successful in controlling its population growth. A more direct way is to increase crop yields by increasing public investment in R&D and irrigation (Fan and Pardey, 1997).

5   Conclusions and Policy Implications

This chapter develops a framework for identifying the determinants of land use in China based on policy and historical events. Separate models for arable land area and multiple cropping are specified to reflect the different decision processes that determine each of them. A panel data set at the provincial level for the years 1965 to 1997 is constructed from various governmental sources for the empirical analysis. In spite of the complexity of modeling land use, the results are quite encouraging, and they provide us with a better understanding of the driving forces behind the changes in China's grain production.

It is not surprising that empirical evidence reinforce our hypotheses that industrialization and urbanization are important contributory factors to the conversion of farmland to other uses. There results also underscore the fact that the 'industrialization' and 'grain self-sufficiency' policies, both proposed in fifties, are inherently in conflict. Prior to the economic reform in the 1980s, these two objectives were enforced through the household register system that kept a large rural population in place. Since the reform, the two goals have become more balanced, largely by increasing land productivity through the practice of multiple cropping.

The empirical results show an inverse U-shape relationship exists between land use intensity and industrialization. On the one hand, industrialization brings down non-labor input costs for agricultural production, promoting the practice of multiple cropping. On the other hand, industrialization, especially the rapid development of rural enterprises, offers more non-farm job opportunities, raising wages and making intensive farming unattractive as surplus labor is exhausted. The results also show a strong negative link between urbanization and land use intensity. Initially the total sown area in a province may expand slightly due to greater cropping intensity. Eventually, as the province further industrializes and urbanizes, the total sown area will shrink undermining the objective of grain self-sufficiency.

Until recently, the primary way for government to control farmland loss and increase sown area was through administrative orders, but the efficiency loss from doing so may have been high. However, there are several better ways to deal with the potential decline in sown area. First, encouraging freer labor movement across regions will delay the slowdown of cropping intensity in economically advanced provinces. Second, long-term investment in agricultural research should be expanded in order to further increase yields. If the growth rate of yield surpasses the rate of loss in sown area, total grain output will not fall. Third, China should make more use of international trade to exploit its comparative advantage by augmenting the import of land-intensive crops, such as grain, and paying for these with additional exports of labor-intensive commodities.

References

Ash, R.F. and Edmonds, R.L. (1998), 'China's Land Resources, Environment and Agricultural Production,' *China Quarterly*, 156, pp. 836–79.

Brown, L. (1995), *Who will Feed China: Waking-up Call for a Small Planet*, New York: W.W. Norton & Company.

Fan, S. and Pardey, P. (1997), 'Research, Productivity, and Output Growth in Chinese Agriculture,' *Journal of Development Economics*, 53, pp. 115–37.

Fischer, G., Chen, Y. and Sun, L. (1998), *The Balance of Cultivated Land in China during 1988–1995*, International Institute for Applied Systems Analysis (IIASA), Interim Report 98–047.

Heilig, G.K. (1997), 'Anthropogenic Factors in Land-use in China,' *Population and Development Review*, 23 (1), pp. 139–68.

Kanbur, R. and Zhang, X. (1999), 'Which Regional Inequality? The Evolution of Rural-urban and Inland-coastal Inequality in China, 1983–1995,' *Journal of Comparative Economics*, 27, pp. 686–701.

Li, X. and Sun, L. (1997), *Driving Forces of Arable Land Conversion in China*, International Institute for Applied Systems Analysis (IIASA), Interim Report 97–076.

Lin, J.Y., Cai, F. and Li, Z. (1996), *The China Miracle: Development Strategy and Economic Reform*, Hong Kong: The Chinese University Press.

Mao, Y.-K. and Chi Schive (1995), 'Agricultural and Industrial Development in Taiwan,' in Mellor, J.W. (eds), *Agriculture on the Road to Industrialization*, Baltimore: Johns Hopkins University Press, pp. 23–66.

Ministry of Agriculture (MOA) (various issues). *China Agricultural Yearbooks*, Beijing: China Statistical Publishing House.

Smil, V. (1999) 'China's Agricultural Land,' *China Quarterly*, 158, pp. 414–29.

Tang, A.M. (1984), *An Analytical and Empirical Investigation of Agricultural in Mainland China, 1952–1978*, Taiwan: Chung-Hua Institution for Economic Research,

Zhang, X., Mount, T. and Boisvert, R. (2000), 'Industrialization, Urbanization, and Land Use in China,' International Food Policy Research Institute EPTD Discussion Paper # 58.

PART IV: URBAN GROWTH AND PRODUCTIVITY

CHAPTER 12

URBAN ECONOMIC GROWTH

SHUANGLIN LIN*
University of Nebraska, Omaha

SHUNFENG SONG*
University of Nevada, Reno

Abstract

Urban economic growth is the most important segment of China's rapid economic growth. This chapter examines the relationship between per capita GDP growth and investment, foreign direct investment, labor force growth, government expenditures, and urban infrastructures based on the data for 189 large and medium sized Chinese cities for the period 1991–98. Cross-section analyses indicated that several factors, such as foreign investment, paved roads, and government expenditures on science and technology were positively related to per capita GDP growth, while the overall size of government, measured by total government spending share in GDP, appears negatively related to per capita GDP growth. Contrary to the literature on economic growth, total investment share in GDP was insignificantly related to per capita GDP growth. Also, there is no clear evidence of convergence in per capita GDP among Chinese cities.

*   Correspondence: Shuanglin Lin, Lindley Professor, Department of Economics, University of Nebraska, Omaha, Nebraska 68182, USA. Tel: 402–554–2815; Fax: 402–554–2853; Email: shuanglin_lin@unomaha.edu. Shunfeng Song, Professor, Department of Economics, University of Nevada, Reno, Nevada 89557–0207, USA. Tel: 775–784–6860; Fax: 775–784–4728; Email: song@unr.nevada.edu.

This chapter was presented at the International Conference on China's Urbanization, Xiamen, China, June 2001, Xiamen, Fujian, China. The authors thank Wenting Wu, Ke Yang, and Lei Wang for excellent research assistance and Qingyang Gu and Jackie Lynch for their comments and help.

Keywords: China; urban studies; economic growth

JEL Classification Numbers: O11; O53; P2; P52

1   Introduction

During the last 15 years, there has been a renewed interest in the forces that led to economic growth. Romer (1986) argued that per capita income among countries in the world might not converge if the production technology exhibits increasing returns of scale. Lucas (1988) pointed out the externality of human capital and believed that human capital plays a decisive role in economic growth. Barro (1990) and Rebelo and King (1990) argued that government tax and spending policies affect the rate of economic growth. Empirical studies have identified many other important determinants of economic growth. Landau (1983, 1986), Kormendi and Meguire (1985), and Barro (1991) identified that investment in physical and human capital was positively related to economic growth, while government size (measured by the government spending share in GDP) is negatively related to economic growth. Feder (1982) and Edwards (1992) found that the growth rate of exports is positively related to per capita GDP growth. Wacziarg (1998) and Borensztein et al. (1998) showed that the share of foreign direct investment in GDP is positively associated with per capita GDP growth. Canning et al. (1994) found substantial effects of physical infrastructure on economic growth. Most of these empirical results are based on cross-country analyses.

Researches on China's economic growth began with Chow (1993). Chow (1993) analyzed how physical capital formation in the national economy and the five productive sectors of agriculture, industry, construction, transportation, and commerce contributed to economic growth. He found that capital formation played an important role and technical change was absent in the growth of Chinese economy from 1952–80. Lin (2000) analyzed China's economic growth after the economic reform started in 1978 based on data from 30 Chinese provinces. He emphasized the allocation of resource on economic growth and found that provinces that invested more in state enterprises grew slower than provinces that invested more in private enterprises. In addition, he found that openness measured by the trade share in GDP is positively related to per capita GDP growth. So far there have been no studies of economic growth based on the data for the city level.

China experienced rapid urban growth in the past two decades. Non-agricultural population in urban areas increased from 171.45 million in 1978 to 388.92 million in 1999, a 125.5 per cent growth, while during the same period, the nation's total population grew about 30 per cent.[1] As a result, the urban population's share in total population had increased from 17.9 per cent in 1978 to 30.9 per cent in 1999. The number of cities has increased dramatically. In 1980, China had 223 cities, with 15 cities having a population size over 1 million. In 1999, China had 667 cities, with 37 cities having a population size over 1 million.[2] In 1982, 73.7 per cent of industrial output was produced by cities including the affiliated counties (67.6 per cent excluding the affiliated counties). In 1996, industrial output produced by cities along with the affiliated counties accounted for 97.3 per cent of the total industrial output (75.5 per cent excluding the affiliated counties).[3] Most of the foreign investment to China is in the cities. Urban economic growth has become the driving force of China's economic growth. A study of the determinants of urban economic growth is necessary.

The present study marks the first attempt to explain China's urban economic growth. A growth model based on aggregate production function is developed, which yields a number of testable hypotheses. A unique data set of 189 large and medium size cities for the period of 1991–98 is compiled. Cross-section analyses indicated that several factors, such as foreign investment, infrastructure, and government spending on science and technology were positively related to per capita GDP growth, while the size of government, measured by total government spending share in GDP, appears negatively related to per capita GDP growth. Contrary to the literature on economic growth, total investment share in GDP was insignificant relative to per capita GDP growth. In addition, there is no clear evidence of convergence in per capita GDP among Chinese cities.

Section 2 describes urban development in China from a historical perspective. Section 3 presents the model, discusses data for 189 cities data from 1991 to 1998 and defines variables. Section 4 discusses regression results. Section 5 concludes the chapter.

---

1   See *Statistical Yearbook of China*, 1994, 2000.
2   See *Statistical Yearbook of China*, 2000.
3   See *Statistical Yearbook of China*, 1997.

2   China's Urban Economic Development

Urban economic development has experienced three phases since the PRC was founded in 1949. In the first phrase (1952–65), China emphasized the growth of heavy industries. With this development strategy, many rural workers were recruited in state-owned enterprises and industrial cities were developed, especially in the inland areas. During this period, urban population increased faster than the national population and China experienced a steady rate of urbanization. Urban population increased at an annual rate of 4.6 per cent, from 71.63 million in 1952 to 130.45 million in 1965. During the same period, the pace of national population growth was slower (at an annual rate of 1.8 per cent), from 574.82 million in 1952 to 725.38 million in 1965. As a result, the urban population's share of total population increased from 12.5 per cent in 1952 to 18.0 per cent in 1965 (see *Statistical Yearbook of China*, 1994). During this period, China completed the socialist ownership reform in 1957 and experienced the 'Great-Leap-Forward' movement from 1958–60, which unfortunately turned out to be a great-leap-backward. Despite many difficulties, urban economy developed significantly during this period.

The second phase was during the Cultural Revolution (1966–77). In this period, urban growth was stagnant. A major reason was that the government required millions of urban youth to go to rural areas in order to 'undergo peasants' re-education', which was thought important to prevent the younger generation from being affected by capitalist influences and to channel and cultivate new revolutionary successors. In 1966–77, 17 million urban people were resettled in the countryside for political reasons and because of worsening housing shortages, job opportunities, and the infrastructure in the cities (Song and Timberlake, 1996). The growth rate of the national population was higher than that of the urban population between 1965 and 1975. As a consequence, the urban population share stagnated and even decreased, being 18.0 per cent in 1965, 17.4 per cent in 1970, 17.3 per cent in 1975, and 17.9 per cent in 1978 (see *Statistical Yearbook of China*, 1994). Urban economic development was in chaos.

The third phase is the reform era beginning in 1978. Since 1978, China has not only promoted an open-door policy and a 'socialist market economy' but also encouraged urbanization. Many county towns (*xian-zhen*) have been upgraded and classified as cities. The number of cities increased at an annual rate of 6 per cent, from 191 in 1978 to 232 in 1982, and to 667 in 1999, and the urban population share increased from 17.9 per cent in 1978 to 30.9 per cent in 1999, respectively (*Statistical Yearbook of China*, 2000, pp. 95 and 347). During the same period, urban population greatly increased.

In China, cities are classified into three levels according to their administrative status: county-level cities, prefecture-level cities, and central municipalities.[4] In 1993, for example, China had 371 county-level cities, 196 prefecture-level cities, and three central municipalities. These numbers changed to 437, 227, and four, respectively, in 1998.[5] Chongqing became the fourth central municipality in July 1997. Cities at different status are given different levels of authority such as investment decision-making and foreign-funded project approvals. The higher the level, the more directly the city reports to Beijing and the greater is its autonomy and influence.

Urban economy is an important component of the national economy. In 1982, 232 cities accounted for 73.7 per cent of the industrial output including the affiliated counties, while 67.6 per cent excluding the affiliated counties. In 1996, industrial output produced by cities along with the affiliated counties accounted for 97.3 per cent, while industrial output produced by cities excluding the affiliated counties accounted for 75.5 per cent.[6] Most foreign direct investment in China has been in cities. In 1996, the amount of foreign direct investment actually utilized by cities (excluding the affiliated counties) accounted for 76.1 per cent of the national total. Also, in 1996, 63 per cent of the doctors were in cities (excluding the affiliated counties) serving 42 per cent of the population.

Urban economic development has been quite uneven across cities. Table 12.1 shows summary statistics for some large cities in China.[7] Generally

---

4   The definition of city in China is not straightforward. Chinese cities are administrative entities and must be officially designated, with designation criteria being a function of political-administrative status, economic development, openness, and total population of an urban place. Since upgrading status in the administrative hierarchy is usually accompanied by greater autonomy, political power, and access to resources, local authorities are eager to pursue upgrading of their settlements to higher statuses. Such efforts, together with relaxation of designation criteria, have brought a significant growth in China's urban sector in the past two decades. Many county towns (*xian cheng*) were reclassified as cities (*shi*), resulting in a sharp increase in the total number of cities, from 223 in 1980 to 667 in 1999. Some county towns earned the city status even though they population were small. During the past two decades, many cities were upgraded through expanding their territories, or merging two adjacent cities, or combining a city with its surrounding counties.

5   The 227 prefecture-level cities in 1998 include 15 quasi-province-level cities (NBS, 1999). Quasi-Province-level, newly designated, has an administrative status higher than the prefecture-level but lower than the central-level.

6   See *Statistical Yearbook of China*, 1997, p. 332.

7   The data are from *Urban Statistical Yearbook of China*, 1992–99.

Table 12.1 Summary statistics for some large cities in China

City	Population 1998 (10,000)	Per capita GDP 1998 (yuan)	Per capita GDP growth 1991–98 (%)	Investment in GDP 1991–98 (%)	FDI share in GDP 1991–98 (%)	Population growth 1991–98 (%)	Paved road growth 1991–98 (%)	Gov't spending share in GDP 1991–98 (%)
Beijing	981.86	18,139	1.98	37.36	0.86	4.73	6.14	8.96
Tianjin	597.09	17,647	8.18	39.60	2.37	0.39	2.73	11.16
Shijiazhuang	157.17	20,843	12.14	38.09	0.60	2.32	8.94	5.33
Qinhuangdao	67.31	19,490	6.74	42.39	1.00	3.85	0.18	8.36
Taiyuan	223.32	11,570	4.35	33.69	0.37	1.70	5.24	6.35
Hohhot	101.77	9,834	6.36	29.40	0.14	1.83	3.86	10.48
Shenyang	479.99	16,474	9.10	19.49	1.14	0.68	9.15	7.61
Dalian	262.40	24,741	10.03	25.11	2.12	1.18	6.37	10.76
Changchun	282.69	14,595	13.68	25.07	0.33	4.03	5.29	7.85
Harbin	299.16	14,244	8.72	31.18	0.42	0.72	-3.04	9.92
Shanghai	1,070.62	27,771	7.73	51.22	1.56	4.41	15.55	13.27
Nanjing	276.36	22,364	8.83	31.21	0.68	1.31	9.57	6.83
Lianyungang	60.45	14,225	6.80	35.28	0.96	1.86	5.44	9.05
Nantong	63.96	19,383	6.42	31.75	2.44	1.42	5.18	6.28
Hangzhou	171.89	33,088	10.18	23.52	0.63	3.45	9.65	4.11
Ningbo	119.69	29,458	12.34	38.74	1.12	1.28	5.14	10.11
Hefei	127.94	14,829	9.20	30.02	0.87	3.19	16.48	5.90
Fuzhou	143.69	29,370	17.47	26.51	2.11	1.34	6.53	7.32
Xiamen	126.59	33,025	8.74	32.66	4.70	10.34	8.20	11.47
Nanchang	162.11	16,833	12.45	19.95	0.48	2.39	10.37	4.79
Jinan	257.49	21,113	12.55	20.28	0.46	1.33	6.05	5.57
Qingdao	229.58	19,954	9.10	25.67	1.14	1.46	9.39	9.36

Table 12.1 cont'd

City	Population 1998 (10,000)	Per capita GDP 1998 (yuan)	Per capita GDP growth 1991–98 (%)	Investment in GDP 1991–98 (%)	FDI share in GDP 1991–98 (%)	Population growth 1991–98 (%)	Paved road growth 1991–98 (%)	Gov't spending share in GDP 1991–98 (%)
Yantai	156.77	14,710	5.95	16.97	1.43	9.33	5.08	6.32
Weihai	49.64	25,927	9.51	23.72	0.80	8.96	13.78	6.60
Zhengzhou	203.93	13,307	10.51	37.13	0.54	2.33	7.37	6.94
Wuhan	530.24	16,533	9.18	38.88	0.94	4.79	3.62	6.12
Changsha	166.91	20,368	10.76	25.54	0.58	3.03	8.20	6.44
Guangzhou	399.3	32,514	9.97	33.46	1.44	1.40	10.73	10.54
Zhanjiang	130.73	12,206	7.72	31.49	0.93	2.73	3.89	9.74
Shenzhen	114.6	112,480	9.12	31.53	2.32	13.93	10.31	13.79
Zhuhai	40.70	54,764	4.06	31.61	2.74	5.41	17.66	8.75
Shantou	111.32	19,307	12.00	38.07	3.86	3.47	16.18	10.73
Nanning	130.81	14,087	9.80	21.99	0.84	2.66	10.86	6.81
Beihai	49.70	12,331	6.06	26.90	2.73	12.61	12.67	11.08
Haikou	52.79	20,890	9.59	54.25	5.18	4.45	13.68	9.01
Chengdu	325.98	17,737	9.55	35.58	0.20	1.96	9.02	4.84
Chongqing	836.57	8,439	1.38	24.51	0.87	14.6	10.74	10.85
Guiyang	176.59	9,851	5.90	33.82	0.17	1.76	14.14	10.01
Kunming	173.06	24,515	11.73	26.07	0.27	1.51	14.37	6.69
Xian	374.75	12,414	8.73	26.36	0.55	4.22	2.01	5.62
Lanzhou	174.98	12,035	5.05	36.32	0.29	1.90	10.06	6.66
Xining	82.27	6,231	2.83	36.00	0.07	3.23	3.84	7.96
Yinchuan	58.60	10,829	5.04	37.08	0.34	2.53	7.33	7.69
Urumqi	139.19	15,504	4.24	40.71	0.25	2.41	12.49	7.69

speaking, cities in east coast provinces grew faster than cities in the inland provinces, particularly in the west regions. For example, the annual growth rate of per capita GDP was 17.5 per cent in Fuzhou, 18.1 per cent in Putian, and 20 per cent in Quanzhou of Fujian Province; 18.8 per cent in Jining and 13.7 per cent in Weifang of Shandong Province; 12 per cent in Shantou, 12.6 per cent in Huzhou, and 13.4 per cent in Yangjiang of Guangdong Province; while the growth rate of per capita GDP was negative for Jingzhou of Liaoning Province, Jixi of Heilongjiang Province, and Shiyan of Hubei Province, Dongchun of Yunnan Province, and Jinchang of Gansu Province.

Different paces of growth have resulted in large differences in the level of per capita GDP. In 1998, 27 cities had per capita GDP higher than 20,000 yuan, of which Shenzhen and Zhuhai had 112,480 yuan and 54,764 yuan, respectively. On the other hand, 20 cities in our sample had per capita GDP less than 5,000 yuan, of which Guigang of Guangxi Province, and Dongchun of Yunnan Province had only 2,259 yuan and 1,808 yuan, respectively. In 1998, the four cities directly under central government control, Beijing, Shanghai, Tianjing, and Chongqing, had per capita GDP 18,139, 27,771, 17,647, and 8,439 yuan, respectively. Identifying the determinants of urban economic growth is clearly important for urban development.

3   The Model, Data and Definition of Variables

The theoretical framework is based on the aggregate production technology that incorporates labor force, domestic capital, and foreign capital, infrastructures, and government expenditures. The production function exhibits constant returns to scale across all factors. The production function can be written as:[8]

$$Y_t = F(L_t, K_t, X_t, H_t, R_t, G_t) \tag{1}$$

---

8   Previous studies of economic growth focusing on the aggregate production technology include Feder (1983) and Ram (1987). The approach based on the aggregate production function may have one advantage for empirical work over the framework based on the recently emerged theory of endogenous growth. In an endogenous growth model, variables such as investment are endogenous and cannot be used as a regressor in regression models, while in a model, such as the one we presented, investment can be an explanatory variable. In most empirical studies of economic growth, investment is treated as an explanatory variable [see, for example, Barro (1989), Romer (1990), and Levine and Renelt (1992)] in regression analyses.

where Y_t is the real aggregate output, L_t is the aggregate labor force, K_t is the aggregate capital stock, X_t is foreign capital stock, H_t is the stock of human capital, R_t is the stock of infrastructure, and G_t is government expenditures representing a flow of service from the government sector.

Let P_t be the total population, and $y_t = Y_t/P_t$, $k_t = K_t/P_t$, $l_t = L_t/P_t$, $x_t = X_t/P_t$, $h_t = H_t/P_t$, $r_t = R_t/P_t$ and $g_t = G_t/P_t$. Dividing both sides of equation (1) by P_t, we obtain the output per capita, y_t, as a function of per capita capital stock, k_t, per capita foreign direct investment, x_t, the ratio of labor force to the population, l_t, per capita human capita, h_t, per capita infrastructure, r_t, and the government expenditure per capita, g_t:

$$y_t = f(l_t, k_t, x_t, h_t, r_t, g_t). \tag{2}$$

Totally differentiating equation (2) and dividing both sides of the resulting equation by y_t, we find an equation which relates the growth of per capita output to the growth rate of the labor force, the ratio of investment to output, the ratio of foreign investment to output, the ratio of human capital to output, the growth rate of infrastructure, the size of government represented by the government expenditure-output ratio, and the growth of the population, i.e.,

$$\frac{dy_t}{y_t} = f_l \frac{L_t}{Y_t}\frac{dL_t}{L_t} + f_k \frac{dK_t}{Y_t} + f_x \frac{dX_t}{Y_t} + f_h \frac{dH_t}{H_t}\frac{H_t}{Y_t} + f_r \frac{R_t}{Y_t}\frac{dR_t}{R_t} + f_g \frac{dG_t}{G_t}\frac{G_t}{Y_t} \tag{3}$$
$$- \left(f_l \frac{L_t}{Y_t} + f_k \frac{K_t}{Y_t} + f_x \frac{X_t}{Y_t} + f_h + f_r \frac{R_t}{Y_t} + f_g \frac{G_t}{Y_t} \right) \frac{dP_t}{P_t}$$

Letting $\dot{x}_t = dx_t / x_t$ for each variable x, equation (3) can be written as:[9]

$$\dot{y}_t = a_1 \dot{P}_t + a_2 \frac{i_t^f}{y_t} + a_3 \frac{i_t}{y_t} + a_4 \frac{g_t}{y_t} + a_5 \dot{L}_t + a_6 \frac{h_t}{y_t} + a_7 \dot{R}_t \tag{4}$$

where

$$\frac{i_t^f}{y_t} = \frac{dX_t}{Y_t}, \frac{i_t}{y_t} = \frac{dK_t}{Y_t}, \frac{g_t}{y_t} = \frac{G_t}{Y_t}, \frac{h_t}{y_t} = \frac{H_t}{Y_t},$$

---

9   With the production technology specified in equation (1), $f_x = \delta f / \delta x_t = \delta F / \delta X_t$, $f_k = \delta f / \delta k_t = \delta F / \delta K_t$, $f_h = \delta f / \delta h_t = \delta F / \delta H_t$, $f_g = \delta f / \delta g_t = \delta F / \delta G_t$, and $f_l = \delta f / \delta l_t = \delta F / \delta L_t$. Also note that the coefficient of the population growth may not be constant based on the theoretical model. We ignore this for simplicity.

and where $a_1 - a_7$ are shorthand for the quantities written out in full in (3).

It is widely believed that the coastal cities grow faster than the inland cities. The coast cities in the east and south have benefited more from the open-door policies. For example, the earlier special economic zones are all east coast cities. These special economic zones introduced market mechanisms earlier than the other areas. Thus, a dummy variable may be added to distinguish the east coast cities and the other cities. We also add a variable for initial GDP to see whether there existed convergence of per capita GDP among cities.

With a dummy variable for coast cities, *coast*, a variable for initial per capita GDP, y_0, a constant term, a_0, a stochastic component, u_t, equation (4) becomes:

$$\dot{y}_t = a_0 + a_1 \dot{P}_t + a_2 \frac{i_t^f}{y_t} + a_3 \frac{i_t}{y_t} + a_4 \frac{g_t}{y_t} + a_5 \dot{L}_t + a_6 \frac{h_t}{y_t} + a_7 \dot{R}_t$$
$$+ a_8 coast + a_9 y_0 + u_t. \tag{5}$$

Equation (5) states that per capita output growth depends on the growth of the population, $\dot{P}$, the share of foreign investment in output, i^f / y, investment share in total output, i/y, government expenditure share in total output, g/y, the growth rate of the labor force, $\dot{L}$, the ratio of human capital to GDP, h/y, the growth rate of infrastructures, $\dot{R}$, a coast dummy variable, *coast,* and initial per capita GDP, y_0.

a_1, representing the effect of the population growth on the per capital output growth, can be either negative or positive theoretically. On one hand, the population growth increases the labor force, tending to increase output. On the other hand, the population growth tends to reduce the per capita output at a given total output. Thus, the net effect of population growth depends on the productivity of the increased population.

a_2, the effect of foreign direct investment on economic growth, should be positive. According to Leninism, foreign investment is a channel through which the rich imperialist countries explore and rob the poor colonies. Decades after World War II, many developing countries were not enthusiastic about foreign investment. Even some economically successful countries, such as South Korea, had been reluctant to accept foreign direct investment until the recent financial crisis (although it had emphasized exports). Times have changed and most economists have now recognized that foreign investment is beneficial to less developed countries. The benefits of foreign direct investment to a developing country include the following.[10] First, FDI is a transfer of capital from the rich countries to the poor countries, and capital is vital to economic growth. Second, FDI from the developed countries to the developing countries involves a transfer of technology, skills, and know-how. Third, FDI may contribute to employment creation. Fourth, FDI helps the developing countries to access world markets. Fifth, FDI flows tend to be less volatile than other types of foreign capital flows, such as foreign debt.

a_3, the marginal product of capital, should be positive in theory. Nearly all the empirical research on economic growth has incorporated investment-output ratio as an explanatory variable. In the Harrod-Domar theory of economic growth, the growth rate of output is a function of the investment-output ratio (the savings rate). In a Solow-style growth model higher saving results in temporarily higher growth, and in a Rebelo-style endogenous growth model higher saving results in permanently higher growth.

a_4, the elasticity of government spending, can be either positive or negative depending on the effect of government expenditure on the output. Government may invest in the essential projects that private firms are unwilling to support (such as infrastructures). With improved infrastructure, cities can raise the efficiency of the production process. Government spending must be financed by taxes, levies, or borrowings. An increase in taxes and levies extracts resources from the private sector, tending to slow down the economic growth. Thus, the net effect of government spending on economic growth is ambiguous in theory, depending on the productivity of government expenditures. It is generally believed that government sector is less efficient than the private sector, and thus, a larger size of government leads to a slower rate of economic growth. Allocation of government expenditures may also matter for economic growth. For instance, government spending on science and technology may help economic growth, while government spending on consumption may retard economic growth.

a_5, the output elasticity of labor, should be positive theoretically. In the neoclassical growth theory, the long-term growth rate of output depends exclusively on the growth rate of labor force, which is assumed to be exogenous. That is, the higher the growth rate of labor force, the higher the rate of per capita output growth will be. Attention should be paid to the transition economy, such as the Chinese economy, where a large amount of the labor force is employed by state enterprises.

a_6, the output elasticity of human capital, should be positive. Analyses of the role of human capital can be traced back to Adam Smith (1776), where

---

10   See Perkins et al. (2001) for a detailed discussion.

he treated human capital as another type of capital that would bring returns to the investors. For years, Schultz (1961) has emphasized the role of human capital in economic growth and in improving people's living standards. Lucas (1988) pointed out the positive externalities of human capital and argued that human capital is decisive in determining the rate of per capita GDP growth. The higher the rate of human capital accumulation, the higher rate of per capita output growth should be.

a_7, the output elasticity of infrastructure, should be positive. The positive role of economic infrastructure in economic development has been emphasized in economics [see, for example, Canning, Fay, and Perotti (1994)]. Public infrastructures have strong positive externalities. A growth of public infrastructures tends to stimulate private economic activities, such as investment and consumption. Thus, the higher the growth rate of infrastructures, the faster the economy will grow.

a_8 represents the coefficient of the coast dummy variable. It appears that the coast areas in China have grown faster than the rest of the country. Many factors may contribute to the rapid growth in the coast areas. If the variables used in the analysis can fully explain the reasons for the fast growth in the coast areas, then the coast dummy variable will be insignificant. Otherwise, the coast dummy variable will be significantly positive.

The coefficient on the initial per capita output is a_9. Standard neoclassical growth theory predicts that the initial capital labor ratio should have no effect on steady state growth. In the transition to the steady state, however, economies with a lower initial capital-labor ratio, and therefore, lower output per capita, are generally expected to grow faster as a consequence of less diminishing returns under a given technology. Diffusion of technology from developed areas to poor areas would also produce the same result. a_9 should have a negative sign if there was a convergence among the rich and the poor cities.

The data are mainly from various issues of the *Urban Statistical Yearbook of China* (NSB, 1992–99).[11] Other data sources include *China Regional Economy: A Profile of 17 Years of Reform and Open-Up* (NBS, 1997) and various issues of *China Statistical Yearbook* (NBS, 1990–2000). The definitions of variables used in our regression are as follows.

y_0:   Real gross domestic product (GDP) in 1991. GDP for 1991 in current price is from the *Urban Statistical Yearbook of China*, 1992, and it was deflated by the overall retail price index.

---

11   Relevant data on the city level for the years earlier than 1991 are not available.

$\dot{y}$: Growth rate of real GDP from 1991 to 1998. It is calculated as follows: $\dot{y} = [ln(GDP_T) - ln(GDP_0)]/T$, where GDP_0 and GDP_T is the real GDP for the initial year and the end year, respectively, and T is the time span.

i^f/y: The share of foreign investment in GDP from 1991 to 1998. It is calculated as follows: $i^f/y = \frac{1}{T}\sum \frac{X_L}{GDP_t}$ where is foreign investment in year t and T is the time span.

i/y: Average of ratios of total investment to GDP for the period of 1983 to 1994. It is calculated as follows: $i/y = \frac{1}{T}\sum \frac{I_t}{GDP_t}$, where I_t is total investment in year t and T is the time span.

$\dot{P}$: Average annual growth rate of population from 1991 to 1998. It is calculated as follows: $\dot{P} = [ln(POP_T) - ln(POP_0)]/T$, where POP_T and POP_0 are the population for the end year and the initial year, respectively; and T is the time span.

$\dot{L}$: Average annual growth rate of the labor force from 1991 to 1998. It is calculated as follows: $\dot{L} = [ln(L_T) - ln(L_0)]/T$, where L_T and L_0 are the labor force for the end year and the initial year, respectively; and T is the time span.

g/y: Average of the share of government spending in GDP over the period of 1991 to 1998. It is calculated as follows: $g/y = \frac{1}{T}\sum \frac{G_t}{GDP_t}$, where G_t is government spending in year t, and GDP_t is GDP in year t.

illit: The illiteracy rate of the labor force (people who are 15 years or older and who are illiterate or semi-illiterate) in 1995. This variable is used for the human capital variable in equation (6), h/y. Note that the data are from Statistical Yearbook of various provinces in 1996. Three provinces, Guangdong, Liaoning and Guangxi do not have the data available. Shaanxi just has provincial data available but not the data on the city level. We use the data for provincial data for all cities in Shaanxi Province.

$\dot{R}$: Growth rate of road in $\dot{R} = [ln(R_T) - ln(R_0)]/T$, where R_T and R_0 are the infrastructures for the end year and the initial year, respectively; and T is the time span.

coast: Dummy variable with a value 1 for 16 east coast cities and four special economic zones, and 0 for the rest cities.[12]

---

12 The 16 coast cities are: Tianjin, Qinhuangdao, Dalian, Shanghai, Nantong, Lianyungang, Ningbo, Jiaxing, Fuzhou, Xiamen, Qingdao, Yantai, Weihai, Guangzhou, Shenzhen, and Zhenjiang. There are three more cities belonging to this category. Unfortunately, data on the major variables are not available for these three cities.

Table 12.2 shows some basic statistics of the major variables for 189 cities from 1991 to 1998. The mean annual growth rate of per capita GDP was 7.4 per cent. Quanzhou of Fujian Province led all the cities with 20 per cent annual growth, followed by Fuzhou of Fujian and Jining of Shandong, 17.5 per cent and 18.8 per cent, respectively. The mean of population growth for all 189 was 2.4 per cent. Shenzhen led all the cities with 13 per cent growth. The mean of the share of investment in GDP was 31 per cent, with Panzhihua of Sichuan being the highest (75 per cent) and Guigang of Guangxi being the lowest (9.3 per cent). The mean of government spending in GDP was 8.4 per cent, with Yingtan of Jiangxi Province being the highest (25 per cent) and Daqing of Heilongjiang the lowest (2.5 per cent). The mean of the share of foreign investment in GDP was 0.72 per cent. Sanya of Hainan Province led all the cities with 6.1 per cent and many cities in the west had negligible foreign direct investment. The mean of the growth rate of the area of paved roads (square meters) was 9.2 per cent, with many cities in Guangdong such as Maoming, Dongguan, and Yangjiang being the highest. The mean of the illiteracy rate of the population 15 years or older was 10.5 in 1995 for 149 cities.

Table 12.2   Descriptive statistics for major variables: 1991–98*

Variable	Mean	Maximum	Minimum	Std dev.
$\dot{y}$	0.074	0.289	−0.066	0.041
i/y	0.309	0.755	0.093	0.116
$i^f/_y$	0.007	0.061	0.000	0.010
$\dot{P}$	0.024	0.139	−0.038	0.021
$\dot{R}$	0.092	0.445	−0.056	0.076
s/y	0.008	0.019	0.001	0.003
$(g-s)/y$	0.084	0.259	0.025	0.032
y_0	4010	30509	860	3129
coast	0.101	1.000	0.000	0.301
$illit_{95}$	10.54	27.08	1.520	5.520

* y_0 = real per capita gross domestic product (GDP) in 1991; $\dot{y}$ = average growth rate of
real per capita GDP from 1991 to 1998; i/y = average of ratios of total investment to GDP
from 1991 to 1998; $i^f/_y$ = the average of ratios of foreign investment to GDP from 1991
to 1998; $\dot{P}$ = average annual growth rate of population from 1991 to 1998; $\dot{R}$ = average
growth rate of road from 1991 to 1998; s/y = average of the share of government spending
on science and technology in GDP over the period of 1991 to 1998; $(g-s)/y$ = average of
the share of other government spending in GDP over the period of 1991 to 1998; $illit$ =
the illiteracy rate of the population 15 years or older in 1995; $coast$ = dummy variable for
coast cities (see section 3 for a detailed description of the variables).

Table 12.3 shows the correlation matrix of some major variables. While most variables have quite low correlation coefficients, government spending on science and technology and other government spending have a moderate correlation coefficient (−0.664), i.e., when the expenditures on science and technology is high, other expenditures must be low. In our regression analyses, we use three government spending variables, government spending on science and technology (s/y), the total government spending (g/y), and government spending on others (total government spending minus government spending on science and technology), $(g-s)/y$. Since there is a high correlation between population growth and labor force growth, we excluded the latter from our regression analysis.

Table 12.3   Correlation matrix*

v.r.	i/y	i^f/y	$\dot{P}$	$\dot{R}$	s/y	$(g-s)/y$	y_0	coast	illit
i/y	1.00								
i^f/y	0.03	1.00							
$\dot{P}$	0.07	−0.28	1.00						
$\dot{R}$	−0.11	−0.12	−0.26	1.00					
s/y	0.16	−0.33	0.16	0.07	1.00				
$(g-s)/y$	−0.30	0.01	−0.12	0.06	−0.66	1.00			
y_0	−0.17	−0.30	0.11	−0.02	0.48	0.01	1.00		
coast	0.004	−0.27	−0.38	0.13	0.04	−0.13	−0.19	1.00	
illit	−0.12	−0.01	0.04	−0.09	−0.21	0.43	−0.20	0.25	1.00

* y_0 = real per capita gross domestic product (GDP) in 1991; $\dot{y}$ = average growth rate of real per capita GDP from 1991 to 1998; i/y = average of ratios of total investment to GDP from 1991 to 1998; i^f/y = the average of ratios of foreign investment to GDP from 1991 to 1998; $\dot{P}$ = average annual growth rate of population from 1991 to 1998; $\dot{R}$ = average growth rate of road from 1991 to 1998; s/y = average of the share of government spending on science and technology in GDP over the period of 1991 to 1998; $(g-s)/y$ = average of the share of other government spending in GDP over the period of 1991 to 1998; *illit* = the illiteracy rate of the population 15 years or older in 1995; *coast* = dummy variable for coast cities (see section 3 for a detailed description of the variables).

Before we present and discuss our empirical results, it is necessary to clarify some data issues related to our model and estimation. First, our sample years are from 1991 to 1998. China had 479 cities in 1991 and this number increased to 668 in 1998. However, data in 1997 and 1998 are available on most variables only for prefecture-level cities. Due to this limit and in order to examine changes between 1991 and 1998, our sample only includes prefecture-level cities. Second, quite a few cities were redefined in the 1990s. For example, China added nine prefecture-level cities in 1994 and eight more in 1996. To keep data consistent, we excluded cities that were redefined during our sample years. This exclusion reduced the sample size from 229 to 189. Third, we used 1985 as a base year and deflated all nominal values in our sample years into 1985 constant-price values. At the provincial level, deflators are overall consumer price index (CPI) of urban residents. Hence, in our calculation, we have considered the variation of urban resident CPI across regions. Since Chongqing was upgraded into a central municipality only in 1997, we treat it as a city in Sichuan Province. Finally, we have paid special attention to variable definitions used in each statistical yearbook and have adjusted them if there are any changes in definitions.

4   Empirical Results

We will now discuss the empirical results on the relationship between the growth rate of per capita GDP and investment, population growth rate, foreign direct investment, the growth rate of infrastructure represented by the paved road, government spending share in GDP, government spending share in science and technology, education, etc.

Table 12.4 shows the regression results based on the cross sectional analyses of the data for the period of 1991–98. In regressions (1)–(3), the coefficient of the population growth is negative and statistically significant, indicating a higher growth in population in a city led to a slower per capita GDP growth. This result is consistent with most of the empirical findings in the literature. Romer (1990) found that the rate of population growth is negatively related to the growth rate of per capita GDP growth. Johnson (1993) argued that there was no negative relationship between population growth and per capita output growth based on evidence of recent centuries. In regressions (4)–(7), population growth has a negative but statistically insignificant coefficient. Thus, the relationship between the population growth and per capita GDP growth is inconclusive based on the Chinese city data.

It might be striking to see that total investment, i/y, is not significantly related to economic growth in China [see regressions (3)–(7)]. More over, in regressions (1)–(2), the investment variable is significantly negatively related to economic growth. Many recent studies have shown that investment is significantly positively related to the rate of per capita GDP growth empirically.[13] The key characteristic of the Chinese economy is that a large part of the investment is controlled by the government and has been allocated to the state enterprises. Lin (2000) decomposed the total investment in different categories, investment by state enterprises, collective enterprises, and private enterprises, and found that the investment share of state enterprises is negative and significant, while the investment share of private enterprises is positive and highly significant. State enterprises have been using resources inefficiently. Their operating costs are much higher than private enterprises, primarily due to excess employment.[14]

Facing the competition from private enterprises, two-thirds of the state enterprises are operating at a loss. For many provinces the investment share of state enterprises was higher than 50 per cent. This may explain why total investment did not have a significantly positive impact on economic growth. Also, De Long and Summers (1991) showed that equipment investment had a positive and significant relationship with economic growth based on an international data set. Thus, allocation of investment could be crucial to for urban economic growth. Unfortunately, the data on the allocation of investment on the city level is not available.

The coefficient of the share of foreign direct investment in GDP, i^f / y, is positive and statistically significant in all the regressions (1)–(7). That is to say, cities with a higher ratio of foreign direct investment share in GDP grew faster. The effect of foreign investment on economic development has been an important subject of debate for more than a century. Recent studies have demonstrated that foreign direct investment is beneficial to economic growth. It has been found that a 1 per cent increase in the share of foreign direct investment in GDP is associated with an increase in GDP of between 0.3 and 0.8 per cent [see Wacziarg (1998) and Borensztein, Gregorio and Lee (1998)]. Our regression results indicate that a 1 per cent increase in the ratio of foreign direct investment to GDP is associated with more than 0.9 per cent increase in the growth rate of per capita GDP.

Throughout regressions (1)–(7), the infrastructure variable (represented by the growth rate of paved roads) has a positive coefficient and is highly significant, indicating that infrastructure is important for urban economic growth. This finding is consistent with the literature. Ashauer (1989) argued that public expenditures are quite productive, and the slowdown of the US

---

13 See, for example, De Long and Summers (1991, 1992). Levine and Renelt (1992) found that the investment variable is significantly positively related to the growth rate of GDP and is not sensitive to the changes of the specifications of the regression equation.

14 The government discourages state enterprises from laying off workers for political stability. Many state enterprises have to pay half of the wages to laid off workers.

Table 12.4 Growth of urban per capita GDP: 1991–98 [a][b]

Variable	(1)	(2)	(3)	(4)	(5)	(6)	(7)
Intercept	0.085	0.074	0.067	0.067	0.066	0.071	0.087
	(10.7)	(9.27)	(5.65)	(4.65)	(4.63)	(4.23)	(3.91)
i/y	−0.048	−0.042	−0.009	−0.009	−0.006	−0.005	−0.044
	(−2.39)**	(−2.14)*	(−0.40)	(−0.40)	(−0.25)	(−0.24)	(−1.63)
i^f/y	1.319	1.051	1.120	1.032	0.874	0.928	0.910
	(4.63)**	(3.74)**	(3.37)**	(3.37)**	(2.61)**	(2.64)**	(2.03)*
$\dot{P}$	−0.207	−0.242	−0.124	−0.124	−0.182	−0.127	−0.275
	(−1.94)*	(−2.30)**	(−1.03)	(−1.03)	(−1.50)	(−1.01)	(−1.84)+
$\dot{R}$		0.121	0.102	0.102	0.116	0.113	0.132
		(3.24)**	(2.95)**	(2.96)**	(3.30)**	(3.27)**	(2.51)**
s/y			5.543	4.966	5.458	4.883	5.121
			(2.81)**	(2.63)**	(2.91)**	(2.37)*	(1.98)*
g/y			−0.577				
			(−4.66)**				
$(g-s)/y$				−0.577	−0.626	−0.601	−0.542
				(−4.66)**	(−4.99)**	(−4.78)**	(−3.11)**
coast					0.021	0.023	0.019
					(2.19)*	(2.38)**	(1.59)
y_0						−1.21E−06	−1.21E−06
						(−0.89)	(−0.66)
illit							−0.001
							(−0.88)
Obs.	189	189	189	189	189	189	145
R^2	0.09	0.14	0.22	0.23	0.24	0.24	0.25

Notes:

a) y_0 = real per capita gross domestic product (GDP) in 1991; $\dot{y}$ = average growth rate of real per capita GDP from 1991 to 1998; i/y = average of ratios of total investment to GDP from 1991 to 1998; i^f/y = the average of ratios of foreign investment to GDP from 1991 to 1998; $\dot{P}$ = average annual growth rate of population from 1991 to 1998; $\dot{R}$ = average growth rate of road from 1991 to 1998; s/y = average of the share of government spending on science and technology in GDP over the period of 1991 to 1998; $(g-s)/y$ = average of the share of other government spending in GDP over the period of 1991 to 1998; illit = the illiteracy rate of the population 15 years or older in 1995; coast = dummy variable for coast cities (see section 3 for a detailed description of the variables).

b) t-values are given in the parentheses, which are based on White (1980) heteroskedasticity robust covariance estimator. + = statistically significant at the 10% level. * = statistically significant at the 5% level. ** = statistically significant at the 1% level.

productivity was related to the decrease in public infrastructure investment. Munnell (1990) explored the impact of the stock of public capital on economic activity at the state and regional levels in the United States. She concluded that those states that have invested in infrastructure tend to have greater output, more private investment, and higher employment growth. Eisner (1991) pointed out that public infrastructures not only serve as an intermediate good in physical goods production, they can also be final consumption goods. For example, water and sewage systems benefit the environment, better transportation saves time spent on traveling, public parks give people pleasure, etc. Canning, Fay, and Perotti (1994) found substantial effects of physical infrastructure on economic growth based on the international data set. Easterly and Rebelo (1993) found that public investment in transportation and communication is consistently correlated with economic growth. Thus, infrastructures are vital to a nation's prosperity.

In regressions (3)–(7), the coefficient of government spending share in GDP [g/y or $(g-s)/y$] is negative and highly significant, indicating the size of government is negatively related to economic growth. As mentioned earlier, based on cross-country analyses, Landau (1983, 1986), Kormendi and Meguire (1985), and Barro (1991) found government size (measured by the government spending share in GDP) negatively related to economic growth. Barro (1990) argued that when government size is small, an increase in the size of government would increase the rate of output growth; while when the government size is large, a further increase in the government size may reduce the growth rate. Looking at the Chinese data, we found that the government size appears rather small since the mean of government spending share in GDP was only 8 per cent for the period 1991–98. However, we should recognize that the government expenditures in China just include the budgetary expenditures, and there also exist extra-budgetary expenditures (expenditures not included in budgetary expenditures but under the central government's supervision and off-budgetary expenditures (expenditures out of the central government's supervision). Adding all the government expenditures up, the size of government at each level in China may not be small at all.

Interestingly, government expenditures on science and technology is significantly positively related to the per capita GDP growth [see regressions (3)–(7) in Table 12.4]. That is to say, a city government that spent more on science and technology experienced a faster rate of economic growth. The reason is simple. Technological progress can overcome the diminishing returns to capital and maintain sustainable growth of per capita output growth. Our result indicates that allocation of government expenditures matters.

There was no convergence in per capita GDP among Chinese cities during the period under study. In regressions (6)–(7), the coefficient of the initial GDP is negative but insignificant. This should not be a surprise. When an economy starts to take off, some regions will first adopt new technologies and grow faster than other regions. Thus, there will be divergence in per capita output in the beginning. After a period of time, when the technology is available to all regions, the other regions may catch up, and convergence in per capita output may occur. Government policies may narrow the gap between the rich and the poor cities.

The dummy variable, *coast,* in our regressions is indeed positively related to the growth rate of per capita GDP in regressions (5) and (6). The east and south coast cities have benefited more from the open-door policies. For example, the earlier special economic zones, such as Shenzhen that is nearby Hong Kong, are all on the east and south coast. These special economic zones introduced market mechanisms earlier than the other areas and have enjoyed low tax rates and have privilege to trade with foreign countries and accept foreign investment that other areas did not have. Its coefficient becomes statistically insignificant ($t = 1.59$) in regression (7) as the illiteracy rate variable is included. The coast cities generally have higher education level than the inland cities.

When the education variable, *illit,* is introduced, the sample size is reduced to only 145 because many cities do not have the data available. Recall that *illit* stands for the illiteracy rate of people 15 or older. The coefficient of the illiteracy ratio is negatively related to the growth rate of per capita output, but is not statistically significant. Many studies have shown that human capital is important for economic growth [Schultz (1961) and Lucas (1988)]. Lin (2000) shows that the illiteracy rate of employees is negatively related to per capita GDP growth based on provincial data from 1978 to 1994. Further efforts need to be made to find better approximation of human capital accumulation on the city level.

5   Conclusions

In this chapter, we have examined China's urban economic growth using the data from 190 large- and medium-size Chinese cities for the period of 1991–98. Cross-section analyses indicated that foreign investment, infrastructure, government spending on science and technology were positively related to per capita GDP growth, while the size of government (i.e., total government spending share in GDP) is negatively related to per capita GDP growth. These results suggest that government at every level should make more efforts to attract foreign direct investment, speed up infrastructure development, and utilize the limited government revenues more efficiently. Meanwhile the relationship between total investment and the growth rate of per capita GDP appears insignificant, indicating that the allocation of investment of investment might matter for economic growth. To increase the rate of economic growth, the government should encourage and facilitate private investment. In addition, we found no significant evidence that poor cities grew faster than rich cities, indicating that the gap of per capita GDP between the rich and the poor cities had not narrowed in the period 1991–98. Persistent income disparity among cities is not consistent with the government's policy of poverty reduction and it may also cause political instability. Thus, policies stimulating the economic growth in low-income cities appear to be desirable economically and politically.

References

Ashauer, D. (1989), 'Is Public Expenditure Productive?,' *Journal of Monetary Economics*, 23, pp. 177–200.

Barro, R. (1990), 'Government Spending in a Simple Model of Endogenous Growth,' *Journal of Political Economy*, 98, pp. 103–25.

Borensztein, E., de Gregorio, J. and Lee, J.-W. (1998), 'How Does Foreign Direct Investment Affect Economic Growth?' *Journal of International Economics*, 45, pp. 115–35.

Canning, D., Fay, M. and Perotti, R. (1994), 'Infrastructure and Growth,' in Baldassarri, M., Paganetto, L. and Phelps, E. (eds), *International Differences in Growth Rates*, New York: Macmillan Press, pp. 113–47.

Chow, G.C. (1993), 'Capital Formation and Economic Growth in China,' *Quarterly Journal of Economics*, 108, pp. 809–42.

Easterly, W. and Rebelo, S. (1993), 'Fiscal Policy and Economic Growth: An Empirical Investigation,' *Journal of Monetary Economic*, 32, pp. 417–58.

Edwards, S. (1992), 'Trade Orientation, Distortions, and Growth in Developing Countries,' *Journal of Development Economics*, 39, pp. 31–57.

Edwards, S. (1993), 'Openness, Trade Liberalization, and Growth in Developing Countries,' *Journal of Economic Literature*, 26, pp. 1358–93.

Eisner, R. (1991), 'Infrastructure and Regional Economic Performance: Comment,' *New England Economic Review*, September/October.

Fan, C. (1999), 'The Vertical and Horizontal Expansions of China's City System', *Urban Geography*, 20 (6), pp. 493–515.

Johnson, D.G. (1993), 'Can There be Too Much Human Capital--is There a World Population Problem?,'in Asefa, S. and Huang, W.-C. (eds), *Human Capital and Economic Development*, Kalamazoo, MI: W.E. Upjohn Institute for Employment Research, pp. 35–61.

Kormendi, R.C. and Maguire, P.G. (1985), 'Macroeconomic Determinants of Growth: Cross-country Evidence,' *Journal of Monetary Economics*, 16, pp. 141–63.

King, R.G. and Rebelo, S. (1990), 'Public Policy and Economic Growth: Developing Neoclassical Implications,' *Journal of Political Economy*, 98, pp. 126–51.

Landau, D. (1983), 'Government Expenditure and Economic Growth: A Cross-country Study,' *Southern Economic Journal*, 49, pp. 783–92.

Landau, D. (1986), 'Government and Economic Growth in the Less Developed Countries: An Empirical Study for 1960–1980,' *Economic Development and Cultural Change*, October, pp. 34–75.

Levine, R. and Renelt, D. (1992), 'A Sensitivity Analysis of Cross-country Growth Regressions,' *American Economic Review*, 84, pp. 942–63.

Lin, S. (2000), 'Resource Allocation and Economic Growth in China,' *Economic Inquiry*, 38, pp. 515–26.

Lucas, R.E. (1988), 'On the Mechanics of Economic Development,' *Journal of Monetary Economics*, 22, pp. 3–42.

Munnell, A.H. (1990), 'How Does Public Infrastructure Affect Regional Economic Performance?' *New England Economic Review*, September/October.

National Bureau of Statistics of the PRC (NBS), *Statistical Yearbook of China*, various issues, Beijing: China Statistics Press.

National Bureau of Statistics of the PRC (NBS) (1997), *China Regional Economy: A Profile of 17 Years of Reform and Opening-up*, Beijing: China Statistics Press.

National Bureau of Statistics of the PRC (NBS) (1992–99), *Urban Statistical Yearbook of China*, Beijing: China Statistics Press.

Perkins, D.H., Radelet, S., Snodgrass, D.R., Gillis, M. and Roemer, M. (2001), *Economics of Development*, 5th edn, New York: W.W. Norton and Company, Inc.

Rebelo, S. (1991), 'Long-run Policy Analysis and Long-Run Growth,' *Journal of Political Economy*, 99, pp. 500–21.

Romer, P.M. (1986), 'Increasing Returns and Long-run Growth,' *Journal of Political Economy*, 94, pp. 1002–37.

Romer, P.M. (1990), 'Capital, Labor, and Productivity,' *Brookings Papers on Economic Activity: Microeconomics*, pp. 337–67.

Song, F. and Timberlake, M. (1996), 'Chinese Urbanization, State Policy, and the World Economy,' *Journal of Urban Affairs*, 18 (3), pp. 285–306.

Wacziarg, R. (1998), 'Measuring the Dynamic Gains from Trade,' *World Bank Policy Research Working Paper*, No. 2001.

White, H. (1980), 'A Heteroskedasticity Consistent Covariance Matrix Estimator and a Direct Test of Heteroscedaticity,' *Econometrica*, 48, pp. 817–38.

CHAPTER 13

AGGLOMERATION ECONOMICS IN CHINESE CITIES: AN EMPIRICAL STUDY

ZUOHONG PAN*
Western Connecticut State University

FAN ZHANG*
Peking University

Abstract

In this chapter, we have tried to identify possible agglomeration economies in Chinese urban areas. Over 120,000 firm-level production data cross 28 industries from the Third National Industrial Survey, along with the urban population data of 200 cities were used. The results revealed strong and significant agglomeration economies in Chinese urban areas. The estimated average agglomeration elasticity is around 0.051, implying a 3.6 per cent gain in firm productivity for every doubling of the city size. The breakdown analysis suggests that the major source of the agglomeration advantage comes from localization effect – benefits from concentration of firms of the same industry within one geographical area, rather than urbanization effect – externalities from urban development itself. The Maximum size study also suggests that, while most of the Chinese cities have yet to grow to demonstrate the full strength of agglomeration economies, many Chinese industries have reached the 'optimal' industry size within a 'given' urban area.

Keywords: Agglomeration elasticity, localization economies, urbanization, and urban productivity

JEL classification: R10

*   Correspondence: Zuohong Pan, Associate Professor of Economics, Western Connecticut State University, Danbury, CT 06810. Email: panz@wcsu.edu. Fan Zhang, Associate Professor of Economics, Beijing University. Email: zhangfan2001@yahoo.com.

We are grateful to Professor Ken Small and referees of this book.

URBAN TRANSFORMATION IN CHINA, edited by Aimin Chen, Gordon G. Liu and Kevin H. Zhang

1   Introduction

China is in a process of fast urbanization. Further reform could free hundreds of millions rural labors and pour them into the urban area at a much faster speed. How fast is the optimal speed of urbanization in China? The real constraint is the capacity with which the cities can absorb this large labor supply from rural areas in a very short period. And this capacity is in turn determined by the cities' ability to produce efficiently.

Agglomeration, the clustering of economic activity, is a powerful force in daily economic life. With agglomeration economies, certain types of economic activities are more productive undertaken in urban areas. Economists have modeled this urban productivity as a technological relationship – a region's production function.

Most of empirical studies of agglomeration focused on city size as determinants of productivity. For US cities, Sveikauskas (1975) and Segal (1976) estimated a 5–6 per cent increase in industrial productivity with every doubling of urban size. In the developing country context, Shukla (1996) estimated an average of 9 per cent increase in productivity for each doubling of city size using Indian data.

Studies that followed focused on distinguishing two separate types of agglomeration economies, namely urbanization and localization. Urbanization economies are related to the general availability of infrastructure, labor and wholesale operations, while localization economies are associated with the availability of infrastructure, labor and facilities specific to a particular industry. Nakamura (1985) explicitly separated urbanization and localization effects using cross sectional data of Japanese cities and showed that light industries receive more productive advantages from urbanization but heavy industries experience these economies more from localization. Using cross-sectional data for the US and Brazil, Henderson (1986) concluded that agglomeration economies are based on localization, not urbanization. But later studies showed different results. Moomaw (1988) used US data and labor-demand equations and found evidence of both localization and urbanization economies. Sveikauskas et al. (1988) found that when the presence of nearby resources and regional differences are accounted for, there is no support for localization effects in the US food processing industry. Using US SMSA (Standard Metropolitan Statistical Areas) average levels of education and work experience as proxies for human capital, Rauch (1993) showed that cities with higher average human capital had higher wages and land rents. Ciccone and Hall (1996) estimated two spatial density models and found that a doubling of employment density increases average labor productivity by around 6 per cent. Using an inverse input demand function and plant-level data, a more recent study by Feser (2001) found urbanization economies in moderate-to-low-technology farm and garden machinery sector and localization economies in high technology measuring and controlling devices sector. Henderson et al. (2001) tried to separate urbanization and localization effects using Korea data in a period of rapid industry deconcentration. They found significant static localization economies in every industry and strong static urbanization economies in the high-tech industry.

The purpose of this chapter is to find out the source of urban productivity in China. We test the relationship of urban productivity and city size and explore the source of urban agglomeration, using flexible production functions and firm level data cross 28 industries in China. China is a large, fast developing country, changing from a command to a market economy and from a rural to an urban society. Using Chinese firm level data enriches the existing literature of empirical studies of urban productivity.

The chapter is organized as follows. Section 2 discusses the data used in our analysis. In section 3, we use major cities' firm level data to construct constant-elasticity urban production functions for different industries. Then in section 4 we analyze the sources of agglomeration economies and the contribution of localization vs. urbanization to economic growth. Section 5 develops a variable-elasticity model to analyze the optimal size of urban areas in China. Section 6 gives our conclusions and policy implications.

2   Data

Our study is carried out on an industry-wide basis with firm-level data. The firm level data are from the Third National Industrial Survey (1995) of China done by the State Statistical Bureau of China. The sample of the Survey is 750,000 firms[1] all over China, covering 39 two-digit industries, about 200 three-digit industries, and over 500 four-digit industries. We selected firm-level data of 28 industries relevant to the problem of city productivity for 224 major cities.[2] Table 13.1 provides some descriptive statistics on the size,

---

1   Due to the availability of particular cities' urban population size, selective industry types and missing data in the total sales, number of employees or fixed capital, the final size of sample used in the estimation is 119,790.
2   We dropped industries that are not located in central cities by their nature, e.g., mining.

ownership, and location of the sampled firms, along with the size composition of the sampled cities.

The firm level data are used in conjunction with corresponding regional data, e.g., the city's urban population. The city level data are from 1997 Chinese City Population Table compiled by the China Population Information and Research Center, a division of the State Family Planning Committee of China.

3   Constant Elasticity Estimates

3.1 Models

This section describes the models used in our empirical estimation of urban productivity for China using firm level data. The estimation is conducted of specific variants of the general urban production function:

$$Q = G(N)F(L,K)$$ Eq. (1)

where F(L,K) is a constant returns to scale production function with L and K denoting labor and capital, respectively. G(N) is a shift function with N standing for city size (proxied in our study by its urban population). The output level Q is proxied, due to the data availability, by total sales, L by the number of employees, and K by the net value of the firms' fixed assets.

The specification of the agglomeration factor G(N) is

$$G(N) = BN^b$$ Eq. (2)

where b is the constant agglomeration elasticity.

In natural logarithmic terms, equation (2) becomes

$$\ln G(N) = \ln B + b \ln N$$ Eq. (3)

F(L,K) is the internal production function that is assumed to be common to all firms in an industry, regardless of location. Although there could be different specifications for F(L,K), we will focus on one of the trans-log flexible function formulations used by Henderson (1986).[3] Combining with agglomeration factor specification, our estimated equation becomes

---

3   In actual estimation, we tried different specifications for F(L,K). The results are very
     similar.

Table 13.1a Summary statistics of size, ownership, and location of the sampled firms

	Number of firms	%
Total	119,790	100.0
By ownership		
State-owned	22,974	19.2
Collective-owned	79,211	66.1
Foreign funded (including Hong Kong, Macao and Taiwan)	14,541	12.1
Shareholding	2,628	2.2
Private	436	0.4
By Size[a]		
Large	10,859	9.1
Medium	29,855	24.9
Small	79,076	66.0
By Location[b]		
East	79,002	66.0
Central	25,722	21.5
West	15,066	12.6

Notes:

a Firm size is classified according to the following employee criteria: large: ≥ 500; medium: 100 to 499; small: < 100. This classification serves only for descriptive purpose. The Chinese official classification system for enterprise size has been changed four times since 1950. The current system is very complicated, with 15 different standards based on types of the industry. A new system proposal is again under serious consideration, based on sales value and size of fixed capital.

b East provinces include Heilonhjiang, Jilin, Liaoning, Beijing, Tianjin, Hebei, Shandong, Jiangsu, Shanghai, Zhejiang, Fujian, Guangdong, Guangxi, and Hainan. Central provinces include Henan, Hubei, Hunan, Shanxi, Anhui, and Jiangxi. West provinces include Neimenggu, Ningxia, Shaanxi, Gansu, Qinghai, Xinjiang, Chongqing, Sichuan, Guizhou, Yunnan, and Xizang.

$$\ln (Q/L) = \ln A + b \ln N + a \ln(K/L) + (\beta/2)[\ln (K/L)]^2 \qquad \text{Eq. (4)}$$

where A, b, a and β are parameters.

In the actual estimation, we also inserted two dummy variables in Eq. (4) to control for other important external influences. An ownership dummy is added to differentiate the impacts of different ownership on the firm's performance. Typically, a state-owned firm is expected to perform less efficiently than other

Table 13.1b Summary statistics of the size of the sampled cities

City classification	Population	Number	%
Super-large	≥2,000,000	17	7.6
Particularly large	1,000,000–1,999,999	65	29.0
Large	500,000–999,999	76	33.9
Medium	200,000–499,999	62	27.7
Small	<200,000	4	1.8
Total		224	100

firms, while a firm related to investment from an overseas source tends to be more efficient. A regional dummy is added to account for the geographic superiority of the firms located in the eastern and coastal region of China.

3.2 Results

In the context of above model specification, we are most interested in the agglomeration effect as measured by parameter b. Table 13.2 reports the results of ordinary least-squares estimation of equation (4) for each of the 28 industries. The meaning of the industry codes is given in Appendix Table 13.A1.

We see strong evidence of agglomeration effects. In 19 of the 28 industries, the estimated parameter b is statistically significant. The result is almost the same with ownership and regional dummy variables added to the estimation (18 industries are significant). Without the dummy variables, the estimated parameters range from 0.028 in Special Equipment Manufacturing (code 36) to 0.188 in Petroleum Processing and Refining (code 25).

In the last row of the table, we show the results of combining the data across all industries. The estimated value of b is 0.060, serving as a reasonable overall measure of agglomeration elasticity. Adding ownership and regional dummies slightly lowers the overall agglomeration elasticity to 0.051. These figures are comparable with US studies: for example, 0.08 in Segal (1976) and 0.06 in Sveikauskas (1975) in the US urban context, and with 0.09 found by Shukla (1996) using Indian data. The elasticity of 0.051 means that if city size doubles, the expected increase in productivity is 3.6 per cent.[4]

It is interesting to observe the overwhelmingly significant impact of the dummy variables. The signs of their value categories also confirmed our hypothesized relationship. The state-owned enterprises tend to lag behind

---

4   Since $(2^{0.051}-1) = 0.036$.

the base firms (collective-owned enterprises) in productivity, while private firms, share-holding corporations and foreign funded enterprises (including enterprises with funds from Hong Kong, Macao and Taiwan), whether in the form of joint-venture, cooperation or whole-ownership, all tend to exceed the performance of the collective-owned firms. Geographically, firms in the eastern and coastal regions showed their natural advantage over firms in other regions, while firms in the west are the least privileged.

It should be noted that where the estimated parameter *b* is negative in sign, it is rarely significant. As a matter of fact, there are only two such cases where that happened — Industries 13 (Food Processing) and 22 (Paper and Paper Products).

4   Localization vs Urbanization

If there are agglomeration economies in urban development, are they due to the sheer size of the city or the concentration of a given industry? This section tries to identify these two separate sources of agglomeration economies in Chinese urban areas.

The localization hypothesis assumes that firms derive benefit principally from spatial proximity to other firms in the same industry, while the urbanization hypothesis consider the specialized system of cities as the main source of agglomeration advantage. To test these hypotheses, we used a revised version of the agglomeration specification employed by Henderson (1986) and Shukla (1996). The agglomeration specification was introduced by

$$G(S,N) = S^a N^b \qquad \text{Eq. (5)}$$

where, N is the urbanization variable, measured by urban population, while S is the localization variable, measured by total district industry sales. Both urbanization and localization elasticities *b* and *a* are assumed to be constant.

Taking logarithms of equation (5) and inserting it and our specification of F(L,K) into (1), we get our estimating equations as

$$\ln (Q/L) = \ln A + a \ln S + b \ln N + a \ln (K/L) + (\beta/2)[\ln (K/L)]^a \qquad \text{Eq. (6)}$$

The estimated regressions for each of the 28 industries are summarized in Table 13.3. It is clear that the general pattern is a stronger and more persistent

Table 13.2 Agglomeration elasticity estimates: constant elasticity

| Code | Without dummies | | With dummies | | | | | | | |
	b	R^2	b	State	Private	Share-holding	Foreign	West	East	R^2
13	0.008	0.140	−0.015	−**	+**	+*	+***	−**	+	0.162
14	0.099**	0.126	0.079**	−**	−	−	+	+	+**	0.156
15	0.027	0.182	0.027	−**	+*	+	−	−	+	0.190
16	0.139	0.470	0.158	+	+	−	+	−	−	0.478
17	0.033***	0.195	0.046**	−**	+*	+*	+***	−**	+***	0.238
18	0.128***	0.157	0.129***	−**	+***	+***	+***	−**	+***	0.204
19	0.026	0.084	0.015	−**	+	+	+***	−**	+***	0.148
20	0.052*	0.093	0.071**	−**	+***	−	+	−**	+*	0.120
21	0.135***	0.098	0.123**	−**	+***	+	+***	−**	+***	0.118
22	0.004	0.218	−0.002	−**	+***	+***	+***	−	+***	0.246
23	0.085***	0.257	0.081**	−**	+***	+***	+	−*	+***	0.274
24	0.039	0.150	0.035	−	+*	+***	+***	−**	+	0.191
25	0.188***	0.228	0.201**	−	+	+	−	−*	−	0.239
26	0.084***	0.184	0.069***	−**	+	+***	+	−**	+***	0.200
27	0.154***	0.162	0.136***	+	−	+	+***	+	+***	0.182
28	0.039	0.307	0.020	−	+	+	+***	+	+***	0.361
29	0.071**	0.199	0.064**	−*	−	+	+***	−	+**	0.216
30	0.063***	0.196	0.054**	−	+**	+***	+***	−	+***	0.212
31	0.042**	0.168	0.052**	−**	+	+	+***	−**	+*	0.191
32	0.105***	0.187	0.104***	−**	+***	+	+	−**	−	0.197
33	0.018	0.188	0.021	−**	+	+***	+***	−**	−	0.223
34	0.006	0.154	0.005	−**	+***	+***	+***	−**	+***	0.169

Table 13.2 cont'd

| Code | Without dummies | | With dummies | | | | | | |
	b	R^2	b	State	Private	Share-holding	Foreign	West	East	R^2
35	0.047**	0.134	0.035**	–**	+**	+**	+**	–**	+**	0.165
36	0.028*	0.118	0.008	–**	+*	+**	+**	–**	+**	0.161
37	0.094**	0.175	0.069**	–**	+*	+**	+**	–**	+**	0.202
40	0.037*	0.174	0.033**	–**	+**	+**	+**	–**	+**	0.197
41	0.083**	0.162	0.086***	–**	+**	+**	+**	+	+**	0.241
42	0.070**	0.097	0.068***	–**	+**	+**	+**	–	+**	0.173
Combined	0.060**	0.175	0.051**	–**	+**	+**	+**	–**	+**	0.197

Note: * indicates significant at 5% level, ** indicates significant at 1% level. Ownership dummy includes five categories: state-owned, collective-owned, private, shareholding corporation and foreign funded (including funds from Hong Kong, Macao and Taiwan); Regional dummy has three categories: east, west and central region.

influence from localization than from urbanization. This is evidenced by the larger estimates and more frequent positive signs for a as compared to b. Only six of the 28 industries are exceptions to this general pattern. They are industries 13 (Food Processing), 20 (Wooden Products), 21 (Furniture), 25 (Petroleum Refining), 31 (Non-Metal Raw Materials) and 32 (Ferrous Metal Metallurgical).

In contrast to Shukla's (1996) findings in the Indian context, then, our findings suggest that the strong agglomeration economies found in China are mainly due to positive externalities realized by firms from others in the same local industry. It may be that urban expansion in China has not reached the point where the business can benefit from the scope economies arising from the clustering of firms across different business lines and from public services like highways, mass transit, schools, and fire protection.

It is informative to see how incorporating localization effect into estimation has changed the result of the agglomeration effect estimation. First, each of the 28 industries now shows a significant agglomeration effect *either* of urbanization or localization, although in many cases it is of the unexpected sign. Second, in many cases where the total agglomeration elasticity based solely on population N is significant (Table 13.2), the corresponding urbanization elasticity (which uses the same population variable) is either insignificant or negative while the corresponding localization elasticity is strongly significant and positive. Furthermore, almost all the significant agglomeration elasticities in Table 13.2 are close in size to the sum of the two corresponding elasticities in Table 13.3. This confirms the reasoning that the agglomeration effect is broken into two components, as intended, and that the dominant impact comes from localization.

5   Variable Elasticity and Maximum Size

The specification of the agglomeration function in the previous section assumes constant agglomeration elasticities a and b, which means that the agglomeration effect increases with city size at a constant rate.

However, the previous research literature suggested that there may be some optimal urban size beyond which economies of scale are exhausted and urban productivity stops increasing, or even declines. In light of the estimated results and observations in the last section, this section examines the optimal size for the industry within a city, by modifying Shukla's (1996) specification and hypothesizing a relationship with a maximum. By studying the issue of

Table 13.3 Localization vs urbanization: estimates

Code	a	b	State	Private	Share-holding	Foreign	West	East	R^2
13	-0.004**	-0.011	-**	+**	+**	+**	-**	-	0.162
14	0.115**	-0.054**	-**	-	-	+	+**	+**	0.168
15	0.072**	-0.052	-**	+*	+	-	+	+*	0.195
16	0.210**	-0.017	+	+	-	+	+	-	0.494
17	0.190**	-0.088**	-**	+**	+**	+**	-	+**	0.268
18	0.170**	-0.023	-**	+*	+**	+**	-	+**	0.226
19	0.159**	-0.088**	-**	+	-	+*	-	+**	0.181
20	0.001	0.070**	-**	+**	-	+	-*	+**	0.120
21	0.011	0.108**	-**	+**	+	+**	-*	+**	0.118
22	0.082**	-0.075**	-**	+**	+**	+**	+	+**	0.253
23	0.167**	-0.133**	-**	+**	+**	+	+	+**	0.296
24	0.078**	-0.058**	-	+*	+*	+**	-	+	0.201
25	0.002	0.199**	-	+	+	-	-**	-	0.239
26	0.104**	-0.044**	-**	+	+**	+	-**	+**	0.208
27	0.114**	-0.021	-	-	+	+**	+	+**	0.193
28	0.139**	-0.059	-	+	+	+**	+	+	0.411
29	0.110**	-0.074**	-**	-	+	+**	-	+	0.234
30	0.126**	-0.056**	-	+**	+*	+**	+	+**	0.224
31	-0.007	0.059**	-**	+	+	+**	-**	+*	0.191
32	-0.003	0.107**	-**	+**	+	+	-**	-	0.197
33	0.627**	-0.045	-**	+	+**	+**	-**	+	0.230
34	0.107**	-0.121**	-**	+**	+**	+**	-	+**	0.174
35	0.114**	-0.116**	-**	+**	+**	+**	-**	+**	0.173
36	0.091**	-0.102**	-**	+**	+**	+**	-	+**	0.166
37	0.067**	-0.039*	-**	+**	+**	+**	-**	+**	0.207
40	0.152**	-0.149**	-**	+**	+**	+**	-	+**	0.214
41	0.143**	-0.062**	-**	+**	+**	+**	+	+**	0.266
42	0.160**	-0.141**	-**	+**	+*	+**	-	+**	0.193

Note: * indicates significant at 5% level, ** indicates significant at 1% level. Ownership dummy includes five categories: state-owned, collective-owned, private, shareholding corporation and foreign funded (including funds from Hong Kong, Macao and Taiwan); Regional dummy has three categories: east, west and central region.

optimal size, we could shed some light on the question whether some of the existing big cities are actually too big, so that they are demonstrating satiated productivity growth or even a decline.

The production function in section 3 is specified in terms of labor productivity. The same specification will be applied here in discussing the issue of optimality. The advantage of that specification over quantity of output (or sale value) is that we could just focus on the impacts of urban expansion on productivity without explicitly formulating the cost effects in our optimality estimation.

5.1 Alternative Modeling for Agglomeration

We use an alternative agglomeration specification in this section to examine the possible optimal size of urban area in China. We first tried a specification with both optimal urbanization and localization effects, but the urbanization effect turns out to be minima in most cases. Since we cannot provide a convincing theoretical explanation of this result without further research, we focus on the variable elasticity just with respect to localization by exploring the following agglomeration specification:

$$G(N) = CS^{a_1 + a_2(\ln S)} N^{b_1}$$ Eq. (7)

Rewrite equation (7) in natural logarithmic terms, we have

$$\ln G(N,S) = \ln C + a_1 \ln S + a_2 (\ln S) + b \ln N$$ Eq. (8)

Where C, a_1, a_2 and b are parameters. The localization elasticity, is the partial derivative of $\ln G$ with respect to $\ln S$ is $a_1 + 2a_2(\ln S)$.

The optimal industry size of the city can be derived by taking the first-order partial derivative of $\ln G$ with respect to industry size S to zero, which gives

$$\ln S = \frac{-a_1}{2a_2} \qquad \text{or} \qquad S = e^{\frac{-a_1}{2a_2}}$$ Eq. (9)

Equation (9) indicates the technologically optimal industry size of an urban area, while holding population size fixed.

5.2 Results

The estimation results are reported in Table 13.4. Although the function $\ln G$ does not have a maximum in all dimensions, it is possible to examine the relationship between productivity and localization for the industries that did register a maximum. There are many industries that did show a significant possibility of the reversal of productivity gain along the localization dimension: 14 of the industries registered positive value for a_1 and negative value for a_2, among which ten are significant.

For all the ten industries that demonstrated significant possibility of an 'optimal' size, we plotted in Figures 13.1 and 13.2 ln$G$ as a function of within-city industry size S. The optimal within-city industry size is computed according to Eq. (9) by using the estimated parameters from Table 13.4. The square marks indicate estimated 'optimal' size in that industry, while triangle represents the sample mean of the represented industry class.

Of the ten significant industries reported in Figures 13.1 and 13.2, eight show their within-city industry averages as having exceeded the 'optimal' size. These are food processing, wooden products, furniture, paper and paper products, petroleum refining, non-metal raw materials, ferrous metal metallurgical, and non-ferrous metal metallurgical. The other two, whose size has yet to exhaust the localization economies, are leather products, and pharmaceutical. It seems that many Chinese industries may have reached the 'optimal' industry size within a 'given' urban area.

6   Conclusion

In this chapter, we tested the relationship of Chinese urban productivity and city size. Using over 119,790 firm-level production data cross 28 industries along with the urban population data of 224 cities, we find strong and prevailing significant agglomeration economies in Chinese urban area. The estimated average agglomeration elasticity is around 0.051, implying that every doubling of city size will provide 3.6 per cent gain in firm productivity. The breakdown analysis suggests that, in the current period, the major source of the agglomeration advantage comes from localization economies – i.e. benefits from concentration of firms of the same industry within one geographical area – rather than urbanization economies, which are externalities from urban development itself. The results also suggest that, while most of the Chinese cities have yet to grow to demonstrate the full strength of agglomeration economies, many Chinese industries have reached the 'optimal' industry size within a 'given' urban area.

The results of this study should of course be taken carefully. Due to the sensitive nature of the estimation, using different proxy variables for the

Table 13.4 Variable elasticity estimates

Ind	a_1	a_2	b	State	Private	Share-holding	Foreign	West	East	R^2
13	1.226**	-0.046**	-0.026	-**	+***	+*	+**	-**	-	0.173
14	0.310**	-0.008	-0.040	-**	-	-	+	+*	+**	0.168
15	0.330**	-0.011	-0.038	-**	+*	+	-	+	+	0.196
16	0.072	0.006	-0.025	+			+	+	-	0.542
17	-0.369**	0.021**	-0.105**	-**	+***	+***	+***	-	+***	0.271
18	0.076	0.004	-0.028	-**	+**	+**	+***	-	+***	0.226
19	0.643**	-0.020**	-0.091**	-**	+	-	+	-	+***	0.185
20	0.846**	-0.038**	0.087**	-**	+***	-	+	-**	-**	0.133
21	0.628**	-0.030**	0.154**	-**	+***	+	+***	-**	+***	0.123
22	1.045**	-0.040**	-0.057**	-	+***	+***	+***	+	+***	0.260
23	0.011	0.007	-0.150**	-**	+**	+***	+	+	+***	0.296
24	0.196**	-0.006	-0.048	-	+**	+*	+**	-	+	0.202
25	0.337**	-0.014**	0.196**	-	+	+	-	-*	-	0.245
26	-0.038	0.005	-0.052**	-**	-	+	+	-*	+***	0.208
27	0.503**	-0.017**	0.040	-		+	+***	+	+***	0.197
28	0.075	0.003	-0.063	-		+	+***	+	+	0.412
29	0.220*	-0.005	-0.066*	-**	-	+	+***	+	+	0.235
30	-0.073	0.008	-0.062**	-	+***	+*	+***	+	+***	0.224
31	0.813**	-0.031**	0.057**	-**	+	+	+***	-**	+	0.196
32	0.423**	-0.017**	0.126**	-**	+***	+	+	-**	-	0.205
33	0.616**	-0.024**	-0.018	-**	+	+***	+***	-**	-	0.239
34	0.064	0.002	-0.125**	-**	+***	+***	+***	-	+***	0.174
35	-0.137	0.010**	-0.141**	-**	+***	+***	+***	-**	+***	0.174

Table 13.4 cont'd

Ind	a_1	a_2	b	State	Private	Share-holding	Foreign	West	East	R^2
36	-0.142	0.010**	-0.131**	-**	+*	+***	+***	-	+***	0.167
37	-0.040	0.004	-0.057**	-**	+***	+***	+***	-**	+***	0.207
40	-0.221**	0.014**	-0.179***	-**	+***	+***	+***	-	+***	0.216
41	0.066	0.003	-0.064***	-**	+***	+***	+***	+	+***	0.266
42	-0.093	0.011**	-0.180**	-**	+***	+*	+***	-	+***	0.195

Note: * indicates significant at 5% level, ** indicates significant at 1% level.

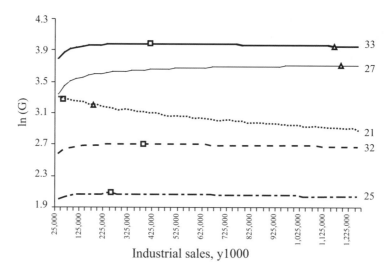

Note: The squares indicate estimated within-city maximum size in an industry; the triangles
       indicate actual average industry size. Maximum size in industry 27 and actual size in
       industry 32 and 25 are far beyond the right-hand border of the graph.

Figure 13.1   Maximum industry size (I)

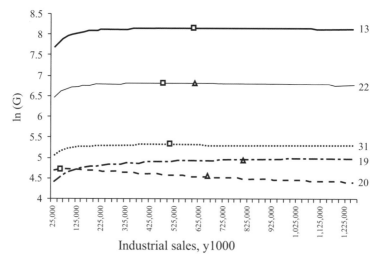

Note: The squares indicate estimated within-city maximum size in an industry; the triangles
       indicate actual average industry size. Maximum size in industry 19 and actual size in
       industry 13 and 31 are far beyond the right-hand border of the graph.

Figure 13.2   Maximum industry size (II)

models could very well change the estimation results. For example, instead of using industry sales as a measure of the 'localization' variable, one could use industry employment; instead of using urban population as the measure of 'urbanization' variable, one could also use population density, etc. Furthermore, using different specification for localization and urbanization effects may also alter the estimation results we derived here. It is our hope that further study on this topic will address these issues.

References

China Population Information and Research Center (2000), *1997 Chinese City Population Table*, available at: http://www.cpirc.org.cn/city97.htm.

Ciccone, A. and Hall, R.E. (1996), 'Productivity and the Density of Economic Activity,' *American Economic Review*, 86 (1), pp. 54–70.

Dixit, A.K. and Stiglitz, J.E. (1977), 'Monopolistic Competition and Optimum Product Diversity,' *American Economic Review*, 67 (3), pp. 297–308.

Feser E.J. (2001), 'A Flexible Test for Agglomeration Economies in Two US Manufacturing Industries,' *Regional Science and Urban Economics*, 31, pp. 1–19.

Fujita, M., Krugman, P. and Venables, A. (2000), *The Spatial Economy: Cities, Regions, and International Trade*, Cambridge, MA: MIT Press.

Grilliches, Z. and Ringstad, V. (1971), 'Economics of Scale and the Form of the Production Function,' in *Contributions to Economic Analysis Series*, Amsterdam: North-Holland Publishing Company.

Henderson, J.V. (1974), 'The Size and Types of Cities,' *American Economic Review*, 64, pp. 640–56.

Henderson, J.V. (1986), 'Efficiency of Resource Usage and City Size,' *Journal of Urban Economics*, 19, pp. 47–70.

Henderson, J.V., Lee, T. and Lee, Y.J. (2001), 'Scale Externalities in Korea,' *Journal of Urban Economics*, 49, pp. 479–504.

Marshall, A. (1920), *Principles of Economics*, MacMillan, London.

Moomaw, R.L. (1920), 'Agglomeration Economies: Localization or Urbanization?,' *Urban Studies*, 19, 25, pp. 150–61.

Nakamura, R. (1985), 'Agglomeration Economies in Urban Manufacturing Industries, A Case of Japanese Cities,' *Journal of Urban Economics*, 17, pp. 108–24.

Pan, Z. and Zhang, F. (2002), 'Urban Productivity in China,' *Urban Studies*, 39 (12), pp. 2267–81.

Rauch, J.E (1993)., 'Productivity Gains from Geographic Concentration of Human Capital: Evidence from the Cities,' *Journal of Urban Economics*, 34, pp. 380–400.

Segal, D. (1976), 'Are There Returns to Scale in City Size?,' *The Review of Economics and Statistics*, 58, pp. 339–50.

Shukla, V. (1988), *Urban Development and Regional Policy in India–An Econometric Analysis*, Bombay: Himalaya Publishing House.

Shukla, V. (1996), *Urbanization and Economic Growth*, Delhi: Oxford University Press.

State Statistical Bureau of China (1995), *The Third National Industrial Survey*, Beijing: State Statistical Bureau Press.

Sveikauskas, L. (1975), 'The Productivity of Cities,' *Quarterly Journal of Economics*, 89, pp. 393–413.

Sveikauskas, L., Gowdy, J. and Funk, M. (1988), 'Urban Productivity: City Size or Industry Size,' *Journal of Regional Science*, 28, pp. 185–202.

Appendix

Table 13.A1 Industry code, industry name, and number of observations

Code	Industry	Observation
13	Food processing	4853
14	Food making	3916
15	Beverage	2332
16	Tobacco processing	96
17	Textile	5955
18	Clothing and other fiber products	6159
19	Leather products	2862
20	Wooden products	3258
21	Furniture	2276
22	Paper and paper products	3396
23	Printing	5736
24	Education and sports products	1693
25	Petroleum refining	636
26	Chemical products	7300
27	Pharmaceutical	1699
28	Synthetic fiber	305
29	Rubber products	1495
30	Plastic products	5371
31	Non-metal raw materials	11222
32	Ferrous metal metallurgical	1698
33	Non-ferrous metal metallurgical	974
34	Metal products	9387
35	General machinery	10134
36	Special equipment	6017
37	Transportation equipment	6993
40	Electronic equipment	7584
41	Electronic telecommunication equipment	3774
42	Apparatus etc. manufacturing	2669

CHAPTER 14

HONG KONG: FROM ENTREPÔT TO MANUFACTURING AND THEN TO PRODUCER SERVICES

ZHIGANG TAO*
The University of Hong Kong

Y.C. RICHARD WONG
The University of Hong Kong

Abstract

In the past 50 years, Hong Kong's economy has undergone two major transformations, first from entrepôt to manufacturing during the period from 1951 to the late 1970s, and then from manufacturing to producer services since the late 1970s. In each case, the transformation was triggered by the change of Hong Kong's relations with Mainland China. The former transformation was due to the sudden and dramatic decrease in China trade following the United Nations trade embargo; and the latter was a response to the open-door policy adopted in Mainland China since the late 1970s. In this chapter, we first give a brief review of Hong Kong's transformation from entrepôt to manufacturing, and then offer an analysis of the recent transformation from manufacturing to producer services.

*   Correspondence: Zhigang Tao, Associate Professor of Economics and Strategy, The University of Hong Kong, Pokfulam Road, Hong Kong. Tel: 852–2857–8223; E-mail: ztao@hku.hk.

This chapter is based on a larger study entitled 'An Economic Study of Hong Kong's Producer Service Sector and its Role in Supporting Manufacturing,' which was generously supported by the Industrial Support Fund of the Hong Kong Special Administrative Government. We thank Michael Enright and participants in the 2001 CES meeting (Xiamen) and the 2001 WEA meeting (San Francisco) for comments and suggestions. We would also like to thank Chi Shing Chan, Yingjuan Du, and Jiangyong Lu for excellent research assistance.

URBAN TRANSFORMATION IN CHINA, edited by Aimin Chen, Gordon G. Liu and Kevin H. Zhang

Keywords: entrepôt, manufacturing, producer services, Hong Kong

JEL classification: F1, O1

1   Introduction

In the past 50 years, Hong Kong's economy has undergone two major transformations, first from entrepôt to manufacturing during the period from 1951 to the late 1970s, and then from manufacturing to producer services since the late 1970s. In each case, the transformation was triggered by the change of Hong Kong s relations with mainland China. The former transformation was due to the sudden and dramatic decrease in China trade following the United Nations trade embargo; and the latter was a response to the open-door policy adopted in mainland China since the late 1970s.

In this chapter, we first give a brief review of Hong Kong s transformation from entrepôt to manufacturing, and then offer an analysis of the recent transformation from manufacturing to producer services.

2   Transformation from Entrepôt to Manufacturing

Since the beginning of British rule in 1843, Hong Kong had been an important entrepôt for trade, mostly British trade, with China. Situated in the outer estuary of the Pearl River, Hong Kong is close to Canton, which for centuries had been China's most important port for trade with Nanyang as well as with India, Africa, and the Western nations. Hong Kong's entrepôt economy was, however, severely damaged during the Japanese occupation from the late 1930s to 1945. The complex network of external economic relations was disrupted. Meanwhile, many of the entrepreneurs, technicians, and skilled workers essential for the entrepôt economy were either dead or scattered in other parts of China. Despite the harsh conditions, Hong Kong quickly restored its role of entrepôt after the Japanese surrender in 1945, through the establishment, reestablishment, and expansion of both British-owned and Chinese-owned trading houses, insurance companies, shipping companies, and banks. Total exports leaped from HK$ 766 million in 1946 to HK$ 4,433 million in 1951. Total imports increased from HK$ 933 million in 1946 to HK$ 4,870 million in 1951 (see Table 14.1).

Hong Kong's postwar recovery was dealt a mortal blow in mid-1951, when China entered the Korean War and the United Nations subsequently imposed a trade embargo on China. As a result, Hong Kong's role as an entrepôt for Chinese trade was abruptly terminated. As shown in Table 14.1, total exports to China dropped from HK$ 1,604 million in 1951 to HK$ 520 million in 1952. Another major event shaping the Hong Kong economy was the return of former residents after the Japanese surrender in 1945 and the huge influx of refugees from mainland China after the victory of the Chinese Communist Party in 1949. As shown in Table 14.2, Hong Kong's population grew from 600,000 in August 1945 to 1.75 million in mid-1947 and then to 2.26 million in mid-1950.

With the loss of Chinese trade, Hong Kong turned to develop its manufacturing industries. The prime movers of the industrialization process were emigrant entrepreneurs from Shanghai, who brought not only capital but also technical and managerial know-how (Wong, 1988). Before the Japanese War, Shanghai had been the industrial center of China. Shortly after the Japanese surrender, Shanghai industrialists ordered a substantial amount of machinery from overseas to rebuild industry in Shanghai. However, by the time the machinery was ready for delivery, the political and economic situation in mainland China had become uncertain, and many Shanghai businessmen decided to offload and store their machinery in Hong Kong. Other Shanghai businessmen were able to move their machinery from Shanghai to Hong Kong before the victory of the Chinese Communist Party. Once in Hong Kong, with the help of bank loans, Shanghai industrialists were able to rent or construct premises and get their businesses started.

Other factors also played important roles in Hong Kong's transformation from entrepôt to manufacturing. First, there had been a huge amount of flight capital entering Hong Kong in late 1940s, sent by refugees fleeing China and also by the Chinese communities throughout Nanyang. According to the estimates by Edward Szczepanik (1958), from 1947 to 1955, the annual injection of foreign capital was about 40 per cent of Hong Kong's national income. Such a large scale of capital injection into Hong Kong certainly helped its industrialization.

Second, the huge influx of refugees, mainly from the adjacent province of Guangdong and from Shanghai, boosted Hong Kong's average rate of population growth from a natural rate of about 3 per cent to an actual rate of 5 per cent over the entire postwar period. A profile of refugees in terms of their prior occupation is shown in Table 14.3. While there were substantial numbers of businessmen (5 per cent as opposed to 2 per cent in Hong Kong), and professionals and intellectuals (10 per cent as opposed to 3 per cent in Hong Kong), most of the refugees were unskilled laborers. Fortunately, there were Shanghai foremen and skilled workers that followed their employers

Table 14.1 Hong Kong's trade by major partners – region and country, 1946–52 (HK$ million)

Region and country		Total	Asia* China	Taiwan	Western Europe Total	United Kingdom	North America Total	United States	World total
1946	Imports	649	323		85	44	131	120	933
	Exports	630	305		32	17	85	84	766
1947	Imports	791	382		304	164	319	299	1,550
	Exports	833	267		129	38	155	152	1,217
1948	Imports	1,003	431		522	301	424	387	2,078
	Exports	1,179	280		138	75	160	152	1,583
1949	Imports	1,302	593		628	388	633	575	2,750
	Exports	1,715	585		222	140	249	234	2,319
1950	Imports	2,140	783	75	745	405	705	655	3,788
	Exports	2,894	1,260	201	342	168	319	309	3,716
1951	Imports	2,476	863	62	1,610	619	461	374	4,870
	Exports	3,646	1,604	139	381	215	179	163	4,433
1952	Imports	2,146	830	45	1,151	470	300	221	3,779
	Exports	2,398	520	207	225	83	133	113	2,899

* Includes Middle East.

Source: Hong Kong Statistics 1947–67 (Hong Kong: Census and Statistics Department, 1969), pp. 97–8, 212.

Table 14.2   Population: mid-year estimates, 1945–50

Mid-year of	Population
1945	600,000
1946	1,550,000
1947	1,750,000
1948	1,800,000
1949	1,857,000
1950	2,262,300

Source: Statistical Planning and Census Department, Department of Commerce and Industry, and Hong Kong Annual Reports.

Table 14.3   Occupations of Chinese refugees in Hong Kong

Occupation	% of immigrant population	
	In China	In Hong Kong
Housewives	33	25
Army and police	16	0
Professionals and intellectuals	10	3
Clerks and shop assistants	10	5
Farmers	10	2
Businessmen	5	2
Industrial laborers	3	13
Hawkers	2	7
Craftsmen	3	12
Coolies and servants	1	11
Others	5	5
Unemployed	2	15
Total	100	100

Source: Hambro (1955), *The Problem of Chinese Refugees in Hong Kong* (Leyden), Tables 29–31, pp. 168–70.

to Hong Kong and subsequently became the cadres for the new Hong Kong factories training the ready pool of unskilled labor.

Third, there existed a mechanism for marketing Hong Kong products overseas. Trading houses with far-reaching contacts overseas had long been established in Hong Kong and had been engaged in the entrepôt trade with China. With the UN enbargo, however, those trading houses turned to develop an alternative trade with local manufacturers. Meanwhile, the Department of Industry and Commerce was supportive in promoting Hong Kong products by arranging Hong Kong participation in various trade fairs and exhibitions in North America and western Europe (Hopkins, 1971).

Due to the combination of the above factors, Hong Kong quickly transformed itself from an entrepôt for China trade to a center of manufacturing industries. As revealed by the 1961 Census, the manufacturing industries employed 40 per cent of the total working population. Exports of locally produced goods had grown from a quarter of total exports in 1953 to about three-quarters in 1961, indicating a much smaller role of entrepôt trade. Gross domestic product data also shows that Hong Kong reversed its slowdown in growth due to the UN embargo and enjoyed spectacular growth in the late 1950s and early 1960s. GDP grew at a rate of 22.6 per cent for the period 1948–49, 5.3 per cent for the period 1950–54, 9.0 per cent for the period 1955–59, and 13.6 per cent for the period 1960–64 (Chou, 1966).

By the late 1960s, the growth of the manufacturing industries was so great that it created an increase in the demand for labor exceeding the increase in supply. Many industrialists were forced to defer their plans for expansion, while some even had difficulty maintaining their existing operations. This set the stage for the second transformation of Hong Kong's economy: from manufacturing to producer services.

3   Transformation from Manufacturing to Producer Services

3.1 Decline of Hong Kong's Manufacturing Industry Relative to its Service Industry

Table 14.4 summarizes the relative contribution of manufacturing and services to nominal GDP in selected years of the past two decades. The percentage share of nominal GDP contributed by services increased from 67.5 per cent in 1980 to an estimated 85.2 per cent in 1997, while the corresponding figure for manufacturing decreased substantially, from 23.7 per cent in 1980 to an estimated 6.5 per cent in 1997.

Similar findings are obtained when the relative contributions to real GDP are used. The percentage share of real GDP contributed by services increased from 74.1 per cent in 1980 to an estimated 83.6 per cent in 1997, while the corresponding figure for manufacturing decreased substantially, from 17.2 per cent in 1980 to 9.0 per cent in 1997.

Table 14.4   Percentage share of services and manufacturing in nominal GDP in selected years

	Services	Manufacturing
1980	67.5	23.7
1985	69.6	22.1
1990	74.5	17.6
1995	83.8	8.3
1996	84.4	7.3
1997*	85.2	6.5

*   1997 figures are our own preliminary estimates.

In the period 1980–97, the share of service sector employment in Hong Kong grew from 42.1 per cent to 79.3 per cent, while the share of manufacturing employment fell from 45.9 per cent to 9.8 per cent (see Table 14.5). A linear extrapolation of the employment trends for this period would imply that by the year 2004, all employment in Hong Kong would be in the service sector. These figures have led to the widespread perception that manufacturing in Hong Kong has declined, and created public concern that the decline of Hong Kong's manufacturing industry relative to the service industry may erode the city's competitiveness.

Table 14.5   Shares of service and manufacturing employment in selected years

	Services (%)	Manufacturing (%)
1980	42.1	45.9
1985	54.0	36.1
1990	62.7	27.8
1995	77.6	13.4
1996	78.8	11.2
1997	79.3	9.8

What has actually happened is that, in the past two decades, Hong Kong has transformed itself from an industrial city into a service hub dominated by producer services. In the late 1970s, when mainland China launched its economic reform and adopted an open-door policy, many Hong Kong manufacturing firms relocated their labor-intensive production processes and lower-value-added activities to the mainland to take advantage of the low production costs available there. However, higher-value-added business activities related to manufacturing – producer services – continued to take place in Hong Kong. The relocation of manufacturing out of Hong Kong is, of course, not limited to the Chinese hinterland; it occurs throughout Asia. The Chinese hinterland is nevertheless home to approximately two-thirds of such manufacturing activity that has been relocated from Hong Kong. It is important to note that such relocation is often accompanied by a manifold increase in the scale of operation, hence stimulating the growth of producer services (Sung, 1998).

3.2 Estimating Hong Kong's Producer Services

Measuring producer services is a challenging problem, because the classification of a service as a producer service or a consumer service is a function not of the service's physical attributes but of its economic purpose. For example, restaurant service is considered a producer service when used by a business executive on assignment. But it is considered a consumer service when used by a tourist on vacation. Thus, only the share of services bought by producers can properly be considered producer services.

We measure the level and growth of Hong Kong s producer services, using a technique first developed by Grubel and Walker (1989). Detailed descriptions of our method are available in Tao and Wong (2001). It is sufficient to provide a general description of the methodology adopted here with reference to Table 14.6, which applies the expenditure-based method for estimating GDP to the service sector. Note that the entries in the consumer services and producer services categories are identical in this classification scheme. This reflects the idea that the same type of service can be used either for final consumption or as embodied service in the production of other goods.

The GDP accounts of Hong Kong contain a consistent time series on the total size of the service-producing sector of the economy, as measured by its value added or GDP. *Consumer services output* refers to all those services used in final consumption. Data on the purchase of consumer services are available from consumer expenditure surveys. These data are reliable and consistent, since they serve as the raw data for the calculation of consumer price and expenditure statistics and contain very detailed records on hundreds of goods and services bought by consumers. Data on *government services output* are Census and Statistics Department estimates and are available from published GDP estimates.

Table 14.6   A goods and service industry taxonomy with service sector classified by use of expenditure

I   Goods-producing sector
Agriculture and fisheries
Mining and quarrying
Manufacturing
Construction
Utilities

II   Service-producing sector
1   Consumer services output
Imports/exports
Wholesale and retail trade
Transport, storage, and communications
Restaurants and hotels
Community and personal services
Finance, insurance, business services, and real estate
2   Producer services output
Imports/exports
Wholesale and retail trade
Transport, storage, and communications
Restaurants and hotels
Community and personal services
Finance, insurance, business services, and real estate
3   Government services output
Government services

We estimate *producer services output* by subtracting consumer and government services output from total service sector output. Producer services therefore contain the output of the industries producing intermediate inputs (e.g., 'business services,' 'wholesale services'). It is important to be aware that they also include as a residual the output of all those industries widely viewed as serving mainly consumers (e.g., restaurants, hotels, transportation). A large fraction of the output of these industries is used by business and government as input into the production of additional goods and services.

Note that many of the services produced by the government serve both consumers and business. Unfortunately, it is not possible to determine the relative magnitude of the two. By not allocating any of the government service output to the category of producer services, our procedure biases downward the estimate of the latter.

To assess the contribution of producer services to the economy, we further have to derive the real values of producer services. We first calculate the real value added of all economic activities (i.e., real GDP) and of the goods-producing sectors – agriculture and fisheries, mining and quarrying, manufacturing, construction, and utilities. We then calculate the real value added of total services by subtracting the real value added of the goods-producing sectors from the real value added of all economic activities. Finally, we obtain the real value of producer services by subtracting the real values of government services and consumer services from the real value added of total services. The price deflator of producer services is the ratio between the nominal value and real value of producer services.

3.3 Changing Patterns of Producer, Consumer, and Government Services

Figure 14.1 illustrates the size of the total service sector and its three components as percentages of real GDP for the years 1980–97. The top line shows the clear upward trend in the basic series. The figure indicates that in 1980 consumer and government services represented 26.8 per cent and 4.7 per cent, respectively, of GDP, while producer services held the largest share at 42.7 per cent. Since then, the share of government services increased to 5.8 per cent in 1997. Producer services trended upward, and by the end of the period had reached 50.0 per cent. Consumer services increased very modestly, to 27.8 per cent by 1997.

Figure 14.2 contrasts the changing pattern of producer services with that of manufacturing. According to this figure, producer services grew very robustly from the late 1980s onwards. At about the same time, Hong Kong witnessed a decline in the manufacturing sector. Manufacturing expressed as a share of GDP fell by about 57.6 per cent, while the rise in the share of producer services was about 16.9 per cent. This is consistent with the hypothesis that the relocation of the manufacturing industries to the Chinese hinterland and the rest of Asia paved the way for the growth of producer services in Hong Kong.

Hong Kong's relocation of manufacturing industries into mainland China was associated with significant investment flows, which then created a demand for China-related trade activities in Hong Kong and gave impetus to the growth of Hong Kong's re-exports. Indeed, Figure 14.3 shows the close relationship between the percentage change of real producer services and the percentage change in the value of utilized stock of foreign direct investments that Hong Kong had made in the Chinese hinterland. Figure 14.4 shows clearly how the

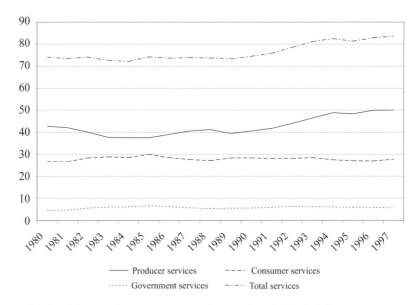

Figure 14.1   Types of services as a share of real GDP (%)

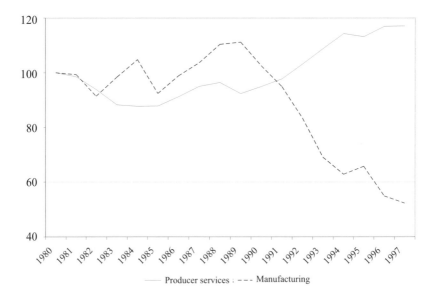

Figure 14.2   Growth of manufacturing and producer services as a share of real GDP (1980=100)

percentage growth of real producer services is closely related to the percentage growth of real re-exports from Hong Kong.

The other reason for the rise of producer services is the increasing role of Hong Kong as an intermediary for trade between mainland China and the world market. As shown in Figure 14.5, there is a close relation between the percentage growth of real producer services and the percentage growth of the real value of all Hong Kong trade with mainland China.

Since China adopted the open-door policy in late 1970s, it has become easier for foreign enterprises to trade directly with China. The transaction costs of establishing a direct trade link have gone down, which in principle should lead to a rise of direct trade between foreign enterprises and Chinese enterprises. What has happened, however, is a rise of indirect trade between foreign firms and Chinese firms via Hong Kong. This is because, along with its open-door policy, China has relaxed its foreign trade system. In late 1970s, the Chinese government deregulated foreign trade, replacing vertical channels of command with horizontal links. The number of trading companies in China has increased at an extremely high rate, reaching one thousand by 1984. The deregulation of foreign trade in China creates a challenging problem for multinationals to spot trading opportunities, find trustworthy trading partners in China, and efficiently carry out transactions in an imperfect legal environment.

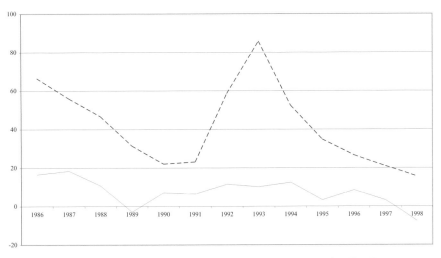

Real producer services - - - China's foreign direct investment from Hong Kong

Figure 14.3　**Real producer services and China's foreign direct investment from Hong Kong (growth rate in percent)**

Being a combination of the East and the West, Hong Kong is in a unique position to play the role of an intermediary. Hong Kong people speak the same language spoken in mainland China, and at the same time they have great ease in communication with Western people. More importantly, a significant percentage of Hong Kong people were originally from various parts of China. There are thus informal links between Hong Kong people and people in all parts of China. This network of friends and relatives allows Hong Kong people to spot trading opportunities and identify trustworthy trading partners, effectively alleviating the information problem of market transactions. In addition, the informal network has created reputation concerns for Chinese firms and their Hong Kong counterparts, and thereby served as a partial substitute for the imperfect contract enforcement in China.

3.4 The Size and Growth of Various Types of Producer Service Industries

According to government statistics, nongovernment services in Hong Kong are further classified into 13 categories. We estimate the percentage contribution to *real producer services* made by different types of service industries (see Table 14.7). The details for estimating various types of producer services can be found in Tao and Wong (2001).

The contributions of wholesale and retail trade to real producer services decreased substantially in the past two decades, falling from 4.3 per cent in 1980–89 to 3.3 per cent in 1990–97 and from 5.2 per cent in 1980–89 to 3.5 per cent in 1990–97, respectively. Restaurants and hotels also decreased their contribution to real producer services from 1.3 per cent in 1980–89 to 1.0 per cent in 1990–97 and from 3.2 per cent in 1980–89 to 2.7 per cent in 1990–97, respectively.

The community, social and personal services and the services derived from the ownership of premises slightly decreased their contributions to real producer services, from 2.0 per cent in 1980–89 to 1.8 per cent in 1990–97 and from 12.5 per cent in 1980–89 to 12.0 per cent in 1990–97, respectively. The percentage contribution to real producer services made by real estate services was more stable, remaining at 11.7 per cent in both periods. Similarly, the transport, storage, and communications services modestly decreased their contribution to real producer services, from 10.1 per cent in 1980–89 to 9.7 per cent in 1990–97.

The contributions of insurance services and business services to producer services increased from 0.42 per cent in 1980 89 to 0.44 per cent in 1990 97 and from 8.2 per cent in 1980–89 to 8.6 per cent in 1990–97, respectively.

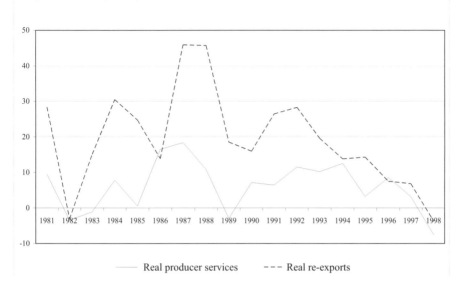

Figure 14.4   Real producer services and real re-exports (growth rate in percent)

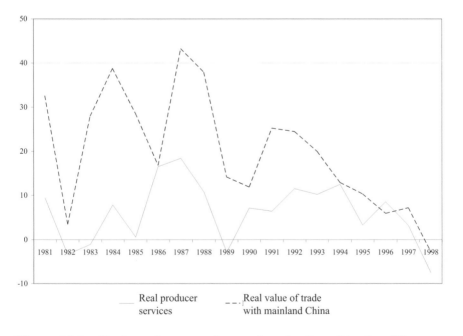

Figure 14.5   Real producer services and real value of trade with mainland China (growth rate in percent)

Table 14.7 Percentage share of various services in total producer services for selected years and periods

	1980	1997*	1980–89	1990–97
Wholesale trade	5.0	2.6	4.3	3.3
Retail trade	5.8	3.0	5.2	3.5
Import and export trade	28.1	37.7	34.1	37.9
Restaurants	1.2	0.8	1.3	1.0
Hotels	2.5	2.3	3.2	2.7
Transport, storage, and communications	8.7	8.8	10.1	9.7
Financing	15.4	19.4	15.7	18.2
Insurance	0.3	0.4	0.42	0.44
Real estate	17.9	11.6	11.7	11.7
Business services	6.0	9.2	8.2	8.6
Community, social, and personal services	1.6	1.9	2.0	1.8
Ownership of premises	10.6	13.4	12.5	12.0
Adjustment for financial intermediation services	–3.0	–10.9	–8.9	–10.7

* 1997 figures are our own preliminary estimates.

The share of real producer services contributed by import and export trade increased substantially, from 34.1 per cent in 1980–89 to 37.9 per cent in 1990 97. The increase in percentage contribution made by financing to real producer services is most substantial: from 15.7 per cent in 1980–89 to 18.2 per cent in 1990–97.

Insurance, financing, import/export trade, and business services have led the growth of total real producer services. The rise of producer services, and especially of the above components, has transformed Hong Kong from a center of manufacturing industries into a hub for managing outsourcing and financial intermediation activities.

4   Conclusion

Hong Kong's economy has been closely linked with that of mainland China. In the past 50 years, it has transformed first from entrepôt to manufacturing after the United Nations embargo on Chinese trade, and then from manufacturing to producer services after the opening up of the mainland Chinese economy since late 1970s. At the time of writing, China has just been admitted to the World Trade Organization. The role of Hong Kong as a center of managing outsourcing and intermediation may well be challenged as a result. It remains to be seen how Hong Kong will cope with the further opening up of the mainland Chinese economy.

References

Chou, K.R. (1966), *The Hong Kong Economy*, Academic Publications.
Grubel, H.G. and Walker, M.A. (1989), *The Canadian Service Industries*, The Fraser Institute.
Hambro, E. (1955), *The Problem of Chinese Refugees in Hong Kong*, Leyden.
Hopkins, K. (1971), *Hong Kong: The Industrial Colony,* Oxford University Press.
Sung, Y.W. (1998), *Hong Kong and South China: The Economic Synergy*, City University of Hong Kong Press.
Szczepanik, E. (1958), *The Economic Growth of Hong Kong*, Oxford University Press.
Tao, Z. and Wong, Y.C.R. (2001), *Hong Kong: From an Industrialized City to a Center of Manufacturing-Related Services*.
Wong, S.L. (1988), *Emigrant Entrepreneurs – Shanghai Industrialists in Hong Kong*, Oxford University Press.

CHAPTER 15

SHANGHAI RISING: RESURGENCE OF CHINA'S NEW YORK CITY?

HANCHAO LU*
Georgia Institute of Technology

Abstract

Shanghai's recent developments are by all accounts impressive and, in some areas, unprecedented. This chapter first looks at the development of China's largest city from a historical perspective. It then outlines Shanghai's major economic developments at the turn of the twenty-first century, including urban development, stock market, key industries, and mega business deals. It is tempting to compare Shanghai with New York City, for the two cities did share things in common, such as a vibrant commercial culture, a long-standing tradition of cosmopolitanism, entrepreneurship, the size of each city to the nation, and so on. The author suggests that Shanghai should be allowed to have more autonomy in business decision-making in order to be able to compete in global markets, as it did in its heyday. What Shanghai needs most is an institutionalized and transparent legal system that can warrant fair play in all business conducts. In conclusion, Shanghai's remarkable achievements in recent years have placed it facing an even greater challenge on its road toward 'China's New York City.'

Keywords: Shanghai, urban development, stock market, key industries, mega business deals

1   Introduction

Shanghai in recent years has been a rising city, both physically and economically. In the decade following 1993 the city was in a frenzy of building

---

*   Correspondence: Hanchao Lu, Professor of History, School of History, Technology, and Society, Georgia Institute of Technology, Atlanta, GA 30332–0345. Tel: (404) 894–6844; Email: hanchao.lu@hts.gatech.edu.

URBAN TRANSFORMATION IN CHINA, edited by Aimin Chen, Gordon G. Liu and Kevin H. Zhang

construction.[1] The old city was literally destroyed and a new city rose from its ruin: the reshaping of the landscape of Shanghai was such that in the late 1990s on average every three months the authorities had to print a new version of the city map.[2] The dynamic behind the mushrooming of high rises was of course economic growth (see Table 15.1). Shanghai doubled its GDP in the five years from 1994 to 1999, and by 2000 it was the only city in China, except for Hong Kong and Shenzhen, that had a per capita GDP exceeding US$ 4,000. A municipality of 0.5 per cent of the area of the nation and just about 1 per cent of the national population contributes 5 per cent of the national GDP, 13 per cent of real estate investment, and 23 per cent of international trade (see Table 15.2). People are now justifiably talking about the possibility of Shanghai's resurgence as China's New York City.[3] The millennium issue of *Time* magazine labeled Shanghai as a rival to New York City for the title of the 'center of the world' in the twenty-first century.

The rise of Shanghai in recent years was first of all driven by the general political relaxation after 1978 that made the economic reform possible. The more immediate source of Shanghai's development was Deng Xiaoping's 1992 'inspection tour of the South,' in which he specifically expressed his regrets that Shanghai had not been designated a Special Economic Zone in the early 1980s – this was, he lamented, his 'major mistake'.[4] On several occasions in the early 1990s, Deng urged the CCP leaders to loosen the reins and let Shanghai surge ahead. His comments have since served as the 'constitution' for Beijing's policy making on Shanghai and have had a direct impact on its development in the past decade.

---

1   For a comparison of various types of new construction in the city, see Shanghai Municipal Statistics Bureau (comp.), *Statistical Yearbook of Shanghai 2000* (Beijing, 2000), pp. 95–6.

2   For a discussion on the social impact of such development, see Hanchao Lu, 'Nostalgia for the Future: The Resurgence of an Alienated Culture in China,' *Pacific Affairs*, 75 (2) (Summer 2002), pp. 169–86.

3   See for example the *Far East Economic Review* correspondent Pamela Yatsko's *New Shanghai: The Rocky Rebirth of China's Legendary City* (New York: John Wiley & Sons, 2001).

4   In one of his speeches, Deng commented: 'In the areas of talented personnel, technology, and administration, Shanghai has obvious superiority, which radiates over a wide area. Looking back, my one major mistake was not to include Shanghai when we set up the four special economic zones. Otherwise, the situation of reform and opening to the outside in the Yangzi River delta, the entire Yangzi River valley, and even the entire nation would be different.' Deng Xiaoping, *Deng Xiaoping wenxuan* (Beijing, 1993), vol. 3, p. 376.

Table 15.1   Shanghai's social and economic development (1980–99)

Indicators	1980	1990	1999
GDP per capita (in US$)	1,837	1,216	3,921
Export (in million US$)	42.66	53.17	187.85
Urban household per capita annual income (*yuan*)	840	2,198	10,988
Life expectancy	73.4	75.8	78.4
Urban population (%)	58	67	74
Percentage of PC ownership by household	0	0	20*
Internet population	0	0	97,100**
Gas supply (household)	663,300	1,131,900	2,574,300
Telephone switchboard capacity (1,000 lines)	159	740	6,450
Year-end installed telephones (1,000)	111	456	4,840

Notes: * In the rural counties the percentage is 1.3; ** Shanghai started to have Internet service on 27 December 1996. This number represents a 187% increase of the previous year.

Sources: *Statistical Yearbook of Shanghai Foreign Economic 1978-1995* (Shanghai, 1996), A *Report of Economic Development in Shanghai 2000* (Shanghai, 2000), *A Report of Social Development in Shanghai 2001* (Shanghai, 2001), *Yearbook of Shanghai Foreign Economic Relations and Trade 2000* (Shanghai, 2000), *Shanghai Science and Technology Yearbook* (Shanghai, 2000).

Table 15.2   Shanghai's major social and economic indicators compared (1999)

Indicators	Shanghai	Nation	Shanghai's share
Land area (1,000 sq km)	63	9,600	0.1
Year-end population (million)	13	1,259	1
GDP (100 million yuan)	4,034	82,054	5
Cargo handled at seaport (million ton)	1,864	10,400	18
Investment in real estate (100 million yuan)	515	4,010	13
Total International trade (US$100 million)	762	3,607	21
Exports (US$100 million)	442	1,949	23
Student enrolment at tertiary level (1,000)	186	4,130	5
Newspaper published (100 million copies)	18	201	9
Public green areas in urban areas (10,000 ha.)	0.39	13.1	3

Sources: Shanghai Municipal Statistics Bureau (comp.), *Statistical Yearbook of Shanghai 2000* (Beijing, 2000); National Bureau of Statistics of the People's Republic of China (comp.), *China Statistical Yearbook 2000* (Beijing, 2000).

Modern economic development in general needs some sort of government initiatives and state interventions and, given China's current political structure, this may be more so in the case of Shanghai. But ultimately the development of a great city relies not on the will of individual strong men, nor on central planing, but on the internal dynamics generated within the city; Shanghai perhaps is no exception. This essay outlines Shanghai's recent history and economic development (with a focus on the city's major economic developments at the turn of the twenty-first century), suggesting that Shanghai's remarkable achievements in recent years have placed it facing an even greater challenge on its road toward 'China's New York City.'

2 Shanghai's Past and Present

Shanghai is a municipality administratively directly under the Chinese central government and occupies an area of 6,341 sq km, nearly ten times the size of Singapore. It includes 13 urban districts of the city proper or central area and nine suburban districts and counties.[5] The central area covers 2,057 sq km – about half the size of New York City – of which more than 300 sq km is built-up and densely populated. This area is expanding as a result of booming construction projects in recent years. The newest urban district is Pudong (literally, East of the Huangpu River), which has developed over the past decade into a world-class advanced business and financial centre. The municipality includes about 30 islands in the Yangtze River and along the coast of the East China Sea, including China's third largest island, Chongming Dao.

Shanghai is located right in the middle of China's long coastal line. Its port is one of the largest in China, accounting for nearly one-fifth of the country's total cargo volumes handled in coastal ports in 1999.[6] Major highways and railroads radiate from this municipality to all major cities and towns. The city has an expanding subway system. In 2000, a state-of-art and fully-modern international airport in Pudong (adding to the Hongqiao international airport in the southwest suburb) started operation, further elevating the city to the status of an advanced modern metropolis.

---

5   As a result of rapid urbanisation in this area, the State Council in 1997–99 has raised the administrative status of three rural counties of the Shanghai Municipality (Jinshan, Songjiang, and Qingpu) to 'suburban districts.'

6   *China Statistical Yearbook 2000* (Beijing, 2001), 536.

In early 2000, the population of the Shanghai urban agglomeration was about 14.7 million, making it China's largest city.[7] The local people speak a Chinese dialect called *Wu*. Most residents also speak *Putonghua* (Mandarin), which is also the language of instruction in all schools from kindergarten to tertiary education. English is the most common second language, with those aged 40 and below being more likely to speak English with a certain level of fluency.

Shanghai began more than 1,000 years ago as a small market town. It grew to a county town in 1292 during the Mongol (Yuan) Dynasty and enjoyed centuries of prosperity as a cotton and textile-based commercial center up to the Opium War (1839–42). Because of the Treaty of Nanjing (1842) and a supplementary agreement signed in 1843, China was forced to open Shanghai to British trade and residence. Other Western countries demanded and received similar privileges. Modern China's largest foreign concessions, known as the International Settlement and the French Concession, were set up north of the original walled Chinese city. In the next 80 years Shanghai developed a distinctly Western character and experienced a period of important commercial, industrial and political development, earning for itself nicknames like the 'Oriental Pearl,' the 'Paris of East,' and the 'Chinese New York'.[8]

Japan occupied the city during the Pacific War. After the war Shanghai again emerged as China's major domestic and international trading, banking, and shipping centre, but the Chinese civil war interrupted Shanghai's growth. After 1949 the new Chinese Communist government, viewing Shanghai as a consumer city with strong ties to the capitalist economy and bourgeois culture that conflicted with Communist ideology, moved quickly to drain capital away from the city to support other areas of China. This pattern largely continued until the economic reforms of the late 1970s. Shanghai, although still the largest and most industrialized city in China, was satirized by some Western observers as the 'world's largest village'.[9]

Although denouncing Shanghai as the bridgehead of Western imperialism, the Chinese central government in fact relied heavily on Shanghai for its

---

7   *Shanghai Almanac 2000*, pp. 58–9. The southwest city Chongqing is now listed as the most populous municipality in China, with a population of 30,234,000. However, 24,318,000 or about 80 per cent of Chongqing's population are rural, while Shanghai's rural population is less than a quarter of the city's total population. Thus, as far as urban population is concerned, Shanghai remains by far the largest city.

8   Hanchao Lu, *Beyond the Neon Lights: Everyday Shanghai in the Early Twentieth Century* (California, 1999), pp. 25–66.

9   Sam Tata and Ian McLachlan, *Shanghai 1949: The End of an Era* (London, 1989), p. 2.

revenue. Shanghai continued to be China's leading industrial centre, satisfying China's domestic demand and providing a substantial portion of its national revenue. In 1978, the Shanghai Municipality ranked first among China's provinces, accounting for 8 per cent of total national income, 13 per cent of gross industrial output and 30 per cent of exports. The city was indeed a cash cow, with 87 per cent of the revenues it generated between 1949 and 1983 being taken by the central government, a figure higher than anywhere else in China. Up to the early 1980s, on average, Shanghai had contributed to nearly one sixth of China's total revenue. As a result, many much-needed investments in infrastructure and urban development in the city were delayed.

Shanghai was declared open in 1984, together with 13 other modestly developed coastal cities and towns designated as 'open cities' to foreign investment. But the designation of Shanghai as an economic development zone at that time, and not a Special Economic Zone (SEZ), downplayed the role of Shanghai at the national level. Overall, Shanghai took a backseat in China's economic reform during the 1980s when the SEZs in Guangdong and Fujian were opened to huge foreign investments and trade. Guangdong's GDP surpassed Shanghai's (at the provincial level) in 1983 and by 1994 was more than twice that of Shanghai.

But by the early 1990s the revitalization of Shanghai as China's leading economic powerhouse had already started. In the wake of the Tiananmen incident of 1989, Jiang Zeming rose from being the mayor of Shanghai to become the general secretary of the Chinese Communist Party (CCP). Premier Zhu Rongji, the prime mover of China's economic reform in the 1990s, had also served as Shanghai mayor. The rise of these Shanghai officials to national leadership apparently accelerated the development of Shanghai. But the architect was, again, Deng Xiaoping himself. In his 1992 'inspection tour of the South', Deng Xiaoping urged the further opening of Shanghai, expressing his regrets that Shanghai had not been designated as a SEZ in the early 1980s. In one of his speeches, Deng commented: 'In the areas of talented personnel, technology, and administration, Shanghai has obvious superiority, which radiates over a wide area. Looking back, my one major mistake was not to include Shanghai when we set up the four special economic zones. Otherwise, the situation of reform and opening to the outside in the Yangtze River delta, the entire Yangtze River valley, and even the entire nation would be different.'[10] Beijing's conservative policy on Shanghai in the early 1980s had more profound reasons than just a personal mistake or neglect (even if

---

10   Deng Xiaoping, *Deng Xiaoping wenxuan* (Beijing, 1993), vol. 3, p. 376.

the person was Deng). First, the SEZ was experimental. Given the importance of Shanghai in the national economy, it would be too risky to put this key city on experiment. Second, Shanghai was the leading treaty port where the core of the city was the foreign concessions known as the International Settlement and the French Concession. It would fit uncomfortably with the image of the city's colonial past. Indeed there was a hot debate among the leadership on this issue, and both the *People's Daily* and Shanghai's *Liberation Daily* deliberately carried articles about the history of *zujie* (foreign concessions) in China. It would be too dramatic a turn in the early 1980s to let Shanghai go this far.[11]

However, a decade later, two developments made a difference. First, the SEZs in south China were largely successful. China now had sufficient experiences for spread the model northward and, given its favorable geographic location and economic caliber, Shanghai would be an ideal place for promoting the model further. Second, the Tiananmen event of 1989 dramatically slowed down the reform and in the immediate aftermath of the incident, it seemed like that the reform would be brought to a halt. To revitalize and boost the reform, Beijing needed a breakthrough, which should be a symbol as well as a real move to show the world its determination to continue the reform. Shanghai was an excellent and indeed the only place that was capable to carry on the task.

The opening of Shanghai's Pudong area for investment and development signaled the city's return to the forefront of Chinese economic reform. Plans are underway to make Shanghai the 'dragonhead' of development of the Yangtze River Basin. These include developing the city into an international center of finance, export processing, business services and high-tech industries. Today, Shanghai is the scene of one of the world's most ambitious development projects and fastest growing metropolitan economies. The per capita GDP of Shanghai in 2000 increased 10.8 per cent to US$4,180.[12]

One of the most important advantages of Shanghai is the city's trained human resources. For more than a century, the city has been China's leading intellectual powerhouse and the cradle of modernity (or Westernization). Although such a tradition was severely suppressed during Mao's times, it is now undergoing a renaissance. In particular, a comprehensive strategy of

---

11 But by the mid-1980s more liberal scholars started to suggest that even the foreign concessions in old China might have had some positive influence on China, see Xiong Yuezhi, 'luelun Shanghai zujie de shuangchong yingxiang' ('On the Dual Influences of Shanghia's Foreign Concessions'), *Wenhui bao* (*Wenhui Daily*), 11 November 1986.

12 Data provided by the Institute of Sociology, Shanghai Academy of Social Sciences, February 2001.

revitalizing the city by promoting science and education is being implemented. The number of university students were increased steadily during the 1990s and had by 1999 doubled that of the early 1980s. Science and Engineering enjoyed an unchallenged position, with nearly half of all recent university graduates coming from science and engineering institutions.

Another stronghold Shanghai has is in the area of high technology. The city has 915 science and technology research institutions and a total of 743,000 professionals and technical workers in its state-owned enterprises and institutions. Its annual expenditures in R&D account for 1.6 per cent of the city's GDP. In 1999 Shanghai reported 1,252 major scientific and technological achievements, of which 41 were cutting-edge inventions and 457 were of world-class standard. Although research personel and R&D in the private sector are insignificant at this stage, along with the city's continuous development, they are expected to increase significantly in the years to come.

3   The Emergence of Asia's Third Largest Stock Market

One of Shanghai's main missions in China's modernization program is building itself up into the country's financial hub. In this regard Deng himself endorsed Shanghai, as he pointed out in early 1991: 'Finance is very important, it is the core of modern economy. If finance were in good shape, everything else would be in good shape. Shanghai in the past was a financial centre where currencies were exchanged freely, and we should do the same in the future. For China to obtain international status in finance we should first of all rely on Shanghai.'[13] These words have served as the guiding light in policy making in regard to finance and the setting up of the country's stock market.

China is now planning to merge the clearing system for its two main boards (Shanghai and Shenzhen). Shanghai has been chosen as the site of a unified exchange, effectively making it the financial centre of China. It is anticipated that once the plan is realised all main board settlements will be in Shanghai. The Shanghai Stock Exchange would trade in all of China's current 1,014 stocks and would have a combined market capitalization of around US$500 billion, ranking it the third largest in Asia behind Tokyo and Hong Kong.

Along with the merge, a set of rules are revised to make the Chinese stock market more standardized. For example, the revised rules stipulate that non-bond securities cannot be sold on the day they are purchased; and the

---

13   Deng Xiaoping, *Deng Xiaoping wenxuan* (Beijing, 1993), 3, pp. 366–7.

closing price will be based on the weighted average strike price one minute before closing time. The changes are reportedly intended as preparation for the introduction of a national securities index, to be called the 'China Index'.[14] A merged market would boost liquidity and allow high-tech firms and private start-ups to raise desperately needed capital. Funds are expected to flow into Shanghai after the merger and will impact all financial institutions and supporting industries associated with the publicly traded companies.

In 2000 Shanghai's B shares set the world's best performing benchmark when investors scrambled to pick up companies that were selling unprofitable units and reorganizing their operations in anticipation of China's WTO entry. Starting 1 January 2001, commissions on trading of B shares were lowered from 0.6 to 0.43 per cent. Securities companies also began automated trading, a move seen as leading to increased trading as trading costs are lowered and the buying and selling of shares made easier.

However, there are a number of issues that the Chinese government needs to deal with before a merged stock market in Shanghai could really be integrated into the global trading body. First, lawmakers are still writing China's first communist-era law on portfolio investments and regulators are only starting to learn to police the market. China has recruited a Hong Kong securities regulator to advise its industry watchdog, the China Securities Regulatory Commission. In the transitional period after China joins WTO, the Shanghai stock market will have to complete the drawing out of rules and regulations and tailoring them according to international norms. In particular, the Shanghai bourse would allow foreign funds to invest in the A-share market, which currently remains open only to domestic investors. Such a scheme could be put in place as early as in two years' time and would offer foreigners a channel into China's closed capital market.

Another issue is the listing of more state-owned enterprises (SOEs). Currently, less than 5 per cent of state enterprises are floated and there is much room for more listings. Signs are that more SOEs would go public, in a bid to force them to become sleeker, more efficient and market driven. Shanghai mayor Xu Kuangdi recently asserted that China would follow international practice and not subsidise state-owned enterprises. 'We want to use the method of establishing shareholding companies to rejuvenate the SOEs so that they can become more public and more transparent, so they can be controlled by the investors,' Xu said.[15] If successful, the policy would kill two birds with one stone – privatising the SOEs and injecting vitality to the stock market.

14 *Straits Business Monthly* (no. 117), 10 September 2001.
15 *International Finance News* (*Guoji jinrong bao*), 12 December 2000.

The third issue relates to the B-share market, which lists companies traded in US dollars. So far foreign investors have largely shunned the B-share market, preferring to invest in Chinese companies listed in Hong Kong and New York, where disclosure rules are far tighter. Like the A-share market, greater transparency is needed to attract foreign investors to domestic bourses. Inevitably, after China's accession to the WTO, the Chinese stock market would have to be more open to foreign investors and foreign fund management companies.

4 Boosting Key Industries

Along with the re-emergence of Shanghai as China's financial center, the city is also working towards regaining its position as China's leading industrial base. The city will be home to five major production bases in the first five years of new century while making efforts to have three enterprise groups, led by the Baoshan Iron and Steel Corporation, ranked among the world's top 500 companies. The bases will cover industries such as electronics and information, automobile, power generation, steel, petrochemicals and refined petrochemical.

4.1 Information Industry

One of China's fastest growing internet service providers, Shanghai-Online, has recently installed the Infranet real-time customer management and billing software from Portal Software, making it Portal's first customer in China. Shanghai-Online now has 174 online resources sites and more than 300 database and application services, making it the largest urban information network in China. Currently supporting more than 100,000 customers, the company has been adding 6,000 new accounts every month, and has developed some 700 different pricing plans to meet the needs and budgets of the widest possible range of users. This is a sign of the city's ambitious plan of developing the information industry, which by 2005, would become the most vital and creative pillar sector of the city's industry. More than 130 billion yuan (US$15.66 billion) will be spent in the five-year period on developing integrated circuit, information technology, telecommunications, computer and Internet, vacuum devices, new electronic components, and digital audio-video products and software.[16]

---

16 http://asia.internet.com/1999/11/2602-shang.html; www.muzi.news.com, 1 February 2001.

4.2 Automotive Industry

Shanghai's auto industry is expected to maintain its 18 per cent average annual growth. The city is home to state giant Shanghai Automotive Industry Corporation, which has high-profile ventures with Germany's Volkswagen AG and General Motors Corporation of the United States. Shanghai GM's plant capacity is 100,000 vehicles per year, though production will not be anywhere near that for some time. The current line speed is 30 jobs per hour, netting about 27 vehicles per hour. That compares with a typical US line speed ranging from 40 to 60 vehicles per hour (depending on the product).[17] This leaves great potential for development.

4.3 Power Plant Project

Shanghai will focus on the production of complete sets of power plant equipment and automatic elevators. Waigaoqiao Thermal Power Project, a US$1.9 billion power project launched recently, aims to further power plant development to meet the burgeoning electricity demand created by explosive growth in Shanghai. The World Bank recently approved a US$400 million loan to the project, which will increase energy supply in an environmentally sustainable manner, promote power sector reform and private sector investment, and boost further economic growth in areas currently constrained by power shortages.

4.4 Steel Industry

Shanghai's steel industry is one of the major industries the city has built up after 1949 and it has been growing steadily in recent years. The production of pig iron, steel and steel products grew about 10 per cent annually from 1996–99. China's Ministry of Metallurgical Industry (MMI) has encouraged mergers and takeovers in an effort to streamline China's massive and moribund steel sector and to create over the next decade a batch of steel groups to form the cornerstone of the industry. According to official sources, in the 2001–2005 period, Shanghai will invest 40 billion yuan to manufacture steel for automobiles, shipbuilding, electrical power supply, oil pipes, stainless and high-grade construction steels, all of which are the city's main areas of focus in the steel industry. By 2005, total output value of these sectors is expected to exceed 100 billion yuan.

---

17   www.auto.com/ Industry News, 26 October 2000.

4.5 Materials

Major investment in petrochemicals, natural gas and refined chemicals will be stepped up, in the hope that production of ethylene, crude oil processing and synthetic materials will contribute to long-term development of the materials industry. Electronic information, petrochemical and fine chemical, integrated circuits, vacuum apparatus, fine chemicals, new types of engineering plastics, compound materials and new types of integrated materials will claim priority. According to the newly established Shanghai New Materials Association, the output value of the industry will reach 60 billion yuan (US$7.25 billion) by 2005, doubling the 2000 figure.

Industry estimates show that the city's new materials industry growing at an annual 30 per cent starting from 1996 and may realize an output value of 30 billion yuan in 2000, up fourfold. More than 600 enterprises are presently engaged in research and production of new materials in the city, and a number of new materials they produce, including artificial crystal, steel fiber and container steel plates, have been able to reach world-class level.

As mentioned, by 2005, revenue from the city's new materials industry is likely to top 60 billion yuan and will make up 20 per cent of the domestic market share. Direct export will be US$500 million. Construction of 30 state and municipal new materials technology R&D centers is underway.

5   Three Mega Deals in Shanghai

5.1 The AT&T Deal

For a long time, China has banned foreign investment in the telecom business, citing concerns about the exposure of State secrets and the inability of domestic telecom operators to compete effectively against foreign competitors. Up to 2000 China only allowed foreigners to buy minority stakes in China Mobile (Hong Kong) Ltd and China Unicom Ltd, the Hong Kong-listed wings of the country's two mobile phone carriers. After nearly eight years of negotiation, AT&T Corp was given the green light to launch the first foreign telecommunication joint venture in China, partly in line with China's pledge to open the sector under WTO rules. Again, Shanghai will serve as the laboratory for the experimental venture.

The top US long-distance phone provider has won approval to take a 25 per cent stake in Shanghai Symphony Telecom Co., a broadband service provider to be launched in the fast-developing Pudong district. The remaining shares will be held by the Shanghai branch of state giant China Telecom and by Shanghai Information Investment Inc., a firm controlled by the Shanghai city government.

The deal is the latest sign that China is willing to comply with market opening commitments it made to members of the WTO. In the mid-1990s foreign investors poured US$1.4 billion into more than 40 telecommunication service joint ventures with state carrier China Unicom Group. But the government declared the ventures 'irregular' in 1998 and forced the companies to unwind. Thus, the AT&T deal marks the only telecom service joint-venture the country has presently with a foreign company.

5.2 The World's First Commercial Maglev Railway

Starting from early 2001, the city is building a 20–25 mile long magnetic levitation railway linking Shanghai's financial district to its new airport in Pudong. The German-made Transrapid maglev train is able to carry 600 passengers with a speed of 430–500 kph. The US$1 billion deal involves China building the track for the system while Transrapid supplying the trains and switching equipment. The target completion date for the first of two tracks is 1 January 2003.

Practically, the maglev is still not a fully developed technology and it also faces growing competition from traditional rail systems. As the Shanghai project will be the first commercial maglev in the world, it is quite experimental in nature. However, if successful, the payoff could be bigger than just a quick ride to the airport. Overnight, Shanghai would become a center for maglev development. And the railway would stand as an outstanding proof of the dare and vision of this booming, energetic city.

A test maglev train in northwestern Germany had delighted Premier Zhu Rongji, who took a ride in July 2000. The Chinese government then signed a 1.6 million mark (US$733,000) agreement with Germany's Transrapid consortium for a feasibility study and said it could eventually lead to a deal worth US$20 billion to the consortium. The image is seductive and futuristic: a train floating above its track races along at jet plane speed. Shanghai now has pledged itself to buy into that dream.

The maglev technology uses powerful magnets to hold a train a few millimeters from the track and propel it with little noise or vibration. It could be an alternative to congested highways. The United States, Japan and other countries are considering building maglev lines. In the US, seven regions in

California, Florida, and elsewhere are competing for an experimental maglev. In Japan, developers hope to have it considered for a new Tokyo-Osaka line. Both Germany and Japan have spent decades and billions of dollars developing the maglev, yet neither has put it to commercial use.

5.3 The Country's Largest Chemical Complex

China has started building the nation's largest chemical complex, a multi-billion-dollar park in a southwest suburb of Shanghai city (north of Hangzhou Bay). Aiming at becoming a key chemical base in East Asia, the park is a big step for the future of China's petrochemical industry. The first phase of the 23.4 sq km park will cost about 150 billion yuan (US$18 billion).

A US$400-million polycarbonate plant, a joint venture between Germany's Bayer AG and Shanghai Tianyuan Group Corporation, will begin production of insulating material and coatings by 2003. Germany's BASF AG, US-based Huntsman Corporation and five Chinese companies, including China Petroleum & Chemical Corporation, will jointly build a plant to make raw material for polyurethane. The US$1-billion plant will start production by 2004.

The Chinese government expects that by 2005 about 60 billion yuan worth of project would be invested in the park. A joint venture between Shanghai Petrochemical Co., China Petroleum Corporation and BP Amoco plc to produce ethylene should go onstream by 2005. The US$3.4-billion plant will have a capacity of 900,000 metric tons per year.

6   Some Speculations

Shanghai's recent developments are by all accounts impressive and, in some areas, unprecedented. It is tempting to compare Shanghai with New York City, for the two cities did share things in common, such as a vibrant commercial culture, a long-standing tradition of cosmopolitanism, entrepreneurship, the size of each city to the nation, and so on. However, one must note that even during Mao's time Shanghai was China's largest and most industrialized city and its position in the urban hierarchy of China was an equivalent to New York City in that of the US. Today, as China is playing an increasingly important role both politically and economically in global setting, such analogy requires new qualifications. The most critical one is that Shanghai must reach international norms and standards in all socioeconomic and political realms and, moreover, like New York, the city must be innovative and avant-garde in the cultural arena.

Shanghai still has to fully establish the rule of law in all aspects of the society in order to have institutionalised accountability, transparency, and free flow of information in conducting business. The city is still hindered by a national legal system that is ranked among the least transparent in Asia by international surveys. While a national reform on legal system may be a long-term goal that is not easy to achieve, Shanghai should be allowed to have more autonomies in business decision making in order to be able to compete in global markets. Historically, Shanghai's heyday in the past was largely due to the fact that the central authorities had little control over the economy of the city. The city therefore was able to develop under a local authority that was essentially business-oriented and legal-minded. Unfortunately, such autonomy was a product of colonialism and doomed to disappear. Sadly, while the national shame of foreign domination had gone, there was no adequate measure to replace it other than Maoist political zeal. Today, the revolutionary zeal has yielded to pragmatism and commercialism, but sound and fully modernized institutions are yet to be established. What Shanghai needs most is an institutionalised and transparent legal system that can warrant fair play in all business conducts.

The lingering central controlling economic system is a double-edged sword in Shanghai's recent development. One should note that the rise of the Pudong New Area was at the beginning bolstered just by a single administrative order directly from Beijing. The quick flow of capital and real estate investments into that area therefore can be seen primarily as the result of government conduct, not a market-driven innovation. Government-backed trade barriers also created the monopolies that guarantee profits. Shanghai's automobile joint venture with Volkswagen, for example, produced vehicles in the 1990s at a cost that was twice the international price, and was only profitable because of trade barriers.

On the other hand, the central controlling economic system, although being much relaxed, still hampers the city's development. It is now a well-known fact that, as a part of national phenomenon, the city's state-owned enterprises are weighing down the economy. Even in the areas that have been reformed for two decades, the central government is still holding the leash pretty tightly. A recent example is the stagnation of the newly founded Shanghai Diamond Exchange. In the spring of 2001, nearly half a year after its grand opening in which Mayor Xu Kuangdi ceremoniously struck a giant gong to symbolize an auspicious beginning, not a carat of diamond had changed hands in the market. The reason is simple: Beijing levied taxes that add up to 36 per cent to a diamond's cost, which was ten times the global average and the highest imposed anywhere in the world; and the Shanghai office could do virtually nothing about it.[18]

China's entry into the World Trade Organization (WTO) will blunt this double-edged sword and bring new opportunities as well as uncertainties to the Chinese economy. Inevitably, as a powerhouse of that economy, Shanghai will face unprecedented challenges. Given the city's indomitable struggle for modernity in the past century, one may hope that such challenges will serve as a sort of catalytic force and Shanghai will be baptized into a truly world-class city in the near future.

---

18 *Asiaweek*, March–April 2001, pp. 62–3.

About the Editors

Aimin Chen is an Associate Professor of Economics at Indiana State University. She publishes extensively on reforms of Chinese firms, Chinese urban housing and urbanization, as well as China's WTO entry. She was the president of the Chinese Economists Society (2000–2001) and has been a Series Editor of *The Chinese Economy Series* published by Ashgate Publishing Limited.

Gordon Liu is an Associate Professor of Health Economics at the University of North Carolina-Chapel Hill. His research is focused on economics and outcomes research assessing medical technology and health policy, and publishes extensively in these areas. He was a vice president of the Chinese Economists Society (2000–2001), and currently serves as the co-editor of *Value in Health*, the official journal of the International Society for Pharmacoeconomics and Outcomes Research (ISPOR).

Kevin H. Zhang is an Associate Professor of Economics at Illinois State University. He has published over 50 journal articles and book chapters on international economics, economic development, and regional/urban economics as well as China's urbanization. He was a vice president of the Chinese Economists Society (2000–2001 and 2002–2003) and was co-editor of two books on FDI and globalization in China.

INDEX